Young Children, Videos and Computer Games

For Ann English

Young Children, Videos and Computer Games
Issues for Teachers and Parents

Jack Sanger with Jane Wilson,
Bryn Davies and Roger Whitakker

 The Falmer Press

(A member of the Taylor & Francis Group)
London • Washington, D.C.

UK   The Falmer Press, 1 Gunpowder Square, London, EC4A 3DE
USA   The Falmer Press, Taylor & Francis Inc., 1900 Frost Road, Suite 101, Bristol, PA 19007

First published in 1997

A catalogue record for this book is available from the British Library

Library of Congress Cataloging-in-Publication Data are available on request

ISBN 0 7507 0 702 x cased
ISBN 0 7507 0 701 1 paper

Jacket design by Caroline Archer

Typeset in 10/12pt Times by
Graphicraft Typesetters Ltd., Hong Kong.

Printed in Great Britain by Biddles Ltd, Guildford and King's Lynn on paper which has a specified pH value on final paper manufacture of not less than 7.5 and is therefore 'acid free'.

Contents

List of Figures and Table

Glossary of Terms

Main Types of Console Games

Platform games

These are relatively simple games which usually involve chasing or avoiding characters and obstacles by jumping on to platforms. Typical examples are the *Mario* and *Sonic* games and the *Donkey Kong* games.

Shoot-'em-ups

These are aggressive games in which the central character is required to shoot all other characters or objects that appear on the screen. Examples are *Sunset Riders* and *Space Invaders*.

Beat-'em-ups

These are fighting games where players usually choose to be one of the characters who has particular combative skills which are then used to destroy other characters on the screen. Examples are *Street Fighter* and *Mortal Kombat*.

Sports

These are usually skilful games in which players participate in simulated sporting situations. The most typical examples feature football, tennis and golf. An example would be *Super Tennis*.

Racing

These are skilful games in which the players take part in simulated car races. A typical example would be *Ridge Racer*.

Flight simulation

These are skilful games in which the player flies an aircraft or attacks enemy aircraft. A typical example would be *Tornado / X wing*.

Adventure

These games usually involve some kind of quest in which the character or characters escape to fantasy worlds where they have to avoid various obstacles and traps before reaching their goals. A typical example would be *Doom* or *Zelda 3*.

Role-playing — In these games, the player is required to take on the role of a central character. A typical example would be Dungeon Master.

Puzzle games — These are often quite challenging games which require the player to solve complex puzzles. An example would be *Tetris*.

Conceptual simulations — These are complex decision-making and planning games involving unpredictable variables e.g., building a city or running an organization. Examples would be *Populous, Sim City* and *Theme Park*.

Weird games — This term is sometimes used to cover a miscellaneous group of games which do not fit easily into other categories.

Main Types of Games Machines

LCD games (Liquid Crystal Display) — These are small, pocket-sized, battery-powered machines which feature a single game. The games range from a very simple type to a more sophisticated, complex variety. The simpler games can be played by children as young as 3 years. Prices range from approx. £3 to £20. Sales are gradually declining for this type of machine.

Game Boy — This is a hand-held console made by Nintendo. The introduction of this type of portable machine contributed to the decline in sales of the LCD machines. It has a black and white screen.

Game Gear — This is a hand-held console made by Sega. It has a colour screen and sells at a higher price than the Game Boy.

Nintendo — This is the original 8-bit Nintendo Entertainment System. It is a dedicated games console which is plugged into the TV. Games are purchased separately as cartridges ('carts') that are then inserted into the machine like video tapes.

SNES — This machine is commonly known by its acronym which stands for Super Nintendo Entertainment System. It essentially works on the same principles as its predecessor, the Nintendo, but is a more powerful 16-bit machine. This means that it offers more complex moves, improved graphics and generally more enhanced game play. Games still come in the form of 'carts' which have to be compatible with that type of machine. 'Carts' developed for the Nintendo cannot be played on a Sega machine.

Super Game Boy Adapter

This is an additional item for the 16-bit console, introduced in 1994, which allows the use of Game Boy cartridges. This means that best-selling games (e.g., *Kirby's Pinball Land* and *Wario Land*) can be played on the 'big' screen. The Super Game Boy makes the games more attractive by replacing shades of grey with a four-colour selection.

Sega Master System Sega Megadrive

This is a 16-bit dedicated games console similar to the SNES.

Sega Megadrive 32X

This is the 32-bit version of the Megadrive. It is more powerful and has faster, improved graphics.

Sega Saturn

This is the most recent development from Sega. It operates a CD drive so the games come in the form of CDs rather than 'carts'. This allows the games to become even more complex. A link to a PC is planned for the near future.

Sony Playstation

This is a new development from Sony. It is a CD machine with 32-bit computer power.

Atari Jaguar

Atari machines have been around for longer than any of the Sega or Nintendo hardware. They were very popular in the first wave of games playing in the early 80s. The latest Atari machine to be released is a 64-bit console. It is priced considerably lower than the Sony and Sega (approximately £149) but a CD-rom drive add-on costs as much again. This can be upgraded to play CD-rom videos.

Ultra 64

This is a new machine developed by Nintendo in conjunction with an American computing firm. It is based on a 64-bit computer processor which gives it outstanding effects. It is staying, at least for the moment, with the traditional cartridge game format.

Acknowledgments

The authors of this book would like to thank the British Library Research and Development Department and the British Film Institute for their financial support for this research. Our agreement with them was that the report should be compiled as a book, to reach the widest possible audience.

We would also like to thank the children, their parents and their schools in this study, for cooperating with us in the way they did. We were made welcome everywhere we went, had little problem over access, and were given, at times, frank and honest accounts of family and school life.

Introduction

Boy (9 years):	When I've finished playing on my own, I sometimes turn it on to two players and then just leave the other player there so I can just kick and punch them.
Researcher:	What's the point if there's no-one playing with you who can move the other joystick?
Boy:	Well, I like to be able to work out the death moves — I can do torso removal and it rips the other body in half. (*He laughs loudly*)

Jeux Sans Frontieres

In the flickering isolation of the bedroom or in the less private surroundings of the family sitting room, children are experiencing screen-related events — sometimes with their parents' approval and sometimes under an umbrella of parental ignorance — screen events over which they have degrees of control which often go beyond the on/off and channel switches of television. The growing utilization by the young of interactive screen-based technologies — computer games, personal computers (PCs), video games and videos themselves — has become a matter of national concern. Debate rages over the effects of these technologies on vulnerable young minds. This book embraces this debate and sets it against a different backdrop — the twin contexts of school and home: what happens in the home which is of value or detrimental to the school experience, and vice versa. Given the trumpetings of the information age and the projected skills and competencies people will need in future society, what can be gleaned from domestic and schooling experiences which will throw light upon how our children are going to fare as they mature?

The X Files

The research project upon which this book is based was funded by the British Library and the British Film Institute and took place between 1994–96. The research focused upon around a hundred children from a variety of backgrounds and family profiles. The families concerned were guaranteed anonymity. Schools produced lists of possible subjects for the study but the research team selected individuals and negotiated directly with families from this point. Most children were observed at home and at school, using very carefully drawn up protocols. Their home environments were documented wherever possible. Parents, teachers, siblings and peers were brought into the study in order that a rounded picture of each child's experience of the relevant technology could be established. Interviews were recorded on tape, or videotaped. Environments were photographed and videotaped. Polaroid instamatic cameras were used to produce instant pictures of children in their home environments, playing with technology, in order to help the very young, in particular, talk about their activities. As the project progressed, the team refined their approaches to gathering data. Working in families involves very delicate negotiation on a moment-by-moment basis. Team members often became aware of family tensions, family secrets, family histories and how children navigated these sometimes fraught waters. But gradually each picture emerged in all its complexity. A full account of the research design and methodology is given in Chapter 10.

Home and Away

And so to some prefacing of the issues which became the focus of the research. One of the most obvious was the difference in outlook between parents and teachers regarding computer games and video material. Enough has been said concerning how they now fill the place once dominated by comics, pop music, Enid Blyton and so on, as media for moral concern. In general, schools don't countenance them on the premises. Indeed, schools were impoverished environments as far as all screen-based activity was concerned, whether PC or video recorder based. The initial response of most teachers to questions from our team about these media and popular culture, as a whole, was one of disapproval. It was allied to the feeling that parents would disapprove of such activities in school time, even though, paradoxically, parents obviously actively embraced their use at home. They believed that there was no educational reason to have them on the premises and had little knowledge of those very popular commercial games which contained strong educational elements. Certainly, their impact upon children's behaviour has been noticed by teachers in stylized play in the playground and to a far lesser degree in subjects chosen in written work but such effects were not particularly prominent within our own findings. Rather emotive research for the Professional Association of Teachers (PAT) on the subject, showed that teachers felt there was an enormously detrimental impact on children's behaviour (PAT, 1994). That research certainly pointed up teachers' beliefs but did little to show whether these beliefs were based on any real evidence.

It must be remembered, too, that the vast proportion of teachers working with our chosen age range — and that of the PAT survey — were women. Within this group we found a great deal of evidence to suggest a gendered antipathy to the technologies. Staff who were very comfortable with such technology in the classroom were far rarer than staff who were technophobic. When taken together with the majority of female parents, female role models for these technologies were notably absent in many children's lives. Negative attitudes to video- and computer-related games activities, and indeed most information technology, tend to run quite deep in some of the adult female population.

During interviews, the first response from some parents to entertainment technology was also one of disapproval, but there was a difference. Whilst teachers maintained their disapproval throughout their interviews, some parents shifted position considerably within their interviews once they realized that the researchers were neutral on the issue. They appeared to adopt a role of the 'responsible parent' in the first instance and downgraded any possible virtues in children being engaged with these media: their original assumptions being that the research was setting out to prove that *the technology concerned was harmful.* But during interviews, they often reversed this position. Given that the research team wanted to observe small groups of children trying out and discussing computer games play and video viewing at school, resistance from many schools prevented the activity. Where it did occur, the results were extremely illuminating.

A second issue concerned strong differences in the way that these technologies are valued by parents from different socio-economic backgrounds. There was a greater tendency among middle-class parents to involve themselves in some aspect of their children's play. This would range from heavy censoring of what they could watch, buy or play upon, to involving them in PC networking and the use of CD-roms. Children from other backgrounds were more likely to be left alone with the technology, which, itself would be more likely to comprise games play on dedicated machines and unregulated video viewing. Their parents or guardians were also less likely to be able to understand the basic functions of operating the technology, particularly their mothers or other female adults.

These differences raise key questions concerning how children are seen by parents and teachers. What should childhood involve? What is good for children and what is bad? How much freedom should be allowed them to experience screen-based activities and determine their choice of content? A crude generalization would be that the vast majority of children have little adult intervention or support in their interaction with the technology. They are being expected to grow up without any critical debate from parents or teachers concerning the production, presentation and content of the programs and videos with which they interact.

There are many other issues, documented and teased out in these chapters. Here are some of them. Young children are consumers targeted directly by the manufacturer, often involving products which, if parents knew about them, would cause some disquiet. Manufacturers increasingly are targeting boys, with sport and fighting games, thereby consolidating the maleness of the activities. There appears to be a spin-off in that boys develop a greater affinity for computers and consequent information handling. Parents also seemed to be easily manipulated by their children and manufacturers' hype. Many had a naive belief that all games machines were computers and would help their children become computer literate and, if they maintained any control over their children's play, it consisted in the amount of time they spent on machines and not the content of the activity.

There was an overall feeling that children are being left to drift in a leisure world of growing technological sophistication, where realism is increasing and the boundaries between fact and fiction diminishing. To become critical consumers capable of managing this aspect of their lives will require wholesale changes in the way education is viewed and delivered.

Seeing is Believing

The research into the ways that children use and abuse (or are used and abused by) screen-based technologies, tends to concentrate upon participation time and its possible effects. The greater the time spent with the technology the greater the supposed effect it has upon them. For example, Griffiths (1993) suggests that children, albeit at a later age, can become addicted to the pleasures of game playing. However, survey approaches are notoriously difficult to make accurate. Taken individually, in our research, parents, teachers and children would offer a point of view which would change later, when challenged by the researcher repeating the perceptions of others, or by observational data generated by the researcher. Children in classrooms often talked unrealistically about what happened in their homes. Parents' assertions about their children's viewing habits were sometimes confounded when the observer visited the house. Teachers' understanding of their pupils' home lives proved very sketchy.

To give an example. In the pilot period of the project a parent informed the researcher that she gave careful attention to what the child viewed and read. Educational material was a priority in the household. Survey research often leads to unwarranted leaps of social understanding. The parent in this case would avow, both in interview and on a questionnaire, that she had knowledge and control over her child's behaviour. But in her case, as with many parents once the bedroom door is closed, it was the child who determined what was seen and viewed. The boy showed the researcher videos with an 18 certificate, in a drawer, that his grandfather had given him *for when he was grown up* . . . This child watched his screen, on his own, until late at night.

The research has been fascinating and has led us to wonder at the relative lack of in-depth studies of everyday children in domestic environments. Access to homes tends to prove that the paradox of idiosyncrasy and conformity exists within most families. What is, of course, mainly true, is that families of whatever shape, size and composition, tend to regard themselves as 'normal' with healthy enough attitudes and day-to-day compromises. They tend not to analyse their own behaviours *vis à vis* the rest of the population. They can be aware, in a generalized way, of moral debates and often subscribe to consensus viewpoints in public arenas (including interviews with researchers!), whilst behaving quite at odds with such a consensus in their own homes.

Panorama

It may be helpful to set this research against the background of some relevant research literature. We chose to examine, in particular, research papers relating to children and entertainment technology, play and gender. To some extent this enables us to see the developments of these new forms of children's behaviour in ways which offer comparisons and contrasts with what has gone before. Let us begin with the obvious, the growth of video- and computer-based technology in the home.

The cliché of our times is that the inhabitants of the late twentieth century are living through a period of great technical change. The past decade has seen an acceleration in growth of every aspect of communications technology. Fax machines, mobile phones, telephone answering machines and, most recently, video phones have transformed the simple telephone into a multi-purpose machine. Electronic mail and teleconferencing are now taken for granted in many walks of life and parts of the world (Plant, 1995). The most recent and perhaps most significant advance, in this regard, is 'convergence' which involves the integration of television, telephone and computer technologies, (see Dyrli and Kinnaman, 1994) in interactive packages through which households will be able to communicate with the outside world; from banking to shopping, to mail, to education and training and to entertainment. In addition to word processing, databases, graphics and spreadsheet applications, these systems will function as fax machines, video-conferencing suites, and as video-phones or television sets. What it means is that we may be nearing a situation where TVs and the PC will be inseparable. And the technology will be in most homes and businesses within the first decade of the next century.

Currently, in British households with children, 39 per cent have a home computer, and sales of personal computers for home use in Britain have averaged more than $^1/_2$ million a year for the past four years. A personal computer is seen as a modern status symbol, according to a Gallup survey, ranking alongside the car, and outranking holiday homes, a Rolex watch and gold credit card. The status such hardware gave to children in this study was often immeasurable. The same survey shows that most middle-class parents see home computers as an educational tool that will help their children. Fewer than a quarter of working-class parents agree, seeing computers as mainly for games-playing. Parents are prepared to make sacrifices to buy a personal computer for their children; 23 per cent would give up a foreign holiday, 26 per cent would go out less in the evening (Margolis, 1995).

Buckley (1995) quotes an Inteco forecast suggesting that by 1998, 47 per cent of households in the UK will own personal computers, with 66 per cent of them having CD-rom drives and a further 9 per cent connected to on-line services. Inteco also forecasts that by 1998, 86 per cent of high income families will possess a PC. But what if there is no computer at home? The survey indicates that 61 per cent of homes currently do not have PCs and that even by 1998, 53 per cent will be without access. Are children with books and a TV but no computer, CD-rom or modem condemned to be disadvantaged, the new poor in the Information Age? Will schools be able to make up the deficit?

The usual explanation for this rise in information technology (IT) sales is that consumers relate it strongly to career needs in themselves and as an essential educational tool for their children. Other theories have been suggested to explain the rapid increase in technology in the home. For example, Wavell (1995) and Neustatter (1992) believe that it is the parents' fear of the outside world which is partly responsible, and computers and televisions are provided for the children as forms of entertainment which the youngsters can enjoy 'safely' within the four walls of the home. At the same time, children in this age bracket are taken to school by adults in increasing numbers and are not allowed unsupervised play outside the home. Virtually every British home has at least one television; and now as many as 50 per cent of children aged 10–15 have a set in their room (Griffiths and Dancaster, 1995): 'creating in their bedrooms a whole new and safe adventure playground' (Wavell, 1995).

Part of the explosion of screen-based entertainment has been the emergence of home video and computer games. This is a relatively recent phenomenon but it has rapidly developed into a multi-million pound industry and has spawned a number of lucrative related markets for accessories, tie-in products and magazines. Since their first appearance in the UK approximately 25 years ago, there has been an extraordinary growth rate in the electronic games market and the technology has advanced to meet demands for ever more sophisticated software. The first home 'TV games' were produced commercially in the early 1970s and, with the introduction of the domestic version of the arcade game, Space Invaders, in 1979, soon began to attract mass popularity.

The arrival in the early 1980s of the low-priced ZX Spectrum, a fairly basic computer invented by Sir Clive Sinclair, which plugged into the back of a television set, effectively sparked off the home computer revolution in the UK. It was particularly attractive to male teenagers who were able to program it and play games they had designed themselves. However, its popularity declined with the advent in the late 1980s of consoles designed exclusively for game playing. Atari was the first manufacture to launch this kind of machine in the UK, but Sega and Nintendo quickly followed with their own 8-bit games consoles. In the early 1990s, the next generation of more powerful consoles was released by both the major companies. These new 16-bit machines with vastly improved computer graphics gradually edged out their 8-bit predecessors which have now virtually disappeared from the shops.

A distinction has been made by manufacturers between 'computer games' that are played on personal computers and 'video games' which are essentially the types of games played on dedicated consoles and hand-held machines. This distinction was not understood by the children in our study who referred to both types as 'computer games' so this has been adopted in this book as the generic term for both types of game.

The development of modern consoles and computer games can cost millions of pounds and requires a formidable range of talents on the design team such as game inventors, scriptwriters, musicians, artists and software and hardware engineers. There is fierce competition between the major computer games manufacturers like Sega and Nintendo and this has been intensified by the direct involvement of large media conglomerates such as Walt Disney, Virgin and Sony. There have been signs (the *Economist Intelligence Unit* (EIU), 1995; *Financial Times*, 1994; and the *Observer*, 1995) that computer game and console sales have started to decline and many toy retailers have abandoned the electronic games sector because of unacceptably low profit margins and the fear of being left with unsaleable, obsolete stock. Most games are now sold through large chains, specialist shops and electrical retailers. This decline in sales may have been partly due to the recession in the early 1990s, since both the hardware and the accessories are expensive compared to more traditional games and toys. Game playing can be extremely costly, taking into account the initial outlay on the console plus the additional expense of the games and replacement batteries (Game Boy, for example, uses four batteries in 20 hours and the Game Gear, with its colour screen, consumes batteries at the rate of six in 4 hours). However, much of the decline in sales can be attributed to the rapidly changing technology which has rendered the first generation of 8-bit consoles obsolete and it seems likely that sales of the following generation of 16-bit consoles has reached saturation point (EIU, 1995). In spite of falls in sales, this continues to be a highly lucrative market for the major players and they are constantly seeking ways of refining and developing their products to appeal to the widest possible audience. Two of the giants of the industry have recently poured huge sums of money into sophisticated systems where the software comes in the form of CDs (compact discs) rather than cartridges and the price (approx. £300–£350) reflects the level of technology. At this price, however, people are increasingly being tempted to opt for a more versatile PC system which offers them a much broader range of facilities. Many children in our study seemed to think that a PC was the next logical step up from their basic games console.

There is a relentless drive towards more realistic, life-like screen action, and games are now being designed which incorporate video images of human actors rather than relying on, albeit increasingly sophisticated, computer graphics. Virtual Reality machines have now arrived in the games arcades and it seems that the major manufacturers are envisaging this as the next generation of home entertainment systems for children. This option is becoming increasingly tempting as the price of PCs is falling. Rather disappointing sales of Windows 95, Microsoft's new operating system, has led some analysts to speculate that the PC market may be reaching saturation point in certain countries, particularly America. In the UK, however, high sales are predicted and the sales of computer games designed for CD-rom drives on PCs will quadruple. Computer games are clearly here to stay.

A letter to the *Times* (22 April 1995) from a 70-year-old Oxfordshire woman revealed her to be 'a granny who has become addicted to computer games', and, while undoubtedly there are many adults who enjoy playing, research suggests that the peak age at which interest is evident in the console games is from approximately 10–14 years). Wober and Fazal (1994) reported on the findings of a questionnaire study conducted by the Broadcasters Audience Research Board which showed that it was the 10–12 age group that demonstrated the greatest involvement in computer games. Another survey conducted by the British Market Research Bureau in October 1993 looked at 6437 participants in three age groupings (7–10, 11–14, and 15–19). Both play and ownership of games machines was highest in the 11–14 age group. The picture appears to be slightly different for PC games players who seem to belong mainly to the 16–35 age group. There is a paucity of demographic data (particularly with respect of very young children such as those participating in the present study), but it nevertheless seems clear that computer games are largely the province of the young. It is probably for this reason that there has been so much concern and alarm amongst parents and teachers about the possible harmful effects of exposure to such games.

Given the rapid and far reaching impact of computer games on children's leisure time, it is, perhaps, surprising that so little systematic research has been conducted into the phenomenon. In spite of the lack of strong corroborative evidence, there has been considerable speculation about the possible short- and long-term effects of computer game playing on children's social, cognitive, physical and emotional development. While claims have been made for both positive and negative consequences, it is, perhaps, not surprising that it is the potential detrimental effects which have been aired most widely and which are, therefore, more familiar to parents and teachers.

It is worthwhile including at this point, a note or two about video. The introduction and development of domestic video technology in Britain has been relatively rapid and pre-dated that of video game technology. Its major decade of expansion was truly phenomenal:

> Although the VCR has been around since the 1970s, it was not until 1980 that private ownership began to take off. Compared to 1979, when only negligible numbers of homes possessed a VCR, latest estimates reveal that more than half of individuals and nearly seven out of ten people with children have acquired a VCR. (Levy and Gunter, 1988)

> No other new communication technology has reached such dramatic levels of home penetration. (Communication Research Trends, 1985)

What was initially perceived as an innovative and expensive luxury is now considered a mere commonplace, being found in over 80 per cent of homes. It has played a considerable role in the expansion (indeed, explosion) in home entertainment, consolidating the place of the screen in people's lives. Users can appreciate at least four major applications which are now possible through home video: (1) watching pre-recorded films, concerts, training videos etc.; (2) recording from television to watch programmes at more convenient times; (3) building video libraries; (4) using TV screens for viewing home movies made on camcorders. It is becoming quite clear that what was once perceived as a simple receiver of broadcast signals, i.e., the television set, may now have as much, if not more, purpose as a monitor screen.

As families and individuals have welcomed this new concept of a variety of interrelated entertainments within the home, they have been willing to invest in increasingly sophisticated technologies. They are also willing to increase the number of television sets and video cassette recorders that they possess. It is not unusual for the various members of the family to be meeting their individual screen-based entertainment needs from each of the several different sources in the house simultaneously. And this includes the children. How children use videos, PCs or video-games machines is the question. What content do they prefer and who monitors it? What kind of critical appreciation do they have of its intent? As has been said already, **they** may regard such viewing as a form of play but adults' views can conflict greatly, in this regard.

Children devote much of their time and energy to the business of playing and most adults would probably agree that this is a valuable and worthwhile part of growing up. Where agreement amongst adults can break down is on the question of defining the nature and function of play. A distinction is often drawn in Western societies between 'work' and 'play' with play being seen as a voluntary activity which is absorbing, fun and done for its own sake without any intrinsic reward. This distinction is, however, not as clear-cut as it may first seem. For example, parents waiting for their offspring at the school gates are frequently dismayed to be told by their children that they have 'just been playing all day'. Teachers would almost certainly describe those same activities in rather different terms. Most of us would probably feel that we intuitively **know** what sort of activities can legitimately count as play even if a completely acceptable and comprehensive definition is elusive. Garvey (1977) has provided a useful starting point by compiling a list of features which characterize many instances of play, including those of enjoyment, positive emotions, personal reward, spontaneity, active involvement, and the fact that it is set aside from real life — it is not meant to be taken literally and so it does not lead to the usual consequences that would follow if it were real (i.e., **real** fighting, **real** cooking, **real** nursing).

Parents and teachers generally seem to see play as a healthy and necessary part of the child's world which provides benefits in the form of relaxation, an outlet for imagination and creativity and a preparation and practice for later life skills. Sluckin in 1981, before computer and video technology could possibly have made a significant impact, observed that children's play was often constrained and directed by other children rather than being spontaneous and freely engaged in. Play activities have long been known to include fighting, bullying and taunting behaviours which are neither enjoyable nor intrinsically rewarding, at least for the 'victim'.

It is clear then that the term 'play' encompasses a rich variety of behaviours — not all of them uplifting and of obvious benefit to the child — and that this observation pre-dated the arrival of the computer game on the play scene. This is not to say that children have abandoned so-called traditional games, even though this idea seems to have widespread currency. Peter and Iona Opie, over 26 years ago, noted that this idea is not restricted to the present generation: 'The belief that traditional games are dying out is in itself traditional' (Opie and Opie, 1969). There are numerous examples from our own study of children actively choosing and enjoying familiar, 'old-fashioned' pastimes — skipping, conkers, hide and seek, chasing games on the playground and, outside school, bike riding, playing on swings and slides, board games, dressing-up, playing with dolls, etc. However, we have an unusual paradox developing in play, involving simulated realities on the screen (and later to be intensified via virtual reality) in that on-screen 'play' may leave less to the imagination and has a graphic capability to present extremes of human behaviour. One cannot say that books and comics afford children this degree of explicitness.

There seems little doubt that while some parents (and politicians) do not see screen-based activities as a form of play, others do. Attitudes to play are enmeshed in attitudes to childhood itself. One can find a spectrum of parenting behaviours, in a research study such as this, related to bringing up children. This spectrum ranges from highly protective and controlled domestic environments at one end of the scale, through to the *laissez faire* and the helpless. In schools in this research, the strong tendency was towards protection and control. Within these latter environments, there appeared to be a high degree of disdain for most forms of popular media such as TV soaps, rented videos and computer games. Practically all the teachers in our study were women and therefore antipathy to popular culture could easily be associated with these role models.

We mentioned earlier that gender seems to be an issue in children's use of entertainment technology, particularly that relating to computer games. In brief, research findings then and since suggest that there are indeed areas in which the sexes differ from one another but these differences may not be as great or as deeply embedded as is popularly believed. They include work on physical attributes, personality characteristics and cognitive abilities. Nevertheless, the findings are often contradictory and relate more to popular stereotyping than to valid measurement. However, even if the differences are small, it is a phenomenon worthy of interest, particularly from the point of view of what causes them. The major controversy centres on the debate about the relative contribution of biological factors as opposed to social and cultural factors. Researchers in the field of screen technology are interested in seeing whether boys and girls actually behave differently in their interaction with the technology because of their very gender and/or whether teachers, parents and commercial agents influence them to behave differently. There is also considerable interest in the content of computer games and video material and the possible role it plays in fostering and maintaining gender stereotypes.

For example, the feature of game and video content that was most frequently mentioned by teachers and parents concerned violence and aggression. Past research findings indicate that boys and girls differ both in their levels of aggression and ways of manifesting it. However, research into the effects of violent computer games on levels of aggression in players has so far been fairly sparse and inconclusive. There has been a much longer history of research into the effects of violence on television and there are possiblely enough parallels between the two types of medium to draw similar conclusions. Many researchers would claim that there is a link between aggression on television and aggressive behaviour and attitudes in children but establishing the precise nature of that link is difficult. Even if a link is established, the mechanism by which children are affected has certainly not yet been determined. One influential theory which still holds great sway today (Bandura, Ross and Ross, 1963), has suggested that aggressive behaviour is acquired through a process of social learning. In other words, the child becomes sex-typed through behavioural reinforcement and imitation of appropriate models. However, it would seem likely that this is only one possible process and that different factors operate depending on the circumstances. Another suggestion is that of attitudinal change whereby children become so used to television violence that they come to see aggression as less unacceptable and are, therefore, more likely to engage in aggressive behaviour themselves.

Whatever the answer, studies have generally demonstrated that boys and girls are affected rather differently by exposure to screen events. It is difficult to carry out methodologically sound research on this question, both in the field of television and video games, because of the number of possible confounding variables. If, for example, social learning is seen to be an important underlying mechanism for absorbing aggression into the behavioural repertoire, there is the problem that most aggressive protagonists on television are male. It would, therefore, be expected within social learning that males are more likely to be affected by these models than girls even though it has been demonstrated that girls, as well as boys, tend to imitate male role models as readily as female models. There is also a difficulty with the theory linking heightened arousal to aggressive behaviour; over-exposure to violent images tends to dampen physiological arousal so that heavy watchers will display lower levels in response to new violence than control subjects. It would, therefore, follow that children who watch the least violence (and this could include girls) are more likely to be aroused by one exposure than those who watch more. This makes it difficult to interpret findings from laboratory studies where children's play activity is observed after a single exposure to a video game but some interesting findings have been reported. One study did indeed demonstrate that girls showed more general activity and aggressive free play after playing an aggressive video game (Cooper and Mackie, 1986).

Some studies (for example, Winkel, Novak and Hopson, 1987) have shown that personality factors may be more important than gender differences in predicting behaviour following from playing on games with a violent content. They found that girls who were reserved and self-assured were more likely to be aggressive than those who were warm-hearted and guilt prone. Links have also been demonstrated between the amount of time spent playing on computer games and levels of aggression (for example, Fling, Smith, Rodriguez, Thornton, Atkins and Nixon, 1992). However, as with all such studies, some caution needs to be exercised in the interpretation of the data. It could simply be that more aggressive children are drawn to video-game playing and not that game playing actually causes the aggression in the first place.

In general, as members of a society, we connect media content with consequential behaviour, although we can't prove the causal connections. The vast outlay on the advertising of products on television assumes the link to be there, as does a school's choice of books in a library, a parent's decision to take a child to church or a documentary film about poverty in Bangladesh. What seems to be of relevance in this study is the overall culture of video usage and games playing; the content; who figure in it as significant role models; what sort of environments promote it, and; what seem to be the consequences for the eventual use of information technologies in school and, later, in work.

Following this introduction to the main themes of the book and the contexts of technology, play and gender which underpin these themes, we hope that the following chapters lead the reader into the complexity of the lives of children in a way which illuminates their thinking, their feelings and their day-to-day experiences. What can then be asked concerns the consequences of this illumination for educators and parents.

The Land of H

In the following extracts, a picture is built of the possibilities that abound for screen-based entertainment technology to impregnate the imagination of the child ('H'). Some might argue for the harmful effects and some for the beneficial. We have included extracts of the interviews because they typify the idiosyncrasies that we met everywhere, even if this 7-year-old is massively atypical in his screen-based media interests. H is capable of differentiating visual material in accordance with film classification; he has seen a great variety of films, from children's to adults'; he negotiates with adults over his schooling and his family life; and, most of the time, he is allowed to have his own way. In this last respect he is certainly not untypical. Please note that throughout this book 'R' refers to the researcher during reported conversations.

Part One

H is a pupil in Class 3 of a first school. When first interviewed, his general demeanour deceived the researcher. Gently offhand and sometimes slow in delivery, his apparently casual approach belied a considerable knowledge, a quick mind and, at times a twinkling sense of humour. The first recorded conversation took place in the school staffroom. There were no other people present and no interruptions. This was the first time the researcher (R) and H had spoken to each other, apart from the formal preliminaries. Neither had the researcher discussed H with the headteacher or class teacher. The reason that he had been identified as one of our case studies was no different from that of other pupils responding positively to the initial request for participants: in other words, H had video and computer technology in his home environment.

> *R*: Can you tell me your name?
> *H*: I'm just going to pick up my sensible voice. Erm ... the name's 'H'.
> *R*: Right and how old are you?
> *H*: Nearly 8.

Other information about H, his family and friends was offered during the interview. He lives at home with his mother and father — 'they look after children, but I haven't got any brothers or sisters'. He plays a lot with S, his next-door neighbour, who is $7^1/_2$ years old. H's father is a postman who is away from the house for long periods of time. His granddad and nanny ('my mum's mum') live in a bungalow opposite; just over the [busy] road.

H talked at length about how he used his computers at home — on his own, with S and other friends — and his mother's attitude to personal computers and games. When asked what else he did when he'd finished with, or tired of, his computers, he said that at around 7:00 pm he watched TV, mainly Sky. It was revealed during the course of the research that H had a considerable need for childish things, things that some people might think were 'too young for him'. He then talked about other regular habits:

> *R*: Right. So, in the morning, if you're waking up at 6 ... that's on a Saturday though, is it ... you wake up at 6?
> *H*: No, other days I wake up at half past.
> *R*: Right and then might you watch telly while you are in bed?
> *H*: Might.
> *R*: What else might you do?
> *H*: Well, I normally watch in the morning. They're all about making of the films or how the films are done, or the UK or the USA or the London new chart.
> *R*: They're all on cable TV?
> *H*: Sky.
> *R*: And do you play with your computers at the weekend?
> *H*: Yes, normally.
> *R*: Do you ever play with your parents on the computers?
> *H*: No. My mum doesn't like it. My dad usually goes to the pub.
> *R*: And you watch your videos at the weekend?
> *H*: Yes. Um ... nearly every two hours if the film's good.

Here is the first indication of H's love of the media. Like many children in the survey, he wanted to know how films are made. This seems to be a necessary critical vantage point for young viewers: 'the blood is only tomato sauce' syndrome. H revealed a liking for not only children's (including younger children's) TV programmes, videos and other artefacts, but also for (mainly Hollywood) movies. It was when he was invited to talk about his tastes in films and videos, that an extensive knowledge and vocabulary were revealed.

> *R*: Do you have any videos that are your favourite videos?
> *H*: Yes I have plenty.
> *R*: Tell me about your favourite video.
> *H*: My favourite video is *Curly Sue*.
> *R*: Was that recorded off television?
> *H*: Recorded ... yes.
> *R*: And which channel was that shown on originally?
> *H*: Sky, the Movie Channel.

R: And it lasts ... what ... about an hour and a half?

H: No ... 98 minutes.

R: And who's in it?

H: James Belushi; new star, Alison Porter and Kelly Lynch.

R: Who directed it?

H: Er ... I thinks it's John Hucks.

R: And when was it made?

H: 1991.

R: And how long have you had it on videotape?

H: October 1993.

R: How do you remember it was October 1993?

H: Well, something between October and December, something between then.

R: So it was around your birthday time was it?

H: Yeah.

This amount of factual (and accurate) detail came as a surprise to the researcher. No other children questioned in the research programme had revealed quite such a comprehensive awareness of the media products themselves. He talks here about a favourite 3D cartoon.

R: Tell me again about the bits coming out of the screen. It is ... is it because it's in a 3D cinema?

H: No it's a 3D ... it's a cartoon which is 3D that's all. Um ...

R: Have you ever seen a 3D film?

H: Yes I have.

R: Where, where did you see that?

H: I've got a video, a 3D video.

R: Is it a film with people in it?

H: No, cartoon characters ... 3D ... and there's two real people.

R: Is it a full length or a short film?

H: A short film.

R: And what kind of glasses do you have to put on? Is one lens green and the other one red?

H: Yeah. No, blue and red.

R: Blue and red. And that gives you a 3D effect?

H: Yeah.

R: Does it work quite well?

H: No it doesn't work too well, it looks like it's normal screen, but it **used** to look really ... like it's going to jump at you and there's this big spider what's going to do this and climb upon your face.

R: And why doesn't it work so well now?

H: Well ... um ... when the spider comes ... it just stays ... it just climbs ... it looks like it's just climbing on your floor, not coming in your face.

R: Would you like it to come to your face?

15

H: Huh! Specially not.
R: I mean in the film.
H: Not in real life?
R: No.
H: But . . . um . . . in the glasses. Yes, it would . . . it would be funny.

H demonstrated in this and other conversations his ready and sophisticated ability to distinguish between:

1   Empathizing with characters and situations in 'realistic' situations in the films/videos.
2   Perceiving them as fictional constructs.

In this, he was similar to the majority of the children we met. They were always very excited over differences between screen depictions and reality and how much they were drawn into the plot. It was when H had the opportunity to discuss videos and films of a more adult nature that he appeared consciously to steer a careful path between his knowledge of, and his experience of, certain movies.

R: Are there any other things that frightened you in films?
H: Frightened me, frightened me. (*Long pause*) The videos I'm not supposed to see. I looked at the front cover of them and they frightened me.
R: Right. The front cover on the box? On the video box?
H: Yeah.
R: Like what, do you know?
H: One that my dad's watched and he says it's really horrible.
R: Right, so that's at home?
H: Yes . . . um . . .

And it was at this stage that H started quite naturally (and without any further prompting from the researcher) to introduce the specific classifications of films and videos into the conversation:

H: 18. Well I normally watch Sky films like 12 and 15 and I don't really should have watched them, but I don't watch them anymore.
R: Why did you watch them. Because you wanted to?
H: No; because some nights children stay up late and that was the only thing on. There are some films like 12 and 15 what are not too bad.
R: Like what?
H: Like *Uncle Buck* and . . . um and cutting out those swear words and the rude bits in *Pretty Woman*, it's not too bad; and there is a video when they cut out those bits.
R: Yeah.
H: 'Cos it was on at 7 o'clock till 9.
R: Have you seen any 12 or 15 films that have frightened you?

H: Frightened me? 12. This one's a 12 film that frightened me once . . . erm . . . I saw it last night, I think it was 15; it was a 12. Ah . . . um . . . *The Amy Fisher Story* . . . . It's true . . . true (meaning that it was based on a true story) and there's one called . . . um . . . *Fatal Justice* and . . . er . . . that frightened me a bit.

R: What do you do if you are watching something that's frightening you? Can you switch it off?

H: Yes, but some . . . now I'm a bit used to it. But there's one thing, *Ghostbusters* it's not so spooky frightening, but it is . . . . *Ghostbusters I* and *Ghostbusters II*.

R: What frightened you — the ghosts themselves?

H: No it's just . . . even my mum says, 'Its horrible'. And she said '*Mrs Doubtfire*, it might just have a swear word in; but if you see *Ghostbusters* that's more worse than one swear word.'

R: Do you think she's right?

H: I think she's right. I've been trying for weeks to get it PG . . . and I have. I've got it.

R: Got what?

H: I've made the film PG.

R: How have you done that?

H: Send it to the Cannon Cinema and they decided probably.

R: Oh, right.

There was considerable public pressure in the county to get the initial certification of *Mrs Doubtfire* changed from 12 to PG. The campaign of sending in letters (which H joined in) was successful. Despite H's knowledge of a wide range of films, particularly adult ones, it was noticeable that whenever H had the chance to talk about his favourites he referred to popular children's choices. But he had his sticking point:

H: My second best was *Home Alone 2* because it's funny and anything. I like anything . . . comedy, drama, anything really . . . except for horror.

R: You don't like horror?

H: No I don't . . . I don't . . . like *Freddy's Dead* — that's horrible.

R: Have you seen it?

H: No, I've seen pictures of it. I've seen adverts of it but I would never like to see it.

R: You don't want to see it?

H: No, like . . . and *Puppet Master* I wouldn't want to see that . . . *Friday the Thirteenth* . . .

R: How do you know about these films?

H: Well, I've always looked at the paper and our book and I ever since liked them as well. I went round my granddad's and asked him to record *Suburban Commando* and when he recorded *Suburban Commando* he put it on till 10 o'clock; and at 9:30 . . . no, 9:40 . . . there was these two adverts.

Half past nine, there was *Mr Nanny* advert and half past four . . . Nine forty . . . there was the *UK Top Ten* and it was full of a bit of horror film.

R: UK Top Ten videos?

H: Films.

R: So it would have some adult films as well?

H: Yep.

R: And it would show clips?

H: Yeh.

R: So you saw those?

H: Yeah. Well, there was a film called *Blink* what's new out and *Schindler's List*.

R: Right.

H: And . . . um . . .

R: What do you do if you see something by accident that's a bit frightening? Do you go and talk to somebody about it?

H: Well, my granddad he watched *Patriot Games* and that's a bit frightening. And my mum said she's going to rent out *Piano*, I don't mind seeing that cos it's a bit . . . it's not violent. It's just . . .

In all this talk of what might be called *material unsuitable for children*, the focus was usually on violence and frightening texts. Sex and sexually inappropriate scenes were rarely mentioned: when they were mentioned by H, he passed over them as 'rude bits'. What is worth noting is the way that children are able to build up their stock of knowledge concerning particular films or computer games from peripheral information. They are very used to reading advertisements and — a key issue in this book — adopting consumer roles. They triangulate the information they receive from friends, parents, magazines and television.

Now, to bed-time routines and activities:

R: What time do you normally go to bed?

H: Well, it depends what night.

R: So you don't have a regular bedtime?

H: No, because it doesn't matter what time I go to bed because if I go to bed I can still watch a film because I have got a television and a video in there and a cable box.

R: So you can watch cable?

H: Yeah, I can still watch cable.

R: So you have cable TV at home that has all the satellite channels on it?

H: Yeah, all the satellite channels.

R: So you can . . . you can watch anything you want when you are in bed?

H: Anything. Sometimes if daddy looks in the paper and says that's too rude he cuts it off.

R: Oh, so he can stop it coming to your bedroom?

H: Yeah. But if it's really rude like some rude bits . . . really rude he cuts it off but if he doesn't it's not too rude he never does. He says he will but he never does.

R: So have you ever been in bed and had the telly on later in the evening and something has come on which has been rude or been frightening or . . . ?

H: Or violent.

R: Or violent?

H: Well, once I woke up and my mum was sitting across in the chair watching it. It was a bit violent um I hated it. It was this man and a thing with all spikes in it; it crushed him to bits, it was horrible so I went back to sleep.

R: Right.

H: Some films give me bad dreams.

R: Even though you know they're just films?

H: Yeah, even though.

R: So, if we're in your bedroom with you at night seeing what's on the telly and something comes on that's perhaps a bit violent what do you do, do you switch off or do you go and talk to your mum and dad?

H: Well, I wouldn't mind if there was something good um something kind of mixed . . . like if someone was trying to kill this man if he wants his wife, that's alright but . . . um . . .

R: Why is that alright?

H: Because really it's only film; it's not true. But if a film what has really been horrible disgusting . . . um . . . not disgusting in a disgusting way, but disgusting in a children's way.

And that could very well be the alternative heading for a study of young people and frightening moving images: 'Disgusting in a Children's Way'. They can be very aware of the different conventions that children and adults have in entertainment. H, like many children in the study, spent much of his time unsupervised. His bedroom was his private world. He was able to talk with some expertise about the many special effects to be found in movies. As can be seen below, although he understood how they were constructed and utilized, he was also affected by them within the context of the story. This again illustrates his ability to appreciate screen events in at least two different ways at the same time:

R: And do you know how they do things like that?

H: Yes.

R: How do they do . . . if a man is crushed by spikes how do they do that in films?

H: Special effects.

R: So you know all about that.

H: Yeah, like *The Bodyguard*. It is a bit violent but I still watched it.

The conversation seemed to dwell on the more vivid, violent and memorable aspects of films, which seemed to lead quite naturally into the area of action movies: he revealed he had seen a number of adult action movies, many of which had an

18-certificate. When asked again about which videos he kept, which were in his collection, the ones he described were again human interest and drama films which had children in key roles; children as stars. However, when it came to films which challenged his fear or 'disgust' threshold, H seemed to have no problem with the fact that his appreciation of a 'mature' film text was sometimes different from that of an adult in his family. He was aware of the ways in which a text could be interpreted. This leads into an exploration of the mode of viewing, when such films are on. As in this case:

R: So what do you do when the film might be on?
H: Muck about; go and have a drink probably, and come back to it.
R: And you don't pause it? You let it keep running and go off?
H: Yeah. Well my mum normally gets up. Well . . .
R: But for your favourite films, you'll watch them from the beginning to the end, will you?
H: Yeah.
R: Or will you wander in and out of the room?
H: The ones . . . if I've seen it, if I've seen it twice maybe I would once. The third time, I just sit down and watch it.
R: Why's that?
H: Because it's . . . I don't know why. Just if I didn't like it the second time I would like to the third time though. When I watched the *Man Without a Face* the first time I cried, the second time I didn't and the third time I did.
R: Why is that?
H: Because. I just don't know really.
R: Why didn't you cry the second time?
H: I just . . . I thought 'Well you could cry next time and he didn't have such a bad life after all.'

After saying that one of his favourite videos was *Sleepless in Seattle*, which was a PG, though regarded as an adult film, H was drawn into a discussion of certification. In this he again revealed knowledge which typified the young's preoccupation with rules and their status *vis à vis* other ages. There is kudos in watching films designated for older people but there are also pitfalls. Children are often caught between the opposing forces of showing-up well against their peer group and their own fears and desires to be controlled.

R: Parent Guidance. Right. What do you think about the classification system where they have different numbers on different videos like PG and 12 and 15? Do you think it's a good idea?
H: Well, sometimes I do agree with what should be 15 or 18 or 12 and some films I agree with are 12 what should be PG also.
R: Do you know of any other children who watch films that are 15 or 18?
H: S does; and another one . . . E?

R: Why — don't their parents mind?

H: No.

R: So what has S seen, that's been 18? [S is a boy; E is a girl]

H: I don't know I haven't asked him.

R: But he says he has?

H: He's seen *Troll* . . . *Troll* . . . *Troll* . . .

R: *Troll*?

H: Yes, horrible. Hate it.

R: So he's seen films that are meant for grown ups?

H: Yeah.

R: Right.

H: I think *Troll* shouldn't be 15, it should be 18.

Part Two

The second meeting took place soon afterwards. There was no formal interview. While the rest of the class had reading time, H was working quietly in a corner of the room with his partner (a girl) for the task in hand. It was an opportunity for the researcher to examine H's latest work in the classroom and gain a picture of him from his teacher's point of view. Some word-processed work (produced jointly with one other pupil) was displayed on the wall and there were several interesting sheets in his work tray, including a story entitled 'The Big Chill'. The influences of film are clearly demonstrated in the extract from the five-page story in Figure 1.1.

Underneath the school worksheets in the tray was a current 'Satellite Guide' magazine, without cover. The itemized film pages in the magazine had many individual movies highlighted in blue or black ball-point pen. On one page they included *Peeping Tom*, and *Lethal Lolita* (aka *The Amy Fisher Story*). When asked, it wasn't clear whether those pen marks were made by H or his father. The question was not laboured. His class teacher (T) provided an interesting perspective on H; his personality and his behaviour. She was interviewed by two researchers (R1 and R2) in her classroom while her pupils were elsewhere.

R1: I was particularly interested in the story that H has been writing.

Teacher: He came in yesterday and said, 'Can I write a play?' This is what he does . . . so I said 'Yes'. I don't know what it's about though; I don't know anything about it.

R1: He often writes plays, does he?

Teacher: He sits and writes . . . not often plays . . . **anything** . . . prose, poetry . . . but the last thing he did on the computer was . . . well, I think the disk was faulty and also the memory must have been full . . . because we lost half of it. It was so much! It was pages and pages long and the computer couldn't cope with it.

R1: Was he disappointed?

Figure 1.1: 'The Big Chill'

pete JR ~~have~~ HAVe you seen CAThy
BOTn HAYe you seen CAThy
By ~~any~~ CHANCe.
GiLBeRT we weRe Going To see iF
she was in The BiG BiG crlill
peTe JR come on let's go
Vicky yoRe TO young
GiBeRt NO ILL go in FiRST but
·I Am The tomBeD

Vicky peTe JR OK OK OK OK
we went in
~~peT~~ GiLBeRT KaTHy KaThy KATby
Vicky KAThy KATny KATny ~~l~~ATny
KAThey Help Help Help Help
Vicky GiBeRT Help Help Help
~~He~~ I got TheRe BuE Vicky
was gone wiLh The wiND
KAThy WheReS vick
GiLBeRT She'sGone

Teacher:	He was, yes. And we did try. I mean there might be a little bit of it still there, but it was ... um ... He needed a clean disk really, and he just sat and wrote this long, long, long, long, long, long, long story.
R2:	And this one. (*Indicating 'The Big Chill'*) The title was his as well?
Teacher:	Yes.
R1:	His friend is writing it with him, is she?
Teacher:	Yes. Yes. N and him just decided to do it together, I don't know why.

R1: Does she often work with him?

Teacher: No, no. No, no. It's just something that she thought: 'Oh, that looks good fun . . . I'll try that with him.'

R1: So we don't know if it's based on something they've seen or . . .

Teacher: I should think H is the main ideas input. It's probably something he's seen somewhere. I haven't read it to be honest. (*Laughs*) I don't know . . . he presents them to me pages long and full and I take them and read them and make them into a book . . . (*She walks around the classroom looking for examples of H's work on the walls*) . . . This is one of his. This is a 'Magic Key' story. It's quite short for him. But he did two 'Magic Key' stories, in fact — so he's quite happy to do short stories.

R2: That was with N again . . . a co-production.

Teacher: Do you know. I hadn't realized that. Perhaps they do like working together then and I hadn't made the connection . . . because with thirty-one in the class, you miss things.

R1: How did they have the stimulus material? Was it read to them?

Teacher: Yes . . . these are reading books of theirs and . . . they're long stories. This is the first one. These kids are always in the reading stories right from the early books. There's three of them actually. There's Chip, Kipper and Biff . . . and there's Wilma and Will, who are black kids, and there's Aneena and Nadeem, who are Asian kids — so there's a nice mix . . . a nice cultural mixture. When these two move to a new house, they find a secret room with an old doll's house in and a tree blows down in the garden and underneath there's an old box with a magic key in it . . . and when it starts to glow they go on adventures . . .

R1: And so H and N would have read this themselves . . . as part of their reading scheme . . . and this is their rewriting of the story?

Teacher: No. Some of them use the stories they've read in books. Some of them use their own stories.

R1: To do with Magic Keys?

Teacher: Yes. It was all to do with the Magic Key. As I say, some of them have their own adventures. Some of them simply rewrote a story they'd remembered from their reading books.

R2: And H made up his own presumably, did he?

Teacher: Yes. He usually does . . . yes.

R1: Where would you place H in terms of academic abilities?

Teacher: Oh, he's very very high up . . . yes . . . I think he's very academic.

R1: All round? Number . . . ?

Teacher: Yes . . . he doesn't particularly take much interest in maths. He'll do what he has to and then he'll shoot back and want to write a story. If it's Choosing Time, he says 'Can I write?' He wants to write a story.

R1: What's his artwork like?

Teacher: Um ... a bit ... it's nice, but he doesn't take much interest in it now and it can be very clumsy like that ... but when he did draw, his pictures were very interesting.

R1: In what way?

Teacher: Well, they were well thought out, original ... slightly odd ... you know.

R1: So, he has quite an imagination?

Teacher: Yes, he has. He's fed on films a lot ... and I think he's often watched films perhaps he shouldn't watch ... I don't know ... He goes to the cinema an awful lot with his mum and dad. I think they take him along to Cinema City or wherever and they watch films.

R1: He gave me a very careful version of his life last week.

Teacher: Very likely. He is an extremely able child ... and I would think he's probably in the top three or four in this class.

R1: Really! I totally underestimated him.

Teacher: Yes, he's easy to underestimate because he's stodgy, but I think he is very, very bright and able ... Like with the maths, I'll explain something and he'll go and he's got it and he'll do it as quick as he can just to get back to his writing.

R1: When you talk to some children, they interact a lot with their body and they're attentive and so on ... it seemed to me when I talked to H that he was very passive. He was taking in the information, but he doesn't give a lot away through his body language.

Teacher: No, no, no ... he doesn't.

R1: So is he less dynamic than other children in that sense?

Teacher: No. He's just an original thinker, I think. He doesn't fit in with the routine at all and I let him go his own way. Sort of — if we are sitting on the carpet usually you see H out of the corner of your eye doing something else. The kids are used to it so they don't mind.

R1: So he chose not to come and sit over here? He chose to write?

Teacher: Yes. He chose to go back to do his script, yes.

R1: Was that negotiated with you?

Teacher: In a sort of an unsaid way. Sometimes he knows that if he's doing something specific he can just get on with it, because he's a wonderful reader. He's got absolutely no problems reading. He must have a reading age of at least a 10-year-old, I think. So, I mean, quite often he enjoys quiet reading sessions anyway because he's ... I sort of introduce new books to him every so often ... but when he's got something like this on he really wants to be getting on with that.

R1: How does he get on with the other pupils in the class?

Teacher: Well, they all quite like him, but he's always the one who doesn't have a partner and things like that. But if you say 'Can you ... will you be H's partner?', they all say 'Yes'. They don't say 'No'. He

just doesn't . . . he seems to be very much a loner. He doesn't seem
to need a special friend.

R2: Does he stay in at playtime and write?

Teacher: If he could, he wouldn't go out at all. He'd stay in all the time;

Within this extract there are glimpses of further issues which dominated the research.
There is the loss of work on the computer in the classroom — breakdowns and
inadequate technology, together with inexpert teacher knowledge were common
findings. We have the computer as a source of collaborative work, even with a child
who is regarded as a loner. And there is evidence that an interest in popular culture,
supported by parents and tolerated by the teacher, allows the child expansive expression and great motivation, which can cross over into other work.

Part Three

On each visit to the house, H's mother was welcoming and cooperative. She offered
excellent homemade cake with the tea. H has no siblings, but is used to children
in the house: a good friend of a similar age lives next door and is always dropping
in, and his mother is a childminder, with regular clients. The house is used to the
sounds and activities of children. As well as the TV, VTR and channel decoder in
the living room, there is a personal computer set up with games for easy access.
H's mother obviously likes having children in the house; there are wall charts and
toys for children younger than H inside the house as well as lots of things to play
in, on and with in the garden. She does not share her son's interest in entertainment
technology: she prefers to read rather than watch much television, and does not use
the computer. She does, however, enjoy taking H to the cinema to see children's
films. They often go to the Regional Film Theatre on a Saturday afternoon.

H's father was also friendly and chatty. He was aware of many of his son's
interests; it 'could be' that H got his love of the cinema from his father. When he
was a lad he used to regularly see films, he remembered the certification system
then: U, A, and X. Because they couldn't get into an X-film, he and his friends
would stand outside an exit and listen to the soundtrack. Although he claimed not
to watch many movies nowadays, H reminded him that he'd planned to record Ken
Russell's *The Devils* off television that evening. There were certain favourite films
which he repeatedly viewed: *High Noon* ('a good movie'); *Darling* (H spoke up:
'I've seen that, Dad', 'Yes'); and *Don't Look Now* (H: 'I saw the beginning of that
. . .'). He lived in Canada for ten years, then in America. He went to the Woodstock
Festival. His records and other related ephemera reflect his interests and commit-
ments in those times. It was much easier for him to talk about his life and interests
than it was of those of his son. When the Children's TV programme *Barney and
Friends* was mentioned in passing by H, his father was critical of him watching
such childish stuff.

It was interesting to see the range of artefacts that were arrayed in H's bedroom
and the adjoining upstairs room. A guided tour for the benefit of the researcher and

his camcorder revealed, amongst many other things, a wealth of toys, games, books, magazines, posters and videotapes. On the bedroom door was displayed a large *Sleepless in Seattle* poster. On his neatly made bed — in fact the whole room was very neat despite the number of the contents — were at least eight small cuddly Teddy bears, and nearby a larger cuddly Babar. Over the bed were mobiles and dotted round the room decorative balloons: including ones of *Jurassic Park* and Ernie from *Sesame Street*. By the window, on the wall were five well-posed, well-framed photographs of H at differing ages. Extremely impressive were the neat piles of books on bedside tables as well as very neat, well-packed shelves of books.

When asked which book he was reading at the moment H pulled out, as if at random from a shelf away from his bed which contained many children's books, *The Firm* by John Grisham.

H: I'm up to here. (*He indicated a page four-fifths of the way into the novel*)
R: Do you recommend it?
H: It's OK.
R: Is the film on video yet?
H: Yes. It is.
R: Have you seen it?
H: No. No.

The researcher was not, and is not, clear in his own mind as to how much — if any — of the book H had read. From the floor by the bed, H picks up a copy of *Cable Guide*. Holding it up to the camera the front cover is revealed with the headline 'LOCK UP YOUR MEN!' partially superimposed over the face of a young woman. 'This is new, because my old one has run out'.

R: And what goodies are there in there for this month?
H: Well, my dad's recording *Patriot Games* tonight.

On top of the high bookshelves lay about fifteen boxed board games, including, at the bottom, *Monopoly*. H says that he plays them with 'anybody who comes round'. His parents? Sometimes. His friend next door? Yeh . . . they mostly play *Monopoly*. He proudly holds up his 'piano', an electronic keyboard, though doesn't play it. Neither does he accept the invitation to strum the guitar resting by the other shelves: 'I'm not very good at it. My dad plays.' On one of the shelves is a set of children's educational videotapes: twelve cassettes looking brand new. Has he used them? 'I have watched some of them.' On top of these shelves sits a portable television, facing the top of the bed, a VTR and a decoder. It's indicating Channel Number 32. How many channels can you get altogether? 'It goes up to 36, but some are scrambled.'

Next door is an even smaller room in which are shelved H's father's record collection — many of the albums were collected in the 1960s and 1970s in North America. On one of the shelves are crammed many pre-recorded videocassettes, mainly PG-classification (including *Ghostbusters*, *Starman*, *Parenthood*, *Mr Nanny*,

Bright Lights, Big City (18) and, interestingly, *The Big Chill*). They 'mostly' belonged to H. The chest of drawers holds, amongst other things, videocassettes: many of them with off-air recordings. Between the drawers and a bed-settee is situated a 'Killer Hamster' in sectioned accommodation. On the opposite wall are the shelves and floorspace where H keeps his Sega and Commodore computers with their associated games (including, for the Sega, *Batman Returns*).

Part Four

A week after talking to H in the classroom for the second time and also discussing him with his teacher, the researcher returned to the school. H was very keen to show his latest story, which was handwritten on many sheets of paper. Since it was not in an easily photocopiable state, H was invited to read it out into the hand-held audiocassette recorder. This he did, reasonably fluently. Much of what he said was already written down, but at times he augmented the tale. On this occasion the interaction took place amid the general hubbub of activity in a corner of the classroom. Apart from one interruption by a classmate seeking audio attention, H's reading progressed as transcribed. He preferred to stand. He was pleased with his work.

> *H:* Well, I watched this on television and then I read the novel . . . (*Pause*) . . . and I . . .
>
> *R:* When did you write this?
>
> *H:* A couple of days ago.
>
> (*A little later*)
>
> *R:* Right — what I would like is for you to read me this story. Can you do that? What's it called?
>
> *H:* It's called *IT*.
>
> *R:* *IT*.
>
> *H:* In the film, Tim Cle . . . **Curry** plays the clown.
>
> *R:* Is this based on the film?
>
> *H:* Yes . . . based on the novel by Shep-ten King. (*Pause*)

> *IT* by Shep-ten King;
> Chapter One: 'The Murders'
> In 1600, two hundred children set out on an Easter Egg Hunt that Easter. But there was a castle . . . a big castle. 150 children went in the castle to find Easter Eggs, but they never came out. It . . . It was they whose . . . It: a clown. Why would a clown eat children? He has big teeth and eats children. Fifty of them are alive.

[The story is several pages, in two parts, with several chapters in each part and end.]

> Chapter Three: 'The End of Pennisworth, The Killer Clown'
> When we went in his Castle and Pennisworth was a big spider.

Beth missed a second but . . . Beth missed a second but then she got her stone back and fired and hu . . . and hunted it and it walked away, but we said it might come back in when we're seventy. So we digged into its body and it never came back. And me and Beth . . . 'cos Ben, it's just him telling the story . . . and me and Beth got married and Mick fell in love and he . . . and . . . and Mick got his love of his life back.

R: Wonderful.
H: That's the end.
R: Thanks very much.
H: Right.

The researcher then asked about the source of this material. How recently had H seen the film?

H: Last Tuesday . . . Wednesday. Tuesday **and** Wednesday.
R: Which channel was it on?
H: Sky . . . it was on Sky . . . Sky One Sixteen.
R: What time was it on?
H: It was on 8 o'clock; Tuesday and Wednesday.
R: And what certificate was it?
H: I don't know. I think it was 18.
R: Oh, right. (*Pause*) Was it frightening?
H: Yeh, it was. It was a bit . . .
R: Did you watch it on your own?
H: Yeh. And mum . . . she said, 'I don't want to watch this'.

Stephen King's *IT* is a horror movie originally made for television in two parts. It is available as a three-hour video (certificate-15) for hire or purchase. It has been shown on television. The researcher viewed the video (and skimmed the original novel) with the specific intent of comparison (and contrast) with H's story. Starring Tim Curry as Penniwise (not Pennisworth) the clown; and Richard Thomas as writer, Bill (not Ben), many of the aspects of the plot are as described in H's story. This plot information is utilized in an interesting and imaginative way by H. Ingredients of children's myths (e.g., the castle) are woven into a contemporary adult horror fiction. The combination is effective. There is no doubt that H saw the film; less certain is whether or not he has any familiarity with the novel on which the film is based.

It was apparent from what H said in the several research conversations that took place, as well as from the way in which he spoke about video and film classification, that he had an excellent working knowledge of the content of a wide range of adult films. On the occasions when H was visited in his house, there was some attempt to steer the researcher's eyes away from certain pre-recorded video-cassettes in a bottom drawer. One in particular (with an 18-certificate) that became the topic of conversation was, H told the researcher, a present from his grandfather — 'although I obviously wouldn't be able to watch it until I'm old enough'.

There is some significant evidence contained within the last couple of sections. Firstly, H may watch adult films but he also has cuddly toys. He may use the adult scenario in his stories and film scripts but he mixes them with motifs that interest children of his age. Add this to points made earlier — for example, his established strategy for coming to terms with films which challenge his fears or 'disgust' at the outset — and a picture emerges of someone in control of his experiences. His parents seem to offer mediation some of the time but also allow him free reign at others, to watch what he likes, at whatever hour he likes.

The picture is of a relatively normal child, managing screen-based entertainment technology but within a secure, supportive setting. In this environment he can push the boundaries of his knowledge as far as he, personally, wants. As a consequence he has a keen sense of the need for certification for children at different ages and a strong sense of how films are made and how they relate to his own sense of reality.

Chapter 2

The Digital Curriculum:
Computers in School

Well everything is PC now, isn't it? It's PC — for teaching or programs for them. (Mother of 4-year-old)

Well, it's the computer age now isn't it? Got to be able to use them, haven't they? (Mother of 6-year-old)

Why Have Computers in Schools?

The ability to solve problems and communicate using a computer will be a fundamental facet of literacy for the next century (Heppell, 1995). Consequently, it was significant to see that a school of 200 pupils had 150 computers, 'ranging from a few old personal computers (PCs) to more sophisticated machines'. The children were plugged into video-conferencing and are on-line to the Internet and the Reuters international news agency. This helped them to produce a regular newsletter with down-loaded information from virtually every corner of the world. All 8.5 teachers at the school had laptops on which to prepare lessons, write reports and attempt to remain a few bytes ahead of their pupils. Unfortunately this is not a description you could write of any of the schools that we have observed, but an account in the *Guardian* (*The Guardian Education Supplement*, Thursday 9th January 1996, pp. 12–13). Nor is this a school in an affluent suburban area of South East England. It is, in fact, Orgill School in Egremont, West Cumbria, in the coastal industrial belt of the Lakeland Fells, an area of above average unemployment. The head teacher of Orgill school is quoted in the *Guardian* as saying,

> The children are going to live for another 70 years into the next century and a significant part of their lives will be to do with technology. It is critically important that they have the understanding to be proactive in that world, both in work and leisure.

Computers are changing rapidly and fit the school context more easily than they once did in that they are:

- More powerful than ever before, able to process and store more information
- Miniaturized and portable so that they need no longer be locked away in corners of classrooms

- Cheaper
- Easier to use because of user-friendly developments of Graphical User Interfaces (GUI), such as Windows 95.

Amongst the teachers we met, and all but three were women, those that use more up-to-date IT are reassured by these changes:

> The Apple is friendlier, messages such as 'Are you sure you want to delete that file?' I find reassuring. (Teacher, First School)

But as the technology is changing, so is the market place and teachers perceive the ill effects of the entertainment end of the technology spectrum upon their children. They have become aware that children are fast learning to be independent consumers and apply criteria to whatever they consume. This includes not only technology and its products, but also teaching itself.

R:	Have children changed generally over the last few years?
Headteacher:	Yes, they are different. In a sense because it is now such a visually stimulated world and it's a quick fix, whenever you watch TV, it's all movement and image in a way and a lot of stimulation. And for a lot of that they have to be passive.
R:	How about the children themselves, are they any different?
Headteacher:	Yes, whether its anything to do with computers or social I don't know. They are more difficult, they're more street-wise, they've more sense of themselves as people, they don't give you any respect you have to earn it. You have to work harder to ensure they're listening, lots of them find it more difficult to listen. (First School)

Fitting IT into the Curriculum

It would be true to say that most of the schools we investigated failed to demonstrate any major shift towards a curriculum which embraced IT, and many of the schools seemed content with a target of just having one computer per classroom. Few schools had facsimile machines, and none were actually connected to the Internet, although one school had investigated the service and was likely to subscribe shortly. All had televisions and video recorders but none were used in our presence. But the most worrying aspect was the fact that many schools had teachers with IT skills considerably below some of the 7- or 8-year-olds in their classes. Unlike most secondary schools, colleges, and universities where networks allow students individual access to PCs, most of the surveyed primary schools had only one computer per class of 25–35 children, which does not make for easy classroom management. This, together with a general lack of resources, was often cited by teachers as a major barrier to the inclusion of IT in the curriculum. It also led to apparent conflicts for teachers in relation to the teaching of National Curriculum subjects.

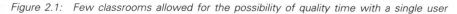

Figure 2.1: Few classrooms allowed for the possibility of quality time with a single user

It was very hard when I was teaching, to fit computers in. I mean if they were supposed to be doing maths, say, what were you supposed to do? Let two children go on the computer while the others got on with the lesson? So those two missed the lesson? And if it wasn't important for them to do the lesson, how could I make it seem important to the other children. (Parent-teacher, First School, Female)

. . . its the managing of the computer in the classroom which is difficult, because if you work in small groups, you need more than one computer because you can't get 4 or 5 kids on it. It would be a lot easier if you had three or four computers in the classroom. Giving all the children a fair time on the computer and getting it into the rest of the curriculum is very difficult. It must be wonderful to have a computer room like the High School. (Headteacher, Rural Junior, Female)

Our observations showed that the power of these single machines in classrooms was such that children were attracted to them, whether or not they had been allocated computer time. Unquestionably they did distract some children from other tasks they were supposed to be doing, adding to the difficulties of the teacher:

The computer is distracting though. When you get to the end of the level the computer often pings, and it attracts the attention of the children, they like the noise. (Teacher, Middle School, City, Female)

33

I think it can be distracting to the other children. I think you get some kids who will hang around the computer, and it is time-consuming to organize so that all children get an equal opportunity. (Teacher, Middle School, City, Female)

The attraction of other children, however, often appeared to lead to stimulating discussion, and on a couple of occasions the level of concentration amongst the children was such that the children seemed unable to even hear the researcher's questions. This was observed in the home as well as in the classroom. It was particularly noticeable when the children were organized in, or naturally coalesced into, small groups, and clearly supported the benefits of working in this manner, particularly on joint problem-solving. These observations supported, for example, the work of Snyder (1994) who undertook some research to compare the performances of two groups, one using a computer and the other pens and paper:

The students in the computer group were more focused and task-oriented. They were also more interactive, cooperative and collaborative than the students in the pen classroom . . . although both classrooms were productive learning environments in which the students were taught genre-based strategies by the same skilled teacher, the positive qualities were more pronounced in the computer classroom. Overall, the development of a more interactive, cooperative and collaborative atmosphere was observed.

Whereas such technology was often a source of difficulty for the teacher, in terms of her expertise and management, it often proved a source of fascination and motivation for children, despite the quality of software sometimes being used. Whilst children within the research were found to spend hours in solo communication with the screen, there was plenty of evidence that they could be as happy in groups. The research we did did not suggest that the technology was, *per se*, anti-social. Some teachers recognized this:

R: What would you say are the advantage and benefits of having the computer in the classroom?
Teacher: I think it is most beneficial when children are sharing or learning together, or, more beneficially, when they are working with an adult. With an adult there is a greater facility for language development. (First School)

For these teachers the same benefits were apparent whether the software was an adventure game, like *Arc Venture*, or when the application was a word-processing package or a database.

On the other hand, many female teachers were extremely uncomfortable with IT equipment, particularly in its practical requirements and functions, adding some embellishment to the stereotyped image of women disliking technology:

Figure 2.2: The computer in the corridor

The whole point of computers, we were told, was to save paper, but it doesn't, it creates paper. I keep telling them you don't need to print it out, you've got it on your disk. We've got a colour printer, it takes hours to print out. I don't know why. (Headteacher)

The most difficult thing with that is to load the paper in the printer, you usually have to load the paper for them. (Teacher, First School)

The pervasive antipathy to computers in the classroom can be seen in the lack of priority often given to the physical placement of the technology in the learning environment for maximum use of its potential. The pictures demonstrate how the teacher fails to consider the positioning of the computer for learning. In one the computer is placed outside the classroom, thus marginalizing its importance and, in the second picture, despite health and safety recommendations that the computer monitor should be at eye level to avoid any possible straining of the eyes or neck, the computer is positioned inappropriately.

In most schools surveyed in the research one teacher was usually given the role of IT coordinator, which might mean anything from having the responsibility for purchasing software, to planning and delivering staff development activities for the school. A lack of prioritized funding for staff development in IT, either on the part of the school or the LEA, and for the purchase of up-to-date technology, together with a general lack of aptitude and interest on behalf of teachers, led most

Figure 2.3: Breaking health and safety rules

schools to a very patchwork provision in this area, as shown in this conversation with a Middle School teacher:

> *R*: You have an IT role for the school?
>
> *Teacher*: Yes, but that doesn't mean I know everything about computers, it just means that I'm interested. I once volunteered to go on a course.
>
> *R*: What do you actually do?
>
> *Teacher*: Well, the whole IT thing here has been very higglety-pigglety. Some staff use computers, some don't and most of our software is so out of date . . . but we are now writing an IT policy. Last year I looked at the IT requirements of the National Curriculum for the school and presented them to the staff. I subsequently organized a program of 'hands-on' IT workshops for my colleagues. We recently spent £2000 on some new software, and I've catalogued it so that we have some kind of maths program, some kind of language program and some adventure programs for each year group. (Middle School)

Not all schools had travelled this far, although most recognized the importance of the subject. Some schools were being pressured into consideration of the needs of their children because they were transferring into cultures which utilized more IT:

> One of the things I've been wanting to do and that we've not been able to do so far, although we will be doing it this year, is to go to them [the

secondary school] and ask them what they do expect and to find out how we can best approach that. There is now guidance from the LEA with suggestions about what they should be doing but, of course, with IT changing all the time it is a very open framework. (Headteacher, Middle School)

The general picture we have formed during the research about the levels of expertise and interest among primary teachers makes us concerned about their ability to respond to new demands within the National Curriculum. It expects children to be really quite skilled with computers well before they reach secondary school (Year 8) at around 11–12 years. From the beginning of academic year 1996–97, information technology will be separated from design and technology. At Key Stage 1 (ages 5–7), teachers will be expected to give children access to computer technology and by Key Stage 3 (age 11 onwards), says the revised document, 'pupils should be taught to become critical and largely autonomous users of IT, aware of the way IT tools and information services can help in their work'. The evidence of our research suggests that this is a forlorn requirement.

Teachers' Knowledge of IT

The problems of lack of teaching expertise in this area resulted in many children of the same age being considerably disadvantaged within the same school year. Where year groups were split, as we observed on many occasions, one group may be taught by a teacher with considerable skills in IT, whilst another may be taught by a technophobe.

R: If you had a teacher who wasn't using IT, would that concern you?

Headteacher: Oh, yes, very much. I mean that's why it's a priority in the school. There are some highly placed members of staff who are resistant to it. In our Year 4 we have one teacher who uses the computer a lot and one who hardly ever looks at one let alone uses it. Which is a problem and the kids' ability depends on the class they have gone into. (First School)

Heppell (1995) suggests 'that a nine-year-old might be expected to make choices about which software tool to use, save and organise their own work and contribute information to (or get answers from) a database'. We suspect that, currently, this is rather an ambitious target, as we doubt whether many young secondary school children could meet his suggested criteria. We found very few teachers who were able to use the technology in these areas. It was more likely that they had a restricted view of usage, which was dominated by seeing the technology as a timetabled block within related subjects, rather than a tool to support all areas of the curriculum:

R: And what do they use the computer for?

Teacher: They use it for sequencing games, counting games, err, things that tie in with our topics . . . and it is mostly, as I say, sequencing. Er, I haven't used it for my language work yet. (First School)

When teachers used it as a tool, it was predominantly as a word processor. This bore out the national survey by the DfEE (1995). Whether it was being used to its full potential is another matter. As Heppell (1995) says:

> There are still too many nine-year-olds stuck in front of an ageing class-
> room computer typing up something they wrote by hand earlier, to spruce
> up the wall display with printouts before the parents evening.

Unfortunately, this type of activity was also too evident in a number of the schools we observed and some teachers had little understanding of IT's greater potential, and some even relied on parents and helpers for there to be any use at all:

R: Do they use it for any type of word processing?
Teacher: I haven't done because I haven't the adults. I haven't had enough adults. I've got 32 children and I have just not had the time. My adults — they've been deployed elsewhere. (First School)

On other occasions, it was only available, together with a range of simple programs, such as *Granny's Garden*, as an awareness-raising exercise in computing.

R: Do they do any word processing?
Teacher: Yes, I do that in a sort of free play. At this stage they just have the program on and they'll, you know like emergent writing, play writing, they'll just go and fiddle on it, just how they choose. By the end of the year most of the children will be able to load a word processor, and be able to print out their work. (First School)

There were also more productive examples of use, which indicated a level of understanding higher than that of Heppell's example above and they demonstrated a better grasp of the word processor's full potential. One of the principle benefits of the word processor is that it allows the child more opportunity for creativity, by eliminating tedious copying of endless drafts of text.

R: What sort of things do you do in the IT field?
Headteacher: We're in the very early days in IT, word processing mainly.
R: So you'd encourage them to write up a story on it.
Headteacher: No, not write it up, but to write it on the computer at Key Stage 2 really. I mean some of them, yes, they write it on paper and then they get it to look nicer by word processing it. But really word processing is not copying it out from written work, it's doing it on a computer. By Year 5, I'm trying to get them

to use the text to move paragraphs about. They can all save
and copy to disk, changing fonts, size etc. (Middle School)

Information handling is another activity which is to be integrated into the National
Curriculum. Students will need to develop their skills by interrogating databases,
such as electronic encyclopaedias, and also by creating their own. Our research
revealed very few instances of this kind of operation. There were some exceptions,
however. For example, one school used a program called *Weathermapper* to record
details of the local weather (see Figures 2.4 and 2.5).

The program shows children how data can be stored, and later retrieved, in a
much more efficient manner than with paper-based systems. For example, a comparison of the weather for a corresponding period in a particular year can be retrieved,
quickly. In addition, the database helps children to develop mathematical skills by
allowing them to classify and then interpret graphical information.

Another example was in a school that decided to use its database software to
automate its library collection. As in the above case, they were able to reap the benefits of automated systems. Being able to produce lists of books on a particular topic,
lists of outstanding items and reserving books were tasks which would have been
extremely tedious and difficult with a manual system.

... instead of having physical cards, which we used to have, they thought
it would be better if we automated the records so we had the kids' names
on, and the author and the title. (Headteacher, Rural Junior School, Male)

Teachers and Entertainment Culture

Computer games take up a whole chapter later in this book (Chapter 8) but, for the
moment, it is worth emphasizing that teachers were disinclined to embrace anything
related to commercial, as opposed to educational, hardware and software. Although
games were viewed generally with scepticism and even hostility by many teachers
there is little doubt that some such as *Sim City* and *Theme Park* do have great
potential. Within games such as these, problem solving is intrinsic to the whole
activity since the solution of the adventure involves learners continually analysing
and interpreting the information currently available to them. Children enjoy them
sometimes to a fanatical degree and it raises the question as to why they are not
used in schools. To some extent, also, children seem to have to develop these very
same skills to read and decode games magazines; another element of the entertainment culture, largely dismissed by teachers.

Games magazines were unknown territory to many of the teachers (and parents) with whom we talked, although teachers admitted to banishing them from
schools without any knowledge of the contents. The assumption was that they were
anti-educational. However, when we discussed them with children we found that
they competed with traditional forms of literature in insignificant ways.

In spite of the endemic violence, sexual or otherwise, which we deal with later

Figure 2.4:   Weathermapper 1

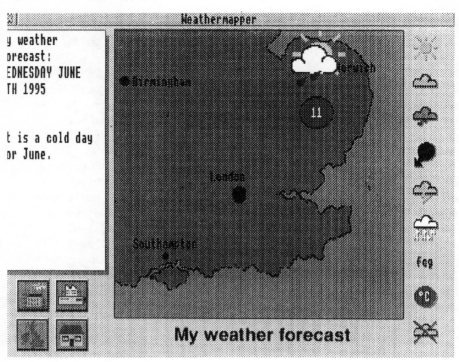

Figure 2.5:   Weathermapper 2

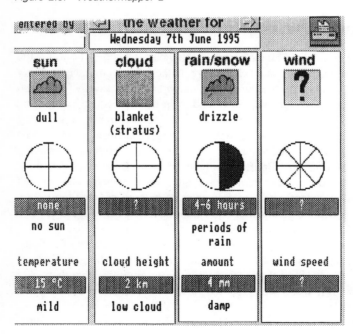

in the chapter on gender (Chapter 8), there were elements of the magazines which could be said to have real curriculum value, at least in the cognitive processes they were challenging. These involved:

- reviewing new games against particular criteria such as graphics, sound, playability, animation, lastability (longevity/life span);
- the very notion of playing the role of a critical consumer (not to be confused with being a critical user);
- managing the varied use of fonts and images to convey information concisely and attractively;
- the representation of moving images via stills;
- the use of percentages to indicate comparative quality;
- the informative nature of tips and cheats (which was an incentive to read instructions, an activity in which few children or adults in the project ever engaged);
- the incentive to read and understand complex conceptualizations in text, if only to impress peers, or persuade parents.

It is hard to convey the essence of these magazines because they vary a great deal and each has its market niche. However, a key element is their clever emphasis upon the reader as 'independent consumer with freedom of choice', even though this can be an illusion created to make marketing more subtle. Thus, text and image is chosen by the child reader in a way that does not take place so much in relation to traditional forms of text, where the linear narrative takes the reader on the author's journey, so to speak. The other major ingredient is the 'secret society' or 'clubby' feel to the productions. This, we would speculate, adds to the private pleasure principle of child users and subtly distances or insulates them in their private worlds from adults. In this, the magazines have a lot in common with mail order techniques which go beyond the mere presentation of the product by adding a dimension of personal identification, offering a series of 'real life scenarios' in which the child, as reader, can figure.

In one or two cases there was a belated realization among teachers that there is much that can be done with the commercial games world to motivate and educate the young.

> We tend not to use any games, although I've got a copy of *Sim City* which is great. When I first came here I inherited all sorts of games, shooting type games for the BBC, which I felt were used for rainy days. We lost those games and Year 5 are going to trial *Sim City*, because it has all sorts of possibilities such as decision-making, problem-solving etc. (Headteacher)

Our observations also indicate that such programs allow the children control of the pace, sequence and depth of progress, and even a choice of learning style, something that the human teacher and educational software often fails to do. For many, the problems encountered within a number of commercial software packages can be very challenging and intellectually demanding. Additionally, and particularly in relation

Figure 2.6: *Elation at winning in a computer game*

to computer games, many children find them such a motivating and interesting experience that they persist with the activity, using trial and error approaches, before quitting or seeking help. This was also true in the educational software that had similar structures to commercial products. There was a noticeable contrast between these forms of software and activities such as word processing, where children would often summon the teacher at the earliest indication of any problem.

> Certainly some of the games can provide more activities than I can provide
> . . . More exciting, more stimulating progams. With the history program,
> the children are actually becoming historians. I know it's not like actually
> going on a dig whatever. Reconstructing pottery into what it was, we
> couldn't possibly do that. (Teacher, First School)

Resources in Schools for IT Development

Johnson, Cox and Watson (1994) believe that IT can have a highly positive impact on children's achievement, but not without substantial demands on teachers and schools. They also confirm the findings of this research when they say that:

> . . . current provision of hardware resources in schools is inadequate to
> enable teachers to take full advantage of the potential contribution of IT
> to pupils learning across the curriculum . . . the majority of schools are not

yet provided with opportunities to take advantage of the potential of the full range of software, a substantial amount of which is currently available in the school or local education authority.

Whilst changes in the classroom are not nearly mirroring the technological changes in our society, there can be little doubt that many schools find it virtually impossible to progress in this area owing to the lack of funding.

> I think the problem is one of resourcing as well. I think children should use them more, far more. If we had a half class with laptop computers, that would cost £15,000 and then you would need that again at a later stage if you're updating. We are also currently looking to lease machines, but ten machines would cost us £5000 per year, and schools are not built easily to hold that number in any one place anyway, in any one room or networked through the school and there are practical problems with that which have to be addressed. But that is a huge amount of money to buy each year when you think that this year ... I haven't had a school meal this year, even though I work right through my lunch hour. By missing out on lunch I can save the school £300 per year. It sounds pathetic I know but £300 is part of another dinner lady, it's three days' supply teaching, and we are scratching around to find that sort of money. So to find £4000 is extraordinarily difficult. The whole situation is totally frustrating. (Headteacher)

This lack of funding wasn't just limited to the actual hardware but the additional, equally important, task of resourcing training for staff to be able to use IT with the children

> Well, it's a time factor really. What those people need is sustained training and inset support. And when you've got such limited resources it's extremely difficult to release the person to be able to go and see another teacher or class where it's working very well. (Headteacher)

On the other hand, there were other schools who, mainly due to their own efforts and support of the parents and local companies, appeared to be rather better resourced, with one school having a small but very effectively used network of three Apple Macs

> *R:* You seem quite well off for IT equipment here?
> *Headteacher:* Well, I think you say that it has been a bit of push of mine. When I left my last school we were just getting into Apple Macs in a fairly big way, and when I came here we had a couple of BBCs. I felt that we were asking children to work on equipment which they would spit at, at home. Children were coming to us with all sorts of facilities and skills already and it was almost like giving them a stone axe, you know go

Figure 2.7: Some schools had better organized networks

and chop that tree down. So we started investing really, I mean the first three we set up in there [the library]. We had an Apple Mac given us as part of LMS [Local Management of Schools], we thought they were very user friendly and we decided to go down this route. We particularly wanted a word processing bay where children could go and produce text or graphics and we felt it was an ideal system so from a variety of sources we got two or three extra machines, and we networked them together, so that was the start of the system.

Headteacher: We've now scrapped our two BBCs which were with Key Stage 1, and we've ordered two Apple Macs with CD-Roms.

R: So how many machines will you have then?

Headteacher: Eight in total, although two will be in the office. This one [in the office] will not be in use all the time by me so what we are intending to do is to use some sessions in here.

R: So there will be one computer between ten, which isn't a bad ratio.

Headteacher: No I don't think it is . . . what we aim to do is to replace them every couple of years, and one way I aim to do this is by selling them off to the staff. 'Cause they're very useful little tools for doing class-based things at home. I do like the network here though.

Perhaps surprisingly, the rural schools in our study seemed better provided for than many of their neighbours in the urban areas.

Headteacher: We'd love to have more equipment but we've no money. We've got the BBC which we obtained years ago from the county, and we've three Apple Macs. Three for the children but we also have one in the office which they use occasionally. We've also got a BBC which the Friends bought and we bought the new Apple Mac last year.
R: So you're reasonably well resourced.
Headteacher: Yes, I suppose we have one computer per eleven children, which is not too bad.

There is also some considerable bitterness amongst teachers that they are being expected to introduce a new skill into the curriculum without the appropriate training. This was a significant issue throughout the research. Technology is changing faster than teachers are being trained. Even small changes in technology specification and software formats can cause teachers frustration, resentment and demotivation. Few teachers like to appear lacking in expertise in front of their children.

The other thing is that as teachers we feel that IT has been introduced on the cheap. No one has had adequate training, there isn't adequate provision of machines in schools or adequate time. It was something [IT] we never covered in Teacher's Training College, and although I can see the need for computers, I am still very uncomfortable with them. Although I've been on a few courses, which have helped me to understand their potential, I never seemed to get the opportunity to put what I had learned into practice. We often had to share computers and by the time I had the opportunity of using the machines again I had forgotten much of what I had picked up on the course. (Teacher, First School)

Kay and Mellar (1994) would suggest that the deficiency of IT training for primary school teachers has still to be fully addressed. Whilst their survey revealed most new teachers having some working knowledge of IT, few were able to visualize the computer beyond the word processor and games.

As described earlier it was evident that a number of teachers in the survey were unhappy with IT and some of the interviews with teachers revealed general antipathy or fear towards the technology:

R: What is your opinion of computer games?
Headteacher: I don't know a lot about them. We don't have a computer at home. I would like a good computer but not one for games. I'm a bit of a Luddite to be honest.
R: Are you happy with computers?

> *Teacher*: I'm happier. At first I found them very pointless in the class-room. I felt that they were used to occupy two children. I couldn't see . . . I felt they were a tool to be used to do a job in much of the way they were used to play games. They were things I could already do that much more efficiently. I found them very time-consuming to do properly at this age and I felt very threatened because I didn't know about them. You couldn't find the game, or you'd lose the game and couldn't get it back. If they went wrong I couldn't access them and get them back and things like that. I didn't want anything to do with computers in the classroom. I was very against them. (First School)

The above teacher's perception of IT changed considerably when she began to explore a computer her family had acquired at home, and demonstrated what could be achieved with a more formalized training programme for teachers. It was surprising how many instances there were within the research, where teachers, despite their mind-sets and lack of staff development, had had extra-curricular encounters with computers in social surroundings, to discover that the technology might have all sorts of benefits. In the following extract from an interview, many of the issues raised in this chapter come to the fore. The teacher concerned learns because her husband and son are at ease with the technology and are there to bail her out, she is able to confront her irrational fears in a non-threatening environment, she is able to maintain a continuous contact with the technology so that she doesn't forget what she has learned previously and she gains the confidence to provide children with the opportunity to become independent users themselves. The exact antithesis of most of our teachers' experience in this phase of education!

> *Headteacher*: To cut a long story short I did some work where we were turning the National Curriculum into child speak and wanted to put it onto disk, I took the Apple Mac home with me and my husband went through it with me and I saw, 'Ah I can see how I can use that to make life easier'. So I sort of got into the Apple Mac and this made me more comfortable with this [the BBC] so I don't worry if I lose a program, I know there is a logic. Because I was more comfortable with it I was able to give the children more freedom with it, and increasingly I have been concerned that they learn how to use the disk, choose the option and the whole process. It isn't just a game.
>
> *R*: So you changed when you had a play with the Apple Mac?
>
> *Headteacher*: Yes.
>
> *R*: And was it just the simplicity of the environment?
>
> *Headteacher*: Yes, and then we bought one at home, and then my husband who is fairly computer literate, and my son is a computer maniac . . . so someone could get me out of a fix.

R:	Do you use the system at home?
Headteacher:	Yes, I do, I'm learning all the time.
R:	Do you use anything other than the word processing packages — like spreadsheets?
Headteacher:	Well my husband is the spreadsheet wizard, so he set the spreadsheet up for me. He showed me vaguely how to do it, but I'm by no means an expert. But I understand the principles. Consequently it is the children who eventually benefit from such developments But they are now independent in such a way that two years ago I wouldn't have dreamt possible. But that's because I'm happier about it and more confident, I'm no longer frightened of them losing it.

Compare this with the number of teachers who we interviewed who were fully aware of the importance of IT for their children but felt helpless in what appeared to be a growing workload, with shrinking resources. For them, training was at best, intermittent, they had to rely upon expert assistance from other staff or parents and they hadn't got continuous contact with the technology:

R:	Are you frightened of IT?
Teacher 1:	No, if I had more time I think I would enjoy it. But what I find is that you are introduced to something, you go on a course or something and you don't use those skills for a while and then you forget everything. And with BBC you get them going and then you get a disk fault which you had a couple of years before. It's that sort of thing. (First School)
Teacher 2:	Yes, it's [the computer] here. It's not on every day. Initially I had a parent that came in to help me to set it all up; and each child went through the business of, er, knowing how to sort out the skills on the keyboard; and I had an adult for that to begin with. Since then it's been on, I suppose, it's on two to three days a week without the adults. The adult who helped me initially has left to do a job. So it means that I have to look after it now. (First School)

The extracts from conversations below are yet another indication of the lack of priority planning given to IT in certain schools, and further demonstrates what little thought had gone into organizing IT within lessons, or even the location of the computers within the classroom: it takes us back to the photographs at the beginning of this chapter.

R:	And you have computer technology in your room?
Teacher:	Mmm — we've got two computers at the moment: one BBC and

R: a new CD-rom which is in here because there's nowhere else for it to go at the moment. It's supposed to go in the library so it has open accessibility to all the children and is used as another resource as far as information gathering and stuff goes.

R: When will it be going into the library?

Teacher: Well at the moment the library is outside my door and it's a kind of . . . corridor . . . so it wouldn't really be used very well there . . . and we're hoping to get some remodelling of rooms going . . . which would mean that the computer could go somewhere that's a little bit more self-contained . . . so hopefully at the end of term.

R: So the CD-rom wasn't just in your room because of your particular expertise in IT?

Teacher: Alas no, no. But it's actually quite nice having it here because I can kind of remind myself how to use an Archimedes and have a go at a CD-rom at the same time. (Reception Class)

Unlike virtually every subject or skill area taught in primary schools, IT is unique in that many of the teachers have fewer skills than a number of the children in their classes. The research also highlighted how some teachers were using the expertise of children in the classroom as consultants to assist in the delivery of IT. Many of these children would have computers at home. IT has also seen an emergence of new languages — jargon and technical terms — which leaves some teachers feeling a little uncomfortable. Whilst believing that the classroom inherently confers parity of opportunity upon children, there was a tendency to handle this problem by establishing the aforementioned class consultants. These individuals may or may not have the necessary skills to help their peers with their problems and some teachers would not have the expertise to predict which were expert and which were not, anyway.

The Way Forward

In this information age, it is crucial that all students are taught how to gather, manipulate, organize and interpret information, and be able to relate it to their current knowledge in terms of its relevance and usefulness. There is a growing realization that IT skills are going to be essential in the very near future, and learning strategies will have to be adapted to meet these needs. 'Learning by doing' and 'making education more fun' will be the key strategies for the new, technologically underwritten curriculum (Davis, 1995). He also quotes projected research which suggests that, within the next few years, people will be spending more time, on average, in front of their computer monitor than their television screen, and believes that education must undergo a drastic 're-engineering', if it is to apply the new learning styles and possibilities presented by multimedia.

But the context is a bleak one. As has been demonstrated above, once children reach school they can be faced with poor hardware and software, ill-trained teachers who are driven on the treadmill of the National Curriculum and queues to use the technology that there is there. Most of the teachers they meet have little interest in the commercial screen-based technologies they enjoy out of school, seeing them as part of popular as opposed to educational culture. If children are having a better time than this it is often because the school has gone outside the formal educational support structures to raise funds for technology and the teachers have managed to develop themselves through non-educational networks.

Buckingham (1993) believes that the crux to success in IT education is to find a way of developing the relationship between what is taught in schools, and the technology that children are exposed to in the home. But for this to happen, we need to look sympathetically at the ways that children use and understand these technologies. This was what originally led us to this enquiry into homes and schools. The evidence of this research suggests that the gap between schools and homes is still vast, that teachers, generally, do not relate the screen-based technologies of the home to IT within schools, that they are falling behind in their own IT skills and that their attitudes to entertainment technology and popular culture are constraining children's maturation in the use of new technology.

Chapter 3

Home Improvements:
Domestic Computers

The Range of Technology in Families

Let us contrast the schools of the last chapter with the homes of most of the children we have studied. Most of them are awash with new technology. At one extreme we observed a family which allowed no television, and an ageing computer was used for carefully vetted games. At the other, we observed a child who had a networked system at home which meant that she could play any computer game or tap into the Internet from any room in the house. This child's parents were in an information-related business but the changing patterns of work may lead to an increase in the number of parents working from home with personal computers (PCs). A number of parents were directly, or idiosyncratically, exposed to computers in a range of different environments.

R: How do you use the computer at work?
Parent: Well, I work at the boiler house at the university and it works all the controls — turning pumps and valves off and on.
R: So, you feel comfortable with computers?
Parent: Yeah, I'm quite happy to have a go.

In the Introduction we gave figures that showed how the PC had become both a status symbol and a 'necessity' in a large proportion (39 per cent) of British homes, particularly among the professional classes (Business Section). But does the availability of this technology in the home actually help the children? Does not having it disadvantage others? Cole (1995) suggests it will have these effects, particularly a computer 'which will help to improve the child's education', and refers to other studies indicating that children with computers at home do better at school than non-users.

It is noticeable how more confident and able the children with computers at home appear. (School Governor)

Others suggested that whilst having a PC at home with a range of applications software would be advantageous, they doubted whether access to computer games consoles would have such an effect. All agreed, however, that the possession of such machines did seem to give children greater confidence when faced with a PC.

Our research also has evidence to suggest that children are also beginning to see the advantage.

> *R*:   Are you the best in the school class at reading?
> *Girl (6 years)*: Yes.
> *R*:   And writing?
> *Girl*:   Yes.
> *R*:   And the computer?
> *Girl*:   Me, they press the wrong buttons and I'm the only one who can use it, 'cause nobody's got a computer at home apart from me. But I've got millions of computers at home.

This is also the first generation of parents who have a lot of technology in the home; and all too often the parents do not know how to use this technology, whether it be a television, video recorder, or computer (November, 1992). As a spokesman for the Atari Corporation also revealed, the computer game is probably the first toy with which the majority of parents have great difficulty in helping or supporting their children. A spokesman for THE Games (UK distributors for Nintendo) also supported this notion, although pointing out that as many as 30 per cent of the callers to their Nintendo hotline are over the age of 18. However, it is not clear whether they are calling on their own behalf, or assisting a younger child. Our research certainly revealed a number of adult computer game players (including two of the authors of this book).

> *R*:   Do you see the computer as relaxation then?
> *Parent 1*: Yeah, me and the lad, we play it between us — football games and he and his sister will play the Sonic games. (Parent)
> *Parent 2*: No, I mean the times I've had it out — that's been there — I have pulled it out to play on it myself and I do enjoy playing it. I just don't have the time so I said to Rose last week — 'I really fancy a game on the computer tonight', but there just wasn't the opportunity. I was working on early shifts and that — it just wasn't the right time of day. (Parent)

Parents have traditionally been able to support their children with reading, writing and maths etc., but many will not have the remotest hope of assisting them with their IT skills, although Atari believed this to be a temporary situation which will remedy itself as progressive generations evolve. However, the speed of technological change must bring this into question, and from an educational point of view one suspects that it is a rather complacent outlook. Closer to the mark is Anderson's (1994) title 'The faster we go the behinder we get', where he discusses the problems associated with the information explosion.

Parents' Perceptions of IT

The parents' knowledge and perceptions of IT vary enormously. Some had little understanding or interest relating to computers. Many demonstrated the same technophobic characteristics demonstrated by many of the teachers we spoke to and observed. Like the teachers, few could perceive the applications of the computer, beyond the word processor and a games console, as shown in this conversation with the mother of a 7-year-old:

R: Do you think that computers should be used more at school?
Mother: Yes I think so, yes. Of course, I don't know anything about it. I haven't given it much thought. They obviously need to learn for when they get older. There's a lot to be learnt.
R: Do computers seem strange to you?
Mother: Yeah, I'm a bit frightened of them really. I don't know anything about them.

And in this conversation with the mother of an 8-year-old.

R: Do you use the computer?
Mother: Well, to be honest, I don't really know anything about them.
R: What do you think it would be useful for?
Mother: Well, games, but you just need to know how to use it these days don't you? Most jobs require it now, don't they?

And in this conversation with the mother of a 6-year-old.

R: What can computers be used for first school children?
Mother: Learning really. Well, I mean play learning really.
R: What about when they get older and go on to other schools?
Mother: Well, more learning I would have thought. Computers aren't going to go away, are they?
R: How should they be using them in the first school?
Mother: Well, they need to know the keyboard and, er, load a disc up and well, you know, the very basics. They know more than we do really.

There is also a perception that school teachers are skilled IT users:

R: Do you think the teachers know about computers?
Mother: I'll give them their due — they're very helpful at that school.
Father: Whenever we've been at the school, they seem to have the computers on, and off they go. They only have to ask the teacher to turn it on.
Father: There's one in each class.
Mother: I suppose when she's at high school doing lots of project work, we

> may need to look again to buy a more powerful machine, perhaps think about a PC then with word processing facilities. (Mother of a 7-year-old)

Others were less convinced:

> So many jobs now use computers. I think if you've got a background of using them at home, you get so much more familiar with it. At school they have them but I'm not sure how much opportunity they get to go on them or get proficient on them. (Mother of an 8-year-old)

Their was also some scepticism as to the value of computers, although we suspect much of it is due to a lack of understanding of the computer's potential and possibly upon parents relying too much on outdated hardware and software. This could also lead to frustration as they come to terms with a new skill.

> What I've found with the musical gear — what d'you call it . . . 'dedicated hardware' . . . this is much better than standard computers. They just tell you what you can do and what sounds you are allowed to use and that is no good. You can't have that sort of limitation put on you when you're trying to create something. It's the same thing with graphics and you've got a certain selection of fonts or something and then the one that you want isn't there. I find that extremely irritating. I'd much rather just draw the thing myself. They have great possibilities — like for library work and storing information and numbers and things but I think in most creative things they are quite tame. (Father of a 6-year-old)

> There's always a limitation to what you can do — I find it so frustrating I think if they're going to use them in schools, they need to be given an inkling to how to do programming. They're working on different levels — you're doing one thing and the computer is doing something else and there's a barrier between you. You've got a whole range of software but you don't have your own choices and I think you should have. There's something I find very limiting about computers — it's always the one thing you want to do that you can't do. (Father of a 7-year-old)

The same person also questioned the value of the computer being used when his daughter had been using a piece of software called 'Banner' to design a logo. Despite supporting more paper and pen activities, however, he said, 'the ironic thing was that it took me 10 minutes to decipher the teacher's note complaining about my daughter's handwriting'.

> I think it would be better for her to have designed and drawn it herself. I don't want to be overly critical of computers — they have their uses, but it's nothing is it to call up a banner on a computer, fiddle about with it a

bit and then print it out. I think the thing is, if they're using it . . . they're studying computers, that's fair enough but if they're using them to study art or graphics or virtually anything else, it's a total waste of time — it has enormous limitations and they can't really express what they want to express . . . I mean, when they were doing a history project, they gave them the old-style pens to use and things — well that's far more valuable. If you've just read about it or seen it on a screen, that doesn't actually amount to much, does it? You need to have the real experience of it. (Father of a 6-year-old)

I mean, fair enough, I think they need the experience of being exposed to a computer — especially the keyboard — I suppose that's quite import- ant but that's enough to be getting on with. I think for any serious pursuit, it's pretty much a dead end . . . I think it's worth schools investing money in computers. Whatever she does [his daughter] as a career in the end, doubtless she'll have to use something like that so obviously it's going to be useful for her if she's already had some experience. (Father of an 8-year-old)

It was noticeable how frustrating the child in the home of the above parent found the experience of using old and clearly corrupted software. The program, on an old Commodore, took a few minutes to load and then crashed a number times. Clearly the child is not going to enjoy many thrills from this type of experience.

It was remarkable how often parents cited the importance of keyboarding skills in the new world of technology, although one of them questioned the efficacy of the QWERTY keyboard. In fact, keyboarding was probably cited as the principal benefit to be gained from exposing children to computers at an early age.

I mean obviously when you're 5 . . . you're . . . do . . . you're not doing a lot of keyboard work, it is mostly mouse-driven . . . but that's not to say that the keyboard isn't important in teaching the distinction between dif- ferent letters. (Father of a 5-year-old)

Other parents were more knowledgeable and were able, in varying degrees, to see beyond the notion of computing as a subject in its own right.

I don't think it's sensible to talk about computer studies — it's more important to talk about how to do particular tasks. In a work situation, you need to know about the task you're actually doing — you go along to a course in computer studies and they're telling you how to set up files and you think 'Hang on, what does this actually mean for us'. I was a governor at first school and they did a two-hour course on the Apple Mac Word Processor. I'd never used one before so I went along and I learnt how to put a disc in and get into the word processing and, basically, that's all I'm interested in. You go on these computer courses and are told all these things and you think, well, how am I actually going to use this? (Mother of a 6-year-old)

Others demonstrated a substantial knowledge (including the pirating of software), of how the computer could assist their children educationally, how it could make the process of learning a more enjoyable experience, and an appreciation of the growing influence of multi-media.

It was only a basic addition and multiplication package but it made it more fun. (Father of an 8-year-old)

Yeah — it's all educational software, but that doesn't mean it isn't fun because she's only 5; so, by definition, the software needs to be engaging in order to be used and as she's so young it's something that . . . she's really going to be taken by, otherwise she isn't going to use it. (Father of a 7-year-old)

. . . because computers are very useful at the moment for jobs. Anyway they learn more if they are enjoying it — it's the quickest way to learn. I think computers at work are a good thing. (Mother of a 6-year-old)

R: How do you define Multi-Media?
Father: Well . . . multi-media is a . . . is a bringing together of sounds, moving pictures, text, graphs, animation . . . with a degree . . . of interactivity. (Father of a 6-year-old)

Mother: I think the CD-roms should be used in first and middle schools more — the main use of computers is for giving children information. Now that the voices are coming in as well, it's really exciting. (Mother of a 6-year-old)

Father: My particular interest is in multi-media and its role in education. To that end, I have a machine which I use for my studies and . . . er . . . I've also got software, multi-media software, on CD-rom, which is for my daughter. (Undergraduate Father of a 5-year-old)

R: What do you think a computer would help Georgia with?
Mother: Well, geography I think. I mean, on Tots TV she knows that Tilly is French from France but she doesn't understand *where* France is. I say that's in another country across the sea. It's good for her to know how other children in other countries live and all that.
R: So would you be interested in having a computer with a CD-rom?
Mother: Well, to be honest, I don't really know anything about them. My husband would probably understand about that but I don't really know. (Mother of a 6-year-old)

One father of a 7-year-old compared the computer to the television. He suggested that with a television, the only interaction is to:

Father: Switch it on, turn it up, turn it over and switch it off. Where as with multi-media . . . the person using it has got to actually, physically, do something. And when they do something they . . . retain more of the information than they do if it is just given to them. With multi-media, really, the sky's the limit.

R: So you think the physical interaction — the ability to actually manipulate keyboards — helps to reinforce learning?

Father: No, I think that that's a by-product. I think that . . . the interaction is actually mental . . . which is . . . manifested in the physical interaction of pressing keys on the keyboard or using the mouse.

Some could see that the problem-solving nature of some computer games could assist children educationally, and described one game as:

Father 1:   That is quite educational really, you have to get a line or more and you mustn't let them stack up to the top otherwise you lose. You gotta try to keep them down at the bottom as much as you can and then, of course, they come down and you can use the buttons to change. Say you get two greens and a red at the bottom or perhaps in the middle, you can press the button — there's a sequence — you press another button for speed. The idea is to stack them in threes or more and that'll drop down.

Father 2:   I think it does, it teaches them reactions. They're aware of lots of things going on.

R: Have your son's reactions improved by playing on those sorts of games?

Father 1:   Yeah, you gotta be alert — there's so many things going on in these games.

Others viewed the games as toys, and there appeared to be a feeling that games are essentially recreational and more constructive software should be sought to further their education:

We have thought about it [buying a PC], we thought it would be educational for the children. The games are just games — just an amusement thing to start off with. Yeah, it would be a good idea 'cos it would help them with their writing and reading and their education.

The latter point is interesting and Nintendo did claim that children read the instructions, and were obviously forced to follow screen instructions occasionally, which would assist them to develop their reading skills. Our research cast some doubt upon that notion, however, as a number of children appeared to pay little regard to the instructions. This could be partly explained by the appalling way in which a number of instructions for computer games are written, as well as computer manuals, generally.

> R: Do you read the instructions before you start to play?
> *Father*:   The best way is to learn the hard way really — just get stuck in.
> R: Do you never read instructions?
> *Father*:   Well, to begin with, I read them to get the basic principles — what the game is supposed to do. After that — well there's a *Thunderbird* game there — we didn't have any instructions — we couldn't find them so we got what the idea of the game was — it's just trial and error. Just play it and find out how it works. I just get the basic layout. I think if they just go off and play it, they'll find out. I think that applies to a lot of things in life. I mean, I keep an eye on them — make sure they're okay, but often they just learn the hard way. Like, riding a bike, I'll say to them 'Don't do that,' but they fall off and they learn the hard way. (Father of 6-year-old)

Information for Parents

It is therefore clear that parents would benefit from some support in the IT area, even to assist in the bewilderingly difficult task of choosing computers and software for their children, if they were in the fortunate position of being able to afford them:

> So we talked about it and decided we'd invest in one of those [PC]. My husband wants to hang on for another 6 months: so much is changing at the moment. (Mother of a 7-year-old)

There are thousands of software titles designed to help young children with their education, word processors for creative writing, graphics packages for artwork, music programs and an ever increasing number of attractive and exciting language programs.

Help is available from the Parents Information Network (PIN), a nation-wide organization aimed at demystifying technology and explaining how it can be used for education. PIN is also working with the National Council for Educational Technology on a series of computer 'fun days' in schools, libraries and community centres. Experts will be on hand to explain to parents what their children are learning and how they can help (Heppell, 1995). November (1992) also outlines a programme in New Mexico, USA, which is designed to help the family to develop their IT skills.

> Regular school bulletins can advise parents on what television programs to watch with their children, computer software to purchase and using these media as an extension of schoolwork. Parents can tape television programs,

using them as a point of departure for family discussions. Families can also attend Family and Computers Together in the School — a six-week course that teaches how technology can enhance communication. (p. 15)

Computer and software manufacturers have tuned in to the potential guilt of parents. Their methods are not unlike those of the encyclopaedia salesmen of thirty years ago: if you don't buy you will be consigning your children to the lower rungs of the educational ladder. Consequently adverts are now appearing daily in the national press promising massive educational achievement if parents buy particular hardware and software. As a result, there is something approaching a 'digital moral panic' (Cole, 1995) among concerned parents, with parent–teacher associations collecting tirelessly for better and newer computers.

The boom in the number of children playing computer games and surfing the Internet is causing toy shops to strip their shelves of traditional stock to make room for the new generation of computers and plug-and-play Internet access kits. One of the biggest attractions of the Internet for children is that it enables them to play computer games with friends, or opponents, anywhere in the world (Cox and Frean, 1995).

Clearly parents need to be aware of these new developments, and one wonders whether they fully appreciate the additional telecommunications cost that are involved in such activities. An hour on a telephone is nothing to a teenager but at peak telephone times, such as immediately after school which is a popular period, this can involve substantial cost. British Telecom, however, launched a service in 1996 called Wireplay which is designed to give substantial discounts to players of on-line games. It is not just for the fans of the typical 'shoot-them-up' computer games. The English Bridge Union is among those working with BT, which expects other conventional games such as chess to be played on the network. Players dial up the service from their home computer, using a modem to connect with the phone line. The service will then act as a match-making facility, putting them in touch with other people wanting to play a particular game (Bannister, 1995).

An overwhelming image researchers were left with, was of how much the children enjoyed using computers. On video footage we have shots of children deep in concentration attempting to solve a problem using the computer. On a number of occasions two children were filmed working on a task, and often the children who were attracted should have been solving a different problem. The computer, and new technology generally, acted like a magnet in attracting children to the extent that in a school where many of the children were from low-income families, even the introduction of a camcorder so disrupted the lesson that it had to be removed from the classroom. One of the most notable revelations, however, during the research, both in the home and at school, was the intense concentration some children demonstrated when using the computer in comparison to other activities. This is also supported by a former teacher on Merseyside, who now runs private classes for toddlers (Knowsley, 1995). Her classes are aimed at a range of ages, but she claims that children as young as 11 months can concentrate for half-an hour without any difficulty with the appropriate programs and hardware.

Negative aspects of computer usage have been expressed from a number of quarters, these include being anti-social, addictive, harmful to health, etc. We feel sure that most would agree with this if the circumstances involved a child being locked away in a scenario described below by Plant (1995):

> Some parents, particularly in the US, are beginning to worry that the social skills of their children will atrophy and that they are becoming psychopathically addicted to cyberspace, holed up in their bedrooms unable to distinguish between reality and fiction or real people and characters in games on the screen. For parents and teachers who have seen this happen to their children, electronic communication appears to be an alienating, potentially dangerous and even sinister development.

Parents could be quite equivocal when it came to the amount of time their children might spend on indoor activities.

> It's you playing against the computer. I can't — it's really difficult. It helps you to learn. I mean if I play, I let Dean have some chances which the computer doesn't. See, it doesn't know if it's playing a little boy or an adult. I can't beat the computer. But it's the same as everything else, the more you practise, the better you'll be. But that doesn't get used very much at all now. (Father of 7-year-old)

> I have some anxieties when children are playing games on their own. I don't have those same anxieties when the children are playing alongside one another and there is some discussion. I know it's partly apocryphal, I suppose, but the idea of children being kept at home in order to keep them away from child molesters outside . . . but the keeping them cocooned in that way and not being allowed to develop some pretty important personal skills. My eldest daughter who's 10, apart from playing the piano, is only interested in reading. She reads endlessly and doesn't get involved in other activities. I'm not quite sure how we've done that to her, and that worries me. (Headteacher and Parent of Junior Rural School)

In reality, young computer buffs could spend a great deal of time with the technology. Our research would also suggest that some children do get aggressive playing computer games, but the question is whether or not the aggression is already in the child, with the game offering a good outlet for the aggression:

> Well he — you can see he gets into it so much and he gets really upset if he doesn't win and — well — he wants to do it for so long. Even the little games — you know — the hand-held ones. I keep those and let them use them occasionally. (Mother of a 6-year-old)

Generally, we also observed that most parents wished to control the amount of time the children were allowed to play the games, and certainly long before any signs of excessive playing or addiction as defined by Griffiths (1993):

R: Do you stop him playing?

Father: Oh yes, I'd stop him. He couldn't play on there two hours or some-thing. He should be doing something more constructive really. I mean they're not allowed just to play. They have to do their school work first and if they've made time, then they can go and play. (Father of a 7-year-old)

Generally, however, parents didn't appear to be quite so rigid in their control as they suggested. However, our conclusions reject the notion that playing with a computer in the home was an anti-social pastime. If anything, there was evidence that games playing in the home is an activity which helps create social interaction. Friends appear to visit each other's houses and chatter away for hours, about strategies, new games and magazines, etc. It may well be that this is more of a problem for parents, who are unable to enter the privacy of the child's world, a world of which they have little or no knowledge.

The Effects of IT on Literacy

There is also a belief in some quarters that playing with a computer will in some way retard literacy, although the information age appears to be contradicting that notion. There are now more hardback books published each year, more novels written and sold than ever before. In 1945 there were eight nationally distributed daily newspapers in Britain, and they sold just under 15 million copies. In the early 1970s there were nine such papers, still selling some 15 million copies. In the mid-1980s the total was ten national newspapers selling 15 million copies and in 1995 there were eleven dailies, selling just under 15 million copies. Total circulations are rising in France and Germany, India and Japan (Jenkins, 1995).

It is clear, therefore, that whether we love them or hate them, computers are very much here to stay. They offer the world of education the possibilities of trans-forming the way children learn, by removing tedious inputting tasks and allowing higher order skills to analyse and interpret data and information. The imbalance between the experiences that many children have at home in comparison to what they receive at school is obviously a worry. Of even greater concern, however, is for those children who have no access to IT equipment at home or at school, and our research reveals that far too many children fall into that category. Where equipment is provided for the children, as appears to be the case at Orgill School mentioned in the previous chapter, then the concern diminishes. We must aim to equip schools to the same standard as almost half the homes in Britain will be equipped, by the end of the century. We must ensure that children are given adequate access at an early age to modern IT equipment, supported by teachers with appropriate skills. If we cannot achieve this then we will be failing half the child population.

Chapter 4

Keeping IT in the Family:
Computer Games and Families

Boy (*9 years*):	I'm not allowed to play . . . well, I am allowed to play *Mortal Kombat* but I'm not allowed to play *Mortal Kombat 2*.
R:	Why's that?
Boy:	Because it's 15. But the first one is just normal. On the Mega Drive it's much more sick because you can uppercut them and the blood goes all over the place and you can throw them onto death pits and you can do death moves on them. Some of them are really disgusting . . . some of them you freeze them and then you jump up and punch them and some of them are when they take their mask off and blow fire and it burns them.
R:	Do you think that games like that are bad for you?
Boy:	If you play it too long.
R:	Why's that?
Boy:	Because your eyes go all funny, your eyes go all square.

Fears about Computer Games

The worries which have been expressed about harmful effects of computer games playing take a number of different forms and have come from various commentators including teachers, politicians, journalists, and psychologists. There are fears that children will become addicted and lose interest in all other activities. The term 'keyboard junkies' has been coined to describe this syndrome (e.g., Neustatter, 1991), although evidence for its existence was at first largely anecdotal. There is now a slowly growing body of evidence to suggest that video and computer games can become addictive (Griffiths, 1993) but the extent of computer game dependency is currently hard to assess. Another major concern is that the violent content of some video games will induce aggressive behaviour in children exposed to it. Provenzo (1991) reported that forty of the forty-seven Nintendo games included in his sample involved simulated acts of destruction and killing and that most of these featured an autonomous individual acting aggressively and alone against an evil force or enemy. His analysis also revealed many examples of stereotypical, racial and gender depictions in the games and he concluded that children playing on such games may be conditioned into racist and sexist attitudes. It is certainly the case that many games contain violent and stereotypical images, but there is currently no unequivocal evidence to support the idea that this produces long-term behaviour changes in those exposed to them.

Other fears have been expressed about the possible physical and social consequences of computer game playing. Case studies have been reported which indicate physical side-effects resulting from excessive game playing. Conditions have included wrist, neck and elbow pain, incontinence and epileptic seizures. There has also been some concern that the high arousal levels sometimes induced by computer games playing can lead to raised blood pressure. New names for syndromes have even been coined which clearly implicate game playing as the causal factor, e.g., 'Nintendonitis' and 'Pac-Man's Elbow'. While there does seem to be evidence for the existence of some of these effects, present research would indicate that they are rare and the causal links have not always been well established. In the case of children who develop incontinence problems, it seems clear that the condition is not caused by computer game playing *per se* but rather because the children have become so absorbed in playing that they are reluctant to stop and go to the toilet.

Other anxieties centre on the fear that children become socially isolated as a result of playing on the games and that they come to see the computer as compensation for lack of human contact and friendship (e.g., Silnow, 1984). It has also been suggested that the time spent on computer games displaces other more 'worthwhile' activities such as reading and indulging in more traditional games and sports. Much of the evidence for these concerns is anecdotal and there is a clear need for more empirical research in this area.

As a counter to these fears, there are many educationalists and researchers in the field who recognize the potential benefits of computer game playing. It is suggested, for example, that computer games could be used in educational contexts largely as a means of motivating less engaged pupils. They can also be used in performance evaluation tests and have already been shown to be reliable and effective in measuring psychomotor skills. In contrast to those critics who see computer games as socially isolating, some writers (e.g., Favaro, 1982) would claim that the playing of these games actually promotes social interaction through cooperation and competition and that they can enhance self-esteem by engendering a sense of mastery, control and accomplishment.

Similarly, some authors would turn the aggression argument on its head and suggest that the violent and destructive elements in computer games serve a cathartic purpose in allowing players to release stress and tension in a contained situation. Another argument, and one espoused by many parents in the present study, is that playing the games allows children access to new technology and gives them the confidence and appropriate skills to work with computers in the future. There are others who have found computer games helpful in a therapeutic context. Ever since the pioneering work of Anna Freud (1928), play has been seen as a useful vehicle for understanding and exposing children's anxieties. Computer games are often now included amongst the repertoire of aids used in therapeutic settings as a means, not only of behavioural observation, but also of communicating and giving rewards (e.g.,

Gardner, 1991; Spence, 1988). However, as is the case with regard to the possible harmful effects, there is currently little solid empirical evidence to lend unambivalent support to ideas about the potential benefits.

So, do computer games turn our children into mindless zombies sitting for hours on end in front of an electronic screen and locked into a distorted, private world of violence and stereotypic images? Or are they simply a harmless and enjoyable, even creative, addition to the wider play and leisure repertoire of children? Are there serious physical, emotional and social consequences of computer game playing or can it actually be used as a positive and beneficial activity?

There is currently a dearth of sound, empirical research in the field of home computer games, particularly that carried out in domestic settings, and many of these issues are unresolved — indeed, the important issues themselves are not all yet clearly defined. It is beyond the scope of the present study to provide definitive answers to these questions, but what we have tried to do, through observations of children in various settings including their own home environment, and through conversations with teachers, parents and siblings, is to enrich and inform the debate.

Computer games are frequently viewed as a sinister and alien arrival into the child's world which displaces more traditional and, therefore, more 'acceptable' forms of play. The recent survey undertaken on behalf of the Professional Association of Teachers (PAT, 1994), mentioned in the introductory chapter, sought the views of UK teachers on the effect of computer games playing on the children in their classes. It elicited comments like the following:

The perseverance of 'living-in' the game prevents children's attention and imagination being caught even by exciting school activities.

Children do not converse or play as they used to.

A noticeable number of pupils show real enthusiasm only for computer-type activities. Anything else is labelled as 'boring'.

Some parents in our own study seemed similarly concerned about the pernicious effects and offered observations like:

I'd stop them if they were on it [games consoles] too long. They should be doing something more constructive really. (Father of 6-year-old and 5-year-old)

I'm funny about it, I suppose. I don't like them playing computer games. X particularly — you see — well he — you can see — he gets so into it and he gets really upset if he doesn't win and — well — he wants to do it for so long. (Mother of 7-year-old and 5-year-old)

My husband might have a different point of view from me but I just think they're [computer games] a complete waste of time. (Mother of 6-year-old and 18-month-old)

Computer Games and Conceptions of Play

Every generation of parents seems to succumb to the idea that contemporary childhood experience is very different from their own. For many of today's parents, this notion encompasses the belief that the childhood experience has been diminished in some way — that the innocence of childhood has been sacrificed on the altar of modern, fast-paced, hi-tec living. Elizabeth Stutz (1995), in a recent unpublished article, seems to typify this nostalgia ('Is electronic entertainment hindering children's play and social skills development?') when she laments the demise of traditional games such as leapfrog, hopscotch and marbles, which she feels not only afforded children opportunities for fun and good exercise but also contributed to their social development.

This represents a view of play which ignores some of the reality. Stutz' interpretation suggests that play is a carefree activity associated only with pleasant emotions. She stresses the cooperative, egalitarian aspect of certain traditional games and the role they play in bringing boys and girls together. Our own contextual observations of children in the school playground suggests that much of the play activity is far from gentle, cooperative and egalitarian. Nor did we find much evidence of boys and girls 'on an equal footing, patiently taking turns'.

> I don't play with the boys — not really. They just get themselves into trouble. (Girl, 9-year-old)

> Some of the boys play ball — well, it's very dangerous because they're playing when this ball — right — two boys and they both have to run up on this bench and then run down from there and you're sitting on the bench and they're running down and you have to jump off the bench quickly because they could hurt themselves or they could hurt you. I'm just sitting on the bench and they just come and jump on you. (Girl, 8-year-old)

> We play spy games. We have a gang and we have top secret meetings. [He names the members of the gang — all boys. I ask if girls are ever included.] No. They're too stupid. (Boy, 8-year-old)

> Some of the girls are OK but only the ones who play football. I hate girls who play Barbie. (Boy, 9-year-old)

> Best of all I like playing outside with my friends and riding on my bike. (Boy, 8-year-old, with Supernintendo at home)

> I've got this great board game called 'Haunted House', I've had it for years but no-one of my friends had heard of it before. Vicky came round and I said 'Why don't we play on it?' and she absolutely loved it and the same happened with Donna. (Girl, 9-year-old)

So are computer games as different from traditional pastimes in their function and usefulness as some critics would suggest? Certainly the children in our study saw computer-based activities essentially as fun, whether the activities took place at home or in school. First School children (4–7 years), in particular, had no doubts about the purpose of the computers in the classroom and their answers emphasized the difference between computer-based activity and the more traditional classroom activities. When we asked a group of 6-year-olds in a First School classroom what kinds of things they did on the computers, we got the following sorts of replies:

> We play lots of games.

> There's *Through the Dragon's Eye* and *Frog* and — well, there's a painting game and a drawing game and some maths games — I'm not sure what they're all called — just lots of games really.

> We play maths on the computer.

Although the younger children seemed to view all contact with the computer as play, they were confused as to its precise role in the curriculum. In conversation with a group of 7-year-olds, one of them said:

> Sometimes we do it on Tuesday afternoons. I think that is technology afternoon and sometimes we do it on Friday afternoons because that is a sort of funtime and we can choose things — you know — activities — and we all like going on the computer.

The confused understandings of both children and staff concerning the use of screen-based technologies in supporting and developing the curriculum are amply illuminated in different chapters in this book. We can now turn to computer games playing in the domestic environment where there is no ambivalence about their role. That's entertainment!

Computer Games Machines in the Home

It has been explained in the Introduction that games machines, in their relatively short history, have already undergone huge developments and change. We found children using a wide variety of games, dedicated consoles and PCs. Some children were still playing on the early Spectrum and Commodore machines, but this was rare and seen as highly disadvantageous in many ways. A good illustration comes from a conversation we had with a 21-year-old young woman and her 8-year-old brother:

> *Sister*:   We've got a very old computer — it's a Spectrum Plus. We must have had it since about 1981. We just got fed up with it in the end.

It was so slow. It just wasn't much fun in the end but we got it out of the cupboard again about three years ago for P. We thought he might get some fun out of it.

Brother: I still play on it sometimes but it's pretty hard for me to set up. I can't do it. I wouldn't know a thing what to do.

Sister: Yes, that's the trouble with the old Sinclairs. There's lots of wires and things to connect up to the aerial and the tape recorder and things and that's a bit complicated for P.

Brother: I'd really like a Nintendo — they're much better.

On another occasion, we watched a 9-year-old girl try to load a game into an old Commodore machine. She puzzled over the appropriate command for some time and tried various things that were unsuccessful. Eventually she remembered the right term but then had to wait 10 minutes for it to load. The tape then clicked off and the child started to appear frustrated. Her father, who was also watching, told her that she had put the tape in the wrong way round so she had to start all over again. While she was waiting for it to load, there was the following conversation with her father:

Girl: I expect it'll do something else now — something else will go wrong.

Father: You can see why it's so frustrating. No wonder she doesn't want to go on it much.

(*The words 'Mission Aborted' have come up on the screen*)

Girl: What's happened now? What on earth does that mean?

Father: Goodness knows. That's just typical.

The usual pattern in homes seemed to be that children exerted pressure on parents to replace outdated models with newer versions. Old consoles and games were frequently consigned to cupboards or passed down to younger siblings rather than sold. Typical of comments about selling 'old' machines was from a mother of an 8-year-old boy:

There's no point in trying to sell it because you wouldn't get much for it. No-one wants to know nowadays so we might as well keep it.

Or from an 8-year-old girl:

We've got one of those Sinclair things as well — you know — what you can put through the telly. It takes so long to load it you just get that you don't want to play on it — you just get really bored before you start.

Or from an 8-year-old boy:

I've got a Nintendo now and so has my brother. We want to sell the old Atari and Spectrum but no-one's really interested. We'd probably have to almost give them away. My dad won't let us do that — he says we might as well keep them. We've lent the Spectrum to our friend. She hasn't got anything so she doesn't mind.

Or from the mother of 7-year-old and 9-year-old boys:

They've got a Master System as well but we've put that away now they've got the Nintendo. I think they've gone out a bit now, the Master Systems.

One family in our study, with two daughters aged 7 and 9, was unusual in that its Spectrum continued to be in regular use. The father often played on specialized railway games that he had to order through a catalogue and would sit up in the evenings for several hours at a time to complete the game. The two girls were aware of their father's interest in the train games but did not play on them because, 'They're too complicated'. They did sometimes play other games on the Spectrum but always under supervision: 'The girls don't ever load the machine, being as they're tapes, they can be a bit temperamental.' It later transpired in the conversation that the two girls 'had been crazing for a Sega'. They had apparently recently been to a friend's house where there was a Sega and the girls had been impressed. The father told us:

I lost them upstairs for almost a couple of hours. I went up to see what they were doing and, I must admit, it looked quite good. It seemed really straightforward — even the youngest was able to play. I can't see me playing on it though. I prefer the Spectrum.

Interestingly, this father, after much 'crazing' from the children, had agreed to buy a second-hand Sega Master System from a cousin who was updating to a newer machine.

There were numerous examples in the study of older games being discarded, forgotten or broken. The very small handheld LCD games which were popular a few years ago seemed to be particular targets for oblivion. Starting from as little as £3, they were targeted by the manufacturers as pocket-money or stocking-filler purchases. They were seen as particularly useful at keeping children occupied on long journeys and were often sold in garage retail outlets, Channel port and airport shops. Children, however, soon became bored with them because of the limited scope of the games. A conversation with a 6-year-old boy produced the following exchange:

Boy: Oh, yes, I remember. I've got those small ones. I don't remember what they're called.

R: And do you like playing on them?

Boy: Well, I don't play on them much. I've only just remembered them again.

R: Where are they?

Boy: I think they must be in my toy box.

> *R*:   Had you forgotten about them?
>
> *Boy*:   Yes, I'd had them for a long time. I used to play with them a lot at first.

Or a conversation at home with a mother and her 8-year-old son:

> *Mother*:   You used to have those really little ones, don't you remember? The little green one and the orange one?
>
> *Boy*:   (*Long pause*) Oh, yes. I remember now. I'd forgotten all about them.
>
> *R*:   Why did you stop playing with those?
>
> *Boy*:   The batteries kept running out and they were really expensive. What I'd really like is a Nintendo — they're much better — they're a better size.

There was a general feeling amongst the children that these little games were no longer worth having. Gameboy, however, still appeared to be relatively popular because it could be easily carried around and offered the opportunity to play different games:

> When I go on holiday to Spain, I'm going to take my Game Boy with me. (Boy, 7-year-old)

> I'm going to Cornwall on holiday soon and I'm taking my Game Boy. My dad will be taking his computer too. (Boy, 6-year-old)

There was also an awareness of the continuing likelihood of changes in the games technology amongst the children, as well as the kudos of owning particular brands as you get older. One 9-year-old boy, for example, when asked if he thought he would continue to play computer games at high school, replied:

> Yeah, but I wouldn't keep this computer though. It will be way out of fashion and my friends will tease me about it.

Most of the children in the study were aware of the range of entertainment systems available and were familiar with the names of the various versions. They were much less clear about the terminology if they had a PC at home, possibly because PCs were seen to be their parents' property:

> It's a big one and has got all sorts of bits round it. It came on a trolley when we bought it. (Boy, 8-year-old)

Computer Games as 'Education'

This problem with terminology was also noticeable in the range of things that were considered to come under the computer game umbrella. Many children and their parents seemed to classify any electronic toy as a computer. We came across many so-called 'educational' electronic games primarily aimed at very young children (roughly the 3–7 years age group) which had usually been bought by parents or other relatives as 'improving' or 'learning' toys. These battery-operated portable games purport to help with spelling, counting, vocabulary etc., but we found that children quickly became bored with them. For example, we spoke to the mother of an 8-year-old boy who had bought him a 'learning one' for his birthday only five months earlier:

> He played with it every day to start with. He really liked it, didn't you A.? He doesn't play with it very often now but it's really good — really educational. It's for learning. It asks questions and you have three tries at the answer — three tries before it tells you. It's quite difficult. It's good for learning.

The boy himself was deeply involved in a game on his Master System while this conversation was going on and did not respond when his mother asked him to go and fetch the 'educational' toy. She went herself in the end and had to rummage down to the bottom of a toy box to find it. We could not see it in operation because the batteries had run out. The boy himself said that he had forgotten all about it and couldn't remember how it worked. He showed no interest at all in renewing his acquaintance with it.

Similarly, in a visit to a 9-year-old girl's bedroom which she shared with her 7-year-old sister, we saw an electronic spelling toy under a pile of toys in a cupboard. In reply to our question about it, the 9-year-old said:

> Oh, that's just a play computer. We don't go on that any more. It's a bit boring. It doesn't really do anything.

There was strong feeling among many of the parents in our study that this type of toy would be of educational value to their children. This is a view encouraged and fostered by manufacturers in their advertising. One can see, for example, a magazine advertisement for the Sega Pico which encourages parents to buy the toy at an approximate price of £150 as 'a valuable investment in your child's future'.

Parents were usually vague about the specific advantages that would accrue from playing with the games. They tended to respond to questions about the perceived usefulness of the toys with statements like:

> Well, it's for learning, isn't it?

> It teaches numbers and things.

> We thought it would help her learn to spell.

> It's supposed to be educational. We saw an advert for it.

Children themselves, however, seemed to find these toys limiting and unsatisfying and poor substitutes for human interaction. There seemed to be little appeal or stimulation for children in a toy that simply corrected a wrong answer or praised a correct answer, often in an uninflected, soulless, robotic voice. We witnessed a number of instances of parents proudly displaying such toys to us only to have the child tap desultorily on a few keys before wandering off to find something more interesting. This lack of interest and engagement did not, however, extend to the video/computer games proper. There we encountered real excitement, animation and involvement.

Critics of computer games, and certainly many of the teachers and some of the parents in our study see them as, at best, a waste of time and, at worst, positively harmful to a child's development. Teachers, in particular, even those who used computer programs in the classroom, were often scathing about the value of games. The following comments were fairly typical:

> *Teacher*: He [a 7-year-old boy in the class] likes playing games. Now, I do have a games disk but I keep it locked away. He'd rather play games than do anything else. As far as I'm concerned, playing games is fine, but that's not what we're here for and I'd like them to learn that the computer has a much wider function than that. The games disk comes out at lunchtime and possibly the end of term.
>
> *R*: Isn't *Arkventure* a game? [*This is a program the researcher had seen being used in the classroom*]
>
> *Teacher*: Yes, it is but they are learning at the same time. With all the best will in the world, zapping space ships is not ever so ... It does have a place with mouse control in particular if they've never used a mouse before.

This first school teacher could at least see some value in the games even though she saw a pretty strong divide between pleasurable and educational use. Most of the other teachers in the study were fairly damning about the games.

> They're pretty mindless. (Female middle school teacher)

> Some children, particularly the loners, spend too long on them. It can't be good for them. (Male middle school teacher)

> I think they're awful. They do nothing for children at all. I have a very low opinion of them — you know, Nintendo and things like that. I say to some of the children at school 'Do you have a home computer?' And they say 'Yes, I've got a Sega' and I say 'No, I mean a real computer.' I ask you. I mean, they actually think a games machine is a computer. (Female middle school teacher)

> It turns them into zombies. (Female first school teacher)

On the basis of our observations of children actually playing on the games, it would be difficult to concur with the suggestion that it is a passive or 'zombie-like' activity. One of the striking features of children in front of the screen is the degree of engagement and animation which they demonstrate. It is precisely the interactive nature of the game playing which so appealed to the participants in our study. Television viewing was often presented to us as a means of relaxation and calming down. Typical comments from parents about television and video watching included:

> I let them watch TV when they first come home from school. I don't mind them doing that. They are so tired, they're not up to much else. (Mother of 7- and 9-year-olds)

> He watches in bed most nights. Well, it helps him to unwind. (Mother of 8-year-old)

> He has to go to bed at 8.00 every night but he'll watch a video while he's in bed most nights. (Mother of 9-year-old)

> He's been off sick from school for the last few days so the only thing he's been up to really is watching videos or telly. (Mother of 7-year-old)

What computer games seem to be offering the children is a means of activating the passive medium of television. They can actually take control of one of the figures in the game and influence the outcomes. Far from being passive and switched off, they need to be totally alert and reactive to events happening on the screen. Parents seem to recognize this aspect of the games playing:

> I think it teaches them reactions. They're aware of lots of things going on. You gotta be alert — there's so many thing going on in these games. (Father of 5- and 7-year-olds)

> I can watch what I like on telly in my room. I watch as long as I like in my bedroom. She [mother] stops me playing computers late, though. She thinks it gets me too excited. (Boy, 9-year-old)

> *R:* Do you play on the computer before you go to school?
> *Boy (8 years)*: No, not now. I'd like to but I'm not allowed any more. My Nan doesn't like it because I get too into it.

The children that we observed playing with games were for the most part totally absorbed. They concentrated exclusively on the screen action and seemed oblivious to people around them.

They frequently shouted out as if they were interacting with another person. One 6-year-old spent a whole hour playing on his Game Boy while a researcher was in the room talking to his parents and older sister. He was completely engrossed and paid no attention to the conversation. He frequently called out things like 'Go, go, go', 'Yes, yes, now'. and 'Go on, blow it up'.

Figure 4.1: A 9-year-old boy sitting on his bed absorbed with his Game Boy

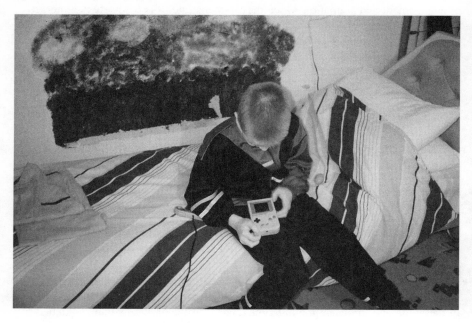

Children Interacting with Games: Realities and Fantasies

An 8-year-old, engrossed on his Master System while a researcher observed him and chatted to his mother, repeatedly whooped with joy as he progressed through the game. He often kept up a commentary to accompany his play, apparently directed purely at himself:

> No, no, not him — I hate him. I hate them things — I don't like them green things — they hurt you. Phew, they didn't get me that time. Oh, oh I'm going to die this time. Look, look, I'm going to get killed. I'm not very good at this bit. This is where I always get stuck. I get one more go and then I'm going to turn it off if I still can't do it.

While instances like this seem to offer evidence for total absorption and involvement in the game, they also provide critics with examples of graphic, violent language associated with game playing. It is faintly disconcerting to hear young children shouting out such messages of destruction with every appearance of relish. However, there seem to be two factors which serve to weaken the case that computer game playing alone is responsible for the children's aggressive verbalization.

Firstly, children have long been known to be fascinated by gruesome images. We found many examples in our study of children enjoying stories that deal with gory and grotesque events — Roald Dahl was a favourite author for many of them.

Figure 4.2: A 7-year-old boy oblivious to the conversation·between his mother and a researcher

During the course of the study, several groups of 8- and 9-year-old children were involved in topic work on the Anglo-Saxons which exposed them to the story of Beowulf and Grendel. Most of the children took enormous pleasure in listening to the story, watching a video version and completing their own subsequent narratives and drawings based on the tale. Pictures and stories about monsters and other frightening things seemed to be fairly recurrent themes in classrooms and bedrooms.

A conversation with a group of 8-year-old girls at school produced the following:

I like games where you get lots of squelchy noises.

Yeah, I've got one like that. You have to blow up these vegetables and they go splat and they just explode and there's this really funny splat noise. [*She produces an impressive squelching noise and the other girls join in.*]

Yes, the noises — I like them. That's the best bit when they splat.

75

Figure 4.3: Monsters created by a group of children for the classroom wall

> I've got a game that's really good. It's funny. It's called 'Aliens Ate my Babysitter'. [*All the girls laugh. When the researcher asked for more details of the game, the girl replied:*] It's not real. I just made that up.

A second factor that suggests that the language use is not as sinister as it may first appear, is the notion that play is divorced from reality. The children in our study seemed to recognize the distinction between reality and fiction, certainly with regard to computer graphics. The words 'die' and 'kill' are used repeatedly but their connection to real death and killing is remote. For example, a 9-year-old girl described by teachers as intelligent, sensitive, well-behaved and hard working, was observed at home playing on a game called *Manic Miner* on an old, black and white screen games machine. She wanted to show the researcher another game and, in order to extricate herself quickly from the current game, she said: 'I'm going to make myself die so I can move on to the next game. Wait a minute and I'll just kill myself.' This was delivered in a completely matter-of-fact tone and clearly had no unpleasant connotation for her. However, this same girl, when talking about watching a recent episode of a television soap in which there had been a fatal aircrash, expressed her distress and said that it had upset her so much that she would not ever want to travel in a plane. This raises a significant issue with regard to children's grasp of reality. We encountered several instances of children being upset by certain TV programmes (e.g., *Casualty, Strange but True*), the disturbance often taking the form of hiding eyes behind a cushion or having subsequent vivid dreams. There were some quite surprising examples of programmes that had been upsetting. For example, the following remarks about the programme *Mr Bean*:

> There was this really horrible thing. You know Mr Bean, well he's really funny but I mean there's this one where he's in the cinema and he's sitting down watching this film and he went to a lady . . . he went — he acts out the knife thing from *Psycho* and does sounds and this lady is going 'Aargh!' and I'm thinking they're going to show a bit from this film, of someone going around the wall like *Psycho*. I've seen *Psycho* and when this man comes in he stabs her to death and she falls on the floor. It's really scary. (Girl, 9-year-old)

This exchange, and other similar ones, suggested that children view films and television programmes rather differently from computer games. They were often able to describe quite unpleasant scenes from games without appearing to be disturbed by them or to find them realistic.

R:	Do you think that games like that are bad for you?
Boy (9 years):	If you play it too long.
R:	Why's that?
Boy:	Because your eyes go all funny; your eyes go all square.

It was interesting that the child interpreted the researcher's question about games being bad for the player solely in terms of possible physical effects. There were children who were aware of the taboos relating to games playing, involving certification, although these were seen as an adult concern which they had to negotiate. There was little understanding on the part of this child that there could be negative socializing effects as well. This is not to say that all children we observed had the same detachment. On rare occasions, we encountered cases where the child seemed preoccupied with the unpleasant aspects of certain games e.g., a conversation with an 8-year-old boy went as follows:

R:	Which games do you like best?
Boy:	Violent ones. Lots of blood. Anything with violence in it.
R:	Why?
Boy:	I just like violence and blood. It gives me great ideas for drawing.

This same child showed similar tendencies in other contexts. We found some drawings in his bedroom of decapitated humans and animals and observed him playing with small model soldiers which he crashed violently together while he yelled and shouted. His mother told the researcher that he often went for bike rides alone in the graveyard situated close to his home and that this was a favourite playground for him. Earlier, before he had been interviewed by any of the researchers or was aware of their interest in him, he was observed in a classroom situation where the children were required to complete a story beginning:

Figure 4.4: An 8-year-old girl's response to 'What makes you feel scared?'

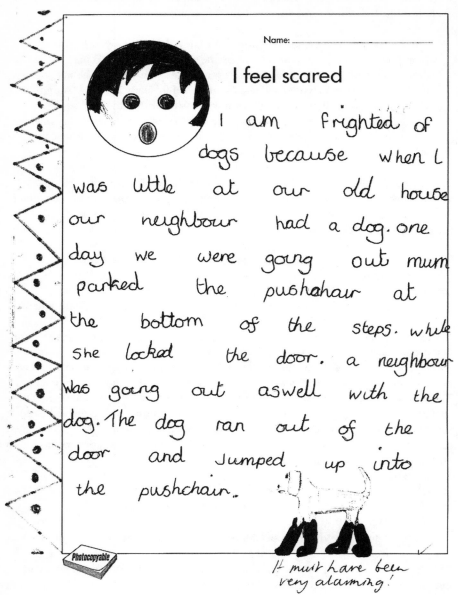

I came down to the kitchen this morning to find a large, wrapped parcel on the table . . .

Most of the children chattered to one another about possible story lines. Several started to recount real or slightly embellished memories of actual presents received in the past through the post. The boy in question, however, immediately began writing with no reference to any other children. After only 10 minutes, he had filled an A4 sheet with writing. This consisted of a gory description of blood oozing from the package which was then opened to reveal a dismembered body. No attempt had been made to explain how this could have come about or to build up any narrative structure — it was all gruesome description. This same boy when asked as a class exercise to write about things that scared him came up with an image of a man in black and drew an ominous looking figure. This contrasted starkly with the offerings of most of the other children in the class who tended to concentrate on real scary events from their lives, see Figures 4.4 and 4.5.

However, it would be difficult to make a case for violent computer games being a causal factor in this child's predilection for death and destruction. There was some evidence of long standing domestic and personal difficulties and he was causing concern for his teachers in a variety of ways. Playing on violent computer games was simply one aspect of this child's rather troubled behaviour.

Another 9-year-old boy who regularly played with games like *Streetfighter* and *Mortal Kombat* told us:

Boy: When I've finished playing on my own, I sometimes turn it on to two players and then just leave the other player there so I can just kick and punch them.
R: What's the point if there's no-one playing with you who can move the other joystick?
Boy: Well, I like to be able to work out the death moves — I can do torso removal and it rips the other body in half. (*He laughs loudly*)

This child also causes some concern at school, in this case because of his aggression, and was observed by researchers in some extremely rough and combative 'play' fighting in a domestic environment. Again it would seem that the computer games served to feed into an already manifest tendency towards aggression. This is not, however, to deny that the content of some games would seem to some unpleasant in its depiction of violent acts and images or to deny that such games have enormous appeal for some children. A review taken from the 'Console Corner' column of a regional newspaper (Yallop EDP, September 1994) is revealing:

Mortal Kombat was released last Friday and has followed its predecessor by going straight to the top of the charts on all console formats. The first Kombat was the biggest selling fight game of last year, having shifted over six million copies world-wide to date. It was also **slightly** controversial

Figure 4.5: An 8-year-old boy's response to 'What makes you feel scared?' (Notice the scarring he has added to the printed face at the top of the page)

Name: _____

I feel scared

I was scared of the man in black cos he was going to put me in a black sack

because one finishing move featured ripping out the opponent's spine. The SNES version cut down on some of the violence and was also noted for green blood — because of Nintendo's insistence that it comply with their family-friendly guidelines. The Mega Drive game was closer to the arcade original and sold more. Nintendo have woken up to the action and this time all 16-bit versions include full moves.

The game is a simple best-of-three against a time limit, using martial arts skills and special magical moves to outwit the other fighter and knock him/her flat. All twelve of the characters from the second arcade machine are featured. New fighters include the mutant Baraka, capable of changing arms into blades (much like the T1000 in the *Terminator 2* film); Kitana who throws and slices with a razor sharp fan; plus supreme Outworld ruler Shao Kahn. All three hidden characters also appear — Noob Saibot, Jade and Smoke.

There are even the new finishing friendship and Babality moves which, instead of bringing the tournament to an end by using a violent move to reduce the other to a has-been, it is possible to either give them an amusing gift or reduce them to a baby before they collapse.

This in an arresting review in several ways. Firstly, 'Console Corner' is a regular feature of this particular newspaper, appearing on a page called 'Kids' Stuff' intended for quite young children and yet the description of the game content is graphic. The language and tone of the piece suggests that the author sees no problem with the violent content. His use of the words '**slightly** controversial' to refer to the inclusion of a move involving 'the ripping out of the opponent's spine' and the phrase 'Nintendo have woken up to the action' suggest that he has little patience with the idea of 'sanitizing' the content of such games. It is also interesting to note the way in which Nintendo had sought, in the first version of *Mortal Kombat*, to reduce the violence level by showing green instead of red blood. This, it is suggested fairly bizarrely, is to conform to the manufacturer's family-friendly guidelines — as though the colour of the blood is a more disturbing factor than the essence of the action. Children clearly do read reviews such as this and doing so appears to affect their own way of expressing themselves about the game, a fact substantiated when we compared the language they used with the language we found in magazines. The piece reproduced below came from the newsletter of one of the middle schools included in our study. It is a fascinating example of precocious journalism on several counts. Firstly, and perhaps most surprisingly, it is written by a girl. Given what is generally assumed about girls' computer game preferences (see Chapter 7), it is probably slightly disconcerting for parents reading the newsletter to encounter such obvious relish from a 9-year-old girl for a violent game. Secondly, the standard of writing, whatever, might be thought about the content, is very high for a child of that age. The journalistic style and use of games jargon suggest that this child is being influenced by magazine and newspaper reviews.

MORTAL KOMBAT 2

Mortal Kombat 2 is the sequel to Mortal Kombat. The difference is, it's a big improvement. Better sound, cool backgrounds, more characters, gory fatalities (where you eat peoples heads and stuff.) The new options: Friendships and Babalities. As I'm a kind person I'll even tell you that Mortal Kombat 2 has three secret characters (Smoke, Jade and Noob saibot) a big improvement than the one secret character in Mortal Kombat. Smoke and Jade didn't remain hidden for long though but only the top Mortal Kombat players have found Noob Saibot. The characters in Mortal Kombat 2 are: Shang Tsung, Kung Lao, Liu Kang, Sub Zero, Reptile, Scorpion, Kitana, Mileena, Jax, Baraka, Rayden, Johnny Cage, Kintaro and the Outworld ruler Shao Khan. The story so far . . . After being defeated in MK1 by Liu Kang, Shang Tsung returned to the Outworld begging the very angry Outworld ruler Shao Khan for another chance to destroy the brave earth warriors which stand between Shao Khans Armies and his rule of Earth. Now about the Friendships and Babalities I mentioned earlier . . . . On the Finish Him/Her screen, instead of just doing another fatality, the Babality option allows you to turn your opponent into a baby! Friendships are quite funny as well, you can make fun of your opponent by dancing in front of him, or offering him a present, while they wobble around about to fall down unconscious! Anyway, Shang Tsung was given another chance to do what he failed to do in Mortal Kombat 1 by Shao Khan, and after being returned to his youth form (also by Shao Khan) stands a good change of living up to his masters orders. Reptile (the secret character in MK1) was seen lurking in the background of the first tournament, is actually a horrible reptile thought to be extinct years ago disguised as a human. Shang Tsungs loyal pet has this time attempted to try his luck in the tournament. Jax, who's strength earned him a stunning reputation in the Outworld has entered the tournament for two reasons, One-to rescue Sonia, taken prisoner by Shao Khan in the last tournament, and two, to show his impressive wrestling skills. Kintaro, a distant relative of Goro, (killed in the last tournament) is out for revenge, and has the strength of Shao Khan and Goro put together. Liu Kang the winner of the last tournament has his home destroyed, and was dragged into the Outworld by Shao Khans armies. He beat Shang Tsung in the final of the last tournament but failed to do away with him. Sub Zero-the mysterious icy ninja, is one of the best fighters out of the brave warriors trying to save earth from the hands of Shao Khan. Falling himself also at the last hurdle of doing away with Tsung, wants to get his frosty hands on Khan now. Rayden watched himself from his temple in the clouds, Shao Khans army storm Liu Kangs home and warned the other earth fighters about it. He himself wants to end Shao Khans rule of the Outworld, Baraka personally lead the army which destroyed Liu Kangs home. He is Shao Khans faithful ruler of all his armies. Kung Lao entered the tournament also for revenge-Shao Khan destroyed his last living relative. Along with his fellow countryman Liu Kang he plans also to destroy Shao Khan.

Mortal Kombat 2 is truly an excellent game, and there is a Mortal Kombat 3, but as of press time its not out. The sound is practically perfect, graphics are ace, the backgrounds are wonderful and the gameplay? Well what can I say? No longer is easy mode a complete doddle, and hard mode is utterly crucifying! I really recommend this game to everyone who is a real megadrive player, because it's truly excellent.

On the whole, we found that children in the 4–9-year-old age group included in our study — particularly the younger ones — did not necessarily express a preference for the violent 'beat-em up' and 'shoot-em up' games. Many of the children said that their particular favourites were based on Disney films and characters. There were frequent observations of children playing with games derived from The Lion King and Aladdin, for example, and many examples of children wishing to acquire these relatively new titles. Platform games, particularly the various versions of *Sonic the Hedgehog*, *Donkey Kong* and *Mario Brothers* were also very popular and, especially with the boys, sport games ranked high on their list of favourites.

R:	What's your favourite game on the Sega?
Boy (6 years):	Football games.
Boy (8 years):	I've got two best games really. I like them the same. It's *Nigel Mansell — World Championship* and *NHL Hockey 93*.
R:	Have you got any fighting games?
Boy (8 years):	Well, not really. I borrowed *Streetfighter* from the video shop but I wouldn't buy it.

Conversation between three 9-year-old boys:

Boy 1:	When I go round my friend's, I always play *Fifa '95*.
Boy 2:	Wicked.
Boy 3:	Yeah, I've got *Fifa '95* on my Amiga.
R:	What do you like about *Fifa '95*?
Boy 1:	You can choose your own teams.
Boy 2:	The graphics and everything — it's just wicked.
Boy 3:	. . . and you're just playing.
Boy 2:	. . . and it's like proper football, you've got like throws and fouls.
Boy 1:	I've got Manchester United, you can go against any team in Europe.
Boy 2:	You can have a league, play offs, cup match . . .
Boy 3:	. . . and you can go against Brazil league . . . any league in the world.

This conversation continued for some time with the boys showing considerable animation. It was obvious that they all found the games highly entertaining and challenging. They enabled the boys to enter into simulated versions of worlds where they are normally marginalized spectators. This kind of evidence also begins to raise the issue of simulated realities where virtue lies in verisimiltude. In sports games and 'beat-em-ups' one of the major criteria, reinforced by the magazines, is whether the game is 'true to life'. The entire computer games movement is directed towards achieving virtual reality. Given the content of some of the merchandise, one can see that current controversies are going to be nothing when compared to those that will erupt in a few years' time. Most of our age group, as said above, retain their delight in products aimed for them. The evidence suggests that this means a continued dominance of Disney and like productions:

Boy (8 years):	My favourite game is *Land of Illusion*. It's Mickey Mouse and you have to go through all these levels. He finds this key, see, and then he has to go through doors. Then there's *Castle of Illusion* — that's Mickey Mouse too. There's three doors, right, in this one and you can choose. You can choose easy or hard but I always choose hard now.
Girl (8 years):	My best are *Taipan* and *Sherwood Forest*.
R:	I haven't heard of either of those. How do you play them?
Girl:	Well, *Taipan* is a trading game and what it is is you can call yourself anything you like — you're on a ship and you've got to buy all these things and, well, I always start off with no money, five guns and no debt otherwise you get — well … the money all goes and you have to give him all the money. I always start off with no money. I kill the pirates by fighting with guns and then I get all their money which you can often do and get quite a lot and then get some really cheap things — opium is the expensivest. And then you sell it somewhere else which is much expensiver and you can go wherever you like. There's loads of places.

Although some of the activities in this game might raise moral questions, observation of the child playing on the game at home revealed it to be a complex strategy game involving quite high levels of anticipation and problem-solving skills.

Choosing Games

There were various criteria that children adopted for choosing games. Surprisingly often, this was quite passive with children simply playing on a set of games acquired in an initial package with the games console. There were some examples, too, of games being given as birthday and Christmas presents and chosen by relatives with little reference to the child's preferences. Few of the children in our study seemed to be reading computer magazines with any regularity, except at the top of the age range, although there were some instances of children being influenced by adverts in those journals. On the whole, computer magazines seem to be aimed at older children. Those in the 4–9-year-old range seemed to prefer the more traditional comics.

I used to get Sonic the Comic but I just get Beano now — it's funnier.
(Boy, 8-year-old)

Peer influence also seemed to be á factor. Often children were constrained in their choice by the retail outlets where they went to purchase. Few of the children were going to specialist shops — indeed many were unaware of the existence of such specialist shops in the locality. Most children were buying games from large chain stores such as WH Smith and Argos or from big toy shops in the local shopping centres.

> I get my games from Boots mostly. Sometimes I look in Games — not very often. (Boy, 8-year-old)

> Usually get them in Argos. I don't like One Step Beyond [a local specialist shop]. It's all messy in there. The games are all jumbled up. When I got the Master System, *Sonic* came with it. Then I got *Sonic 2* for my birthday but I'd like to get another game. I looked in the Argos shop but they hadn't got much. (Boy, 7-year-old)

There were a very few instances of children ordering games through magazines:

> I get this two months sort of catalogue called *Special Reserve* that comes through the post and it tells you about the games. The games are cheaper through *Amiga Program* or through *Special Reserve*. (Boy, 9-year-old)

However, this same boy, when asked if he ever bought games in shops, also avoided the specialist outlets and went to mainstream toy retailers. Children were also sometimes influenced by the picture on the box but many of them had become rather sceptical about this:

> Sometimes in the games they put a really good cover on it and when they put it in the box they put a thing on the back and when you put it into your Nintendo or something it's really boring. (Girl, 9-year-old)

They rarely read the text on the back or asked for a demonstration but could then be disappointed if they experimented with a new game:

> Yeah, when you buy it you don't know what's boring or good because you haven't seen the game before like you've only seen good experts playing the computer. (Boy, 9-year-old)

However, there were some rare instances of children taking more trouble over their choice:

R:	So how do you find out how to play?
Boy (9 years):	I just find out. Sometimes I play on it in the shop or one of my mates has got it — I just start playing.
R:	What makes a game look interesting in the shop?
Boy:	The name.
R:	What then?
Boy:	I ask for help and ask to see it being played.
R:	How long does it take you to choose?
Boy:	About an hour usually.

On the whole, though, we found that children usually seemed to know in advance which game they intended to buy and spent little time in the shop browsing. They knew about particular games from a variety of sources; for example, from playing at friends' and relatives' houses, talking to older siblings, swapping games with friends, TV adverts, TV programmes such as *Gamesmaster* and from hiring them out from rental shops. A conversation with a group of 9-year-olds shows this:

> *R:*　　Do you watch programmes like *Gamesmaster*?
> *Boy 1:*　My sister watches.
> *Boy 2:*　Yeah, I watch that as well.
> *Girl 1:*　I'm not supposed to watch it but I watch it. (*Followed by general laughter*)
> *Girl 2:*　I don't watch anything to do with games. I think it's really boring.

Later in the same conversation:

> *R:*　　Do you think these programmes have good information about games?
> *Boy 1:*　Mmm, and they have a consultation zone on *Gamesmaster* and they tell you about cheats on different games and they have previews to tell you about all new games that have come out . . .
> *R:*　　Would you ever buy a game because you'd seen it on the television or if you'd read about it?
> *Boy 1:*　If it was like good. If it had good ratings.

And from a 9-year-old girl:

> If I ever want to know something, I just ask my brother [older] because he watches all the programmes and he gets *Total* [a computer magazine] every month.

A major draw for the children was the cross-over of games with other media forms such as TV, film and comic characters. They were attracted to titles with which they were already familiar in a different context. Many of the children had seen films and television programmes and were keen to have the corresponding computer game although they were sometimes disappointed by the poorer animation or limited action of the game. Some of the children (although not many in our study) had already had experience of a particular game in an Arcade and were then disappointed by the Sega or Nintendo version:

> They probably thought, well, everyone will see it in the arcade and think, 'Oh, that's really good, I'll buy the game'. And then they end up buying a rubbish game that didn't cost much money to make so the company are making loads of money. (Girl, 9-year-old)

We encountered a few other examples of scepticism but this was relatively rare amongst the children, as shown in this conversation with a group of 9-year-olds:

R: Who do you think designs the games?
Boy 1:   Stupid people. (*General laughter follows*)
Girl 1:   Very stupid people.
Girl 2:   They must be quite smart because most of them know what kids will like to play. Umm, they know that kids will like stuff that's exciting and it's not all the same and everything.

Acquiring Games

As far as the price of the games was concerned, the children were, for the most part, perhaps surprisingly, quite accepting or, in some cases, totally ignorant:

R: Do you think the games are expensive?
Boy (8 years):   Yeah, they cost quite a lot but I think they're worth it. I mean, if a game costs as much as that, it **must** be good.

A conversation amongst a group of 9-year-olds revealed a bit more awareness:

Girl 1:   like they cost so much now. About £40 or £50. (*The others all mutter agreement*)
Boy 1:   Amiga games are getting cheap now because they are . . . well, about £19.99.
Girl 2:   Supernintendo games cost a lot — £50.
Girl 3:   My uncle's got tons of them and he nearly spend £100 once.
Boy 1:   The prices go down once the computers get out of fashion. (*There is general agreement in the group about this.*) Normal Nintendo games will be about £20 soon.
Girl 1:   Yeah, there's this game in the Argos catalogue and it's for £19.99, so . . .
Boy 1:   It's called 1999?
Girl 1:   No, it costs £19.99.
R: And do you think that's cheap?
Girl 1:   Mm.
Boy 2:   Yeah, that's probably the cheapest game you could get — it's less than Game Boy games.
Girl 2:   And you can get them off people that want to sell their games and loads of people.

Many of the children mentioned the idea of getting them second hand from shops, friends or, quite commonly, boot sales, but this was not a preferred method of acquiring games. This was largely because of the obsolescence factor mentioned before — games offered for sale in this way almost inevitably belonged to the previous generation and, therefore, represented outmoded technology. There were other reasons offered for preferring brand new games as shown by this conversation with a mother and her 9-year-old daughter:

> *Mother*:   Dixons do second hand games.
> *Daughter*: Trouble is, if you get a second hand one, you don't know what condition it's like. I mean, why would they buy it and then not want it all of a sudden?

Interestingly, parents often also seemed fairly unconcerned about the price of the games. They recognized that individual games were quite expensive in relative terms but seemed to accept that this was the going price and that there was little they could do in the face of children's requests. The parents who seemed to be most aware of the high cost of games were those who had not allowed their children to have games consoles in the first place. Otherwise there appeared to be an air of resignation about it and parents were reasonably happy to buy games as presents or to let children spend pocket money on them.

Occasionally, we came across examples of children playing on pirate copies of games and, in these cases, parents were usually aware of their origin, as shown by this conversation with the mother of an 8-year-old girl:

> *Mother*:   Our friend gave them this. (*She points to the game her 5-year-old son is playing on a Game Boy*) There are 32 games on the cartridge.
> *Daughter*: Yeah, that's really good. We asked in Dixons and they said they don't do them in this country. I think they must be pirates. Games are usually much more expensive so this is quite good really.
> *R*:   Are they the same quality as the normal priced ones?
> *Mother*:   They seem to be — so, why pay more? (*She and the children laugh*)

There was some evidence of children copying games from one another if they had the appropriate equipment:

> If we won the lottery, the first thing I'd do is get the Amiga 1200. That's the best. The graphics are better and you can get a crack copier. On normal games like Dune 2 I've got, you can't copy that but on the A–1200 you can store a copier into the hard drive and that will crack the original disk and copy it. I know someone who does that. (Boy, 9-year-old, who owns the Amiga 500)

One way that children sought to increase their access to games without actually buying them, was to swap with friends. This, however, was not always sanctioned by parents who were concerned that games would either not be returned at all or be given back in a damaged state.

> He swaps with his friend G sometimes. We're all friends — I see his mother a lot — so that's not so bad. I don't really want him swapping with

other people. They're so dear, the games, you just never know, do you?
(Mother of 8-year-old boy)

In this context, parents were concerned about the value of the games. Teachers, too, gave the high cost of the games as the main reason why they did not wish children to swap at school.

We don't allow children to bring games in to swap them — they're so expensive. On the whole what they do on computers at home is quite separate. (Teacher of 9-year-olds)

Many children, though, would have welcomed the opportunity to have some kind of lunchtime club organized at school where they could swap games and have the opportunity to play. While we did find evidence of a few schools having tried to provide lunchtime computing sessions, there was little encouragement to the children to bring in their own games and sessions had often folded because of problems of time and supervision. There seemed to be a difference in outlook depending on the schools catchment area. Those schools with middle-class children tended to have a moral severity about games.

Parents' Attitudes to Games

We found many examples amongst adults, both teachers and parents, of ignorance about the nature and content of computer games. Teachers, particularly, tended to see them as undesirable and frequently referred to their violent and sexist content although they were rarely able to be specific. A conversation with a teacher of 9-year-olds:

R: Do you know much about the sort of games the children are playing on?

Teacher: Well, I'm not very happy about what they tell me. You know, this one pulling that one to pieces.

There were some exceptions to this and certain teachers acknowledged that there could be benefits in playing, particularly in terms of problem-solving and opportunities for cooperative play, as with this teacher of 7-year-olds:

R: Are you aware of what children are doing at home with computers?

Teacher: Mainly on games but probably not as much as people think. Some children spend too long playing but they can be a good thing. The games for two are a good thing — they can share and cooperate.

As far as parents were concerned, there were those that professed total ignorance of the games and were clearly not interested in becoming more closely acquainted, as shown by this conversation with a mother of 8- and 10-year-olds:

> R: Do you ever play on the games?
> *Mother*: No, not at all. I don't understand what's going on.
> R: Do you ever watch them while they are playing?
> *Mother*: No, not at all, not at all. I'm just not interested. They all seem the same to me — just jumping up and down all the time — otherwise they're fighting. And the noise! I can't stand the noise — it's awful. I wish they could turn it down. I aren't really interested.
> R: How often do they play on the computer?
> *Mother*: I couldn't say. I don't have anything to do with it.

Some of these parents made some attempt to censor their children's television and video viewing but did not feel this to be necessary where computer games were concerned. They seemed to take the view that the games were designed for children and, therefore, did not require any discrimination — as though the responsibility for deciding whether games were acceptable had already been taken by a higher authority. Parents often recognized the names of computer games because of their tie-in to television programmes or film titles and seemed to find them acceptable because of that. *Bart Simpson*, for example, was a game often mentioned by children and parents seemed happy to allow them to play on this game assuming that the content was innocuous. It is possible that they would be quite surprised if they had overheard the following response from a 9-year-old boy to a researcher's question about the *Bart Simpson* game:

> Bart's got his skateboard and he can whack people with his skateboard or get on it and skate, um . . . and his sister uses her saxophone, hitting them round the head and putting them into zombies like playing it with like zombies and everything, like all of them are zombies but she's trying to get them out of it and the baby she's crawling around them and then she uses her dummy to whack people round the face and then she sticks it in their mouths and she uses her bottle like a gun.

While parents rarely censored content, there were many instances of parents curtailing the length of time children were allowed to play, as shown by this conversation with a mother of 7- and 9-year-olds:

> R: Do you mind them playing on it every day?
> *Mother*: No, not really. They enjoy it. I don't mind but I don't let them play too long. It's not good for them.
> R: What's too long?
> *Mother*: (*Long pause*) Well, an hour probably.
> R: Why do you think that's long enough?
> *Mother*: Well, it can't be good for them, can it? I stop them if they're on for too long.

There were some examples of parents who were not only interested but actively involved in playing. Perhaps surprisingly, a few parents played on their own at times when the children were not around:

I used to have one of those little games — you know — what you hold in your hand. It was Pacman — that actually belonged to me. It got broken in the end but we got Pacman for the Master System — that's much better really. (Mother of a 7-year-old)

This comment came from a mother of an 8-year-old daughter and a 10-year-old son who works from home using a PC:

I often don't really feel like starting work so I treat myself to a game of *Tetris* as a way of motivating myself to sit down in front of the computer. I try to restrict myself to one game but I sometimes get carried away once I've started and sit there playing for longer than I intended.

There were mixed reactions among the children towards parental involvement in games playing. They often seemed to enjoy playing with their parents particularly if they were playing as equals but some of the children were surprised to find out that parents played when they were alone.

Girl (7 years): We like playing funny games really where you get different characters and different things to do. It gets boring if you have to keep doing the same things over and over. One time when we were playing *Toejam and Earl* — that's a really good game — we played until 10 o'clock. Well actually it was probably 11 o'clock and it was a school day.

Mother: Yes, she's absolutely right, I'm afraid. It was her who noticed what the time was actually. I'd got carried away — just lost all sense of time.

R: Do you ever play on it when J is at school?

Mother: Yes, I have to confess, I do.

Girl: Do you, Mum? I never knew that.

Mother: Well, sometimes, I just need to relax and unwind and I'll just do it for an hour or so.

Children seemed to like the idea of playing with parents if it gave them the opportunity to win. They appeared to gain in self-esteem and confidence from the feeling that they were more competent at some activity than their parents.

Boy (9 years): Sometimes my mum comes up to play with me. I think there was two times when she's come up but I was so into it, I didn't let her have a go. Dad comes on it.

R: What games does your Dad like?

Boy: He likes fighting games like *Mortal Kombat*. He doesn't like it when I keep on winning. (*He laughs*)

However, parental involvement was not particularly welcomed when parents sought to intervene in play in a controlling way. One father of a 7-year-old boy felt that he had to play with his son otherwise the child would be frustrated by failure:

It's just you against the computer if you're on your own. I mean if I play with D. I let him have some chances which the computer doesn't. See, it doesn't know if it's playing a little boy or an adult.

However, when the child was asked, he clearly would have liked the chance to play on his own and resented this 'help'.

The question of suitability of games is linked to the idea of age restrictions. There is a voluntary code of practice operated by some manufacturers which gives suggested age ratings for computer games. This operates in a rather different way from ratings given to videos and films. The European Leisure Software Publishers Association (ELSPA), in consultation with the Video Standards Council, has introduced a system of age suitability ratings which has 4 categories: suitable for all ages; suitable for 11 years and older; suitable for 15 years and older and suitable for 18 years and older. This system does not indicate the game's level of difficulty but merely whether the game contains depictions suitable for that age group. So, for example, a chess game would be rated as suitable for all ages even though it would be too difficult for a young child to play. The age ratings system was not well understood by parents in our study although some of the children were familiar with it.

> *Boy (9 years)*: I play games mostly. Beat-'em-up games like *Mortal Kombat*.
> *R*: That's got an age restriction on it. How come you've got that?
> *Boy*: Well, my mum knows I don't get nightmares about it or anything. She got it for me.
> *R*: Do you think some children might be scared by it?
> *Boy*: I don't really know. I don't think it should be for people under 7 but for people over 7 it should be OK.

This idea that age restrictions were only appropriate for children younger than themselves was quite a common theme amongst the children in our study. Children sometimes acknowledged that games could be unsuitable but they always felt that they were 'mature' enough to cope.

There were some concerns expressed by parents that computer game playing could pose a health hazard but this was not a common anxiety. When pressed to be more specific, most of them were unsure about the precise damage it could do although some felt that eyesight could suffer, as shown by this conversation with the mother of a 7-year-old:

> *Mother*: I don't want him playing on it for too long.
> *R*: Why is that?
> *Mother*: Well, it's not good for their eyes, is it? One of his friends came round on Saturday and he had to go out into the garden for a while because his eyes had gone all funny.

Or with the mother of 7- and 9-year-old boys:

Mother: I don't think they should play on it for too long.
R: Why is that a problem?
Mother: I always think it can affect their eyes.

Or with a 9-year-old girl and her mother:

R: What makes you stop playing on games?
Girl: Usually my Mum says: 'Do you want to stop now, you've been on it for quite a long time now.'
Mother: Yes, I usually stop her. I don't think she should play on it for too long.
Girl: Sometimes I just get bored with playing anyway — like with *Bart Simpson* — there's lots of aliens and there's like octopuses and you have to sort of run past them and it gets quite hard so it gets quite frustrating and I switch off and go and play in my bedroom. Sometimes it gives me a headache so I just get fed up.
R: Why do you think it gives you a headache?
Girl: Well, I'm not sure really. I think it's looking at the pictures for a long time. I didn't used to wear glasses so I used to watch the pictures without glasses. It's better now I wear glasses.
R: Do you ever get headaches now when you play on the computer?
Girl: Mm — sometimes. Then I stop.
Mother: Yes, it's time to stop when she gets a headache.

Concerns have been expressed, though not by parents in this study, that computer video games playing can induce epilepsy. ELSPA produces an information leaflet for parents which seeks to refute this. However, acknowledging that parents might continue to worry, ELSPA suggests some guidelines for playing:

• Play in a well lit room
• Take regular breaks
• Don't play for hours on end
• Play the full distance possible from the screen
• If possible, use a monitor rather than a TV
• Stop playing should you feel unwell and consult your doctor
• Do not play if you are known to suffer from photosensitive fits

It was interesting to note that, even those parents who felt there were some health hazards involved in games playing, were not taking any clearly defined steps to address their concern. Beyond a vague idea that children should not play 'for too long', they did not seem aware of any other possible precautions. We certainly observed many children playing in dimly lit bedrooms sitting very close to the TV screen.

Occasionally, we came across parents who worried about obsessive use of the computer. For example, the mother of an 8-year-old boy with a 2-year-old sister

... used to find that, for as long as he was playing on the computer, he didn't seem to care about anything else. He'd get up but he wouldn't get dressed, comb his hair or anything. I had to drag him off. People would come to the house and he'd say I'm not coming — I'm playing on my computer. It's not natural for a child to behave like that.

This particular mother found a rather drastic 'solution' to the problem by selling the boy's Master System without consulting him.

> *R:*   Why did you decide to sell it?
>
> *Mother:*   Well, I like computers in lots of ways. I mean, they can be really good, can't they? But when they play on them for hours and hours, well then I don't like it. He used to get so into the computer — he used to get really bad tempered. So, when it got to 'Put that thing away, S, you've been on it for three hours', he just didn't want to know. He got really mad. I'd got a real fight on my hands and I couldn't stand that. So I got rid of it. When he hasn't got a computer, he just finds other things to do.
>
> *R:*   What did you think when your mum got rid of your computer, S?
>
> *Boy:*   I was really angry. (*He glares at his mother and lashes out at her with his foot*)

In spite of the mother's concerns and the boy's obvious aggressive tendencies (he was observed by researchers on several occasions engaged in highly aggressive behaviour involving kicking and punching other children), the mother was in the process of buying a new games console for him.

> He really wants one, he keeps crazing me and — well — what can you do? I expect it'll be different this time.

This idea of powerlessness in the face of children's demands was encountered several times, more particularly with regard to television and video viewing.

Another area of misunderstanding between children and their parents concerned the use of 'cheats'. Children were using these fairly routinely to avoid having to go back to the beginning of a game whenever they lost a life. They saw the use of cheats as a strategy for improving gameplay.

> *Girl (9 years):*   My brother got from his friend this big sheet of paper and sometimes you get codes and I've got it, it's codes for *Mario 2* and it's little boxes and it tells you the codes — all the codes you'll ever need in the whole game.
>
> *R:*   Do you think that makes the games less fun when you use cheats?
>
> *Girl:*   No, it's fun because you get to the end and you feel like good, even if you've cheated, you feel good if you get to the end.

Some parents, on the other hand, focused on the word 'cheat' and saw their use as being somehow morally wrong.

(The boy loads a game into his Master System)

Mother:	You cheat on this one.
Son (8 years):	Yes. I can go on to higher levels. See, you're supposed to go to the next level, but I'm not, I'm going on.
Mother:	Yes, that's because you cheat and go straight on to level 4.
Son:	Oh, no, I'm not. You don't know anything. I'm going on to level **five**. I can go on to level **eight** if I want to. I just found a way.
Mother:	Those people have spent lots of time on doing those other levels and you're not even going to do them.

Another example where adults and children took a different approach was in the use of instruction manuals. Many parents and teachers, unfamiliar with the new technology, sought understanding through a medium with which they were comfortable — namely the written word. Having turned to instruction manuals, however, many of the parents we spoke to confessed themselves completely bewildered by incomprehensible jargon, and this seemed to be an important factor in discouraging any further interest. Children, on the other hand, tended to bypass instructions completely, preferring to get straight into the game or programme and finding out by trial and error or by watching friends and siblings, as shown by this conversation with a 9-year-old boy:

R:	Do you ever read the instructions?
Boy:	I don't bother to.
R:	Why's that?
Boy:	'Cos I just think they're boring.
R:	So, how do you find out how to play?
Boy:	Just press all the buttons.

Or this conversation with three 9-year-old girls:

R:	How did you know that you had to use the whistle?
Girl 1:	My brother told me.
Girl 2:	Yeah, my cousin told me.
Girl 1:	I think he might have read the booklet, because I never read the booklets but he does.
Girl 3:	Well, my uncle told me about the whistle 'cos he's always playing on his. He gave us his Nintendo but he took our Sega.

To conclude this chapter, it can be seen that the place of computer games in the home is a complex one. There is no uniform way that parents handle controversial aspects of the games. In general, we found that children have a way of imposing their wills on parents so that the best intentions parents might have in controlling children's activities, go by the board. What was obvious to us was that many parents don't realize the scope open to them in supporting their children with games which might be deemed to be educational, even though commercial in origin. Nor do many of them realize that games machines are very limited in comparison with PCs. In our study, the undoubted advent of the PC in homes had not yet taken place, presumably because of a mixture of ignorance concerning the technology, the cost of machines and an assumption that PCs were for older children.

Parents were also aware that there was a moral debate concerning computer games and were, at first, loath to express themselves openly about family behaviours. The dissonance between family attitudes, in general, and those of schools, would seem to need bridging in some way. Otherwise, as the first few chapters have shown, the gap between schooling and new technology can only increase.

Chapter 5

Who is Being Framed?
The Use of Video in School

Mortal Kombat to me is not real. It's a bit like Cowboys and Indians we used to play. What worries me most is that I know there are children here, as young as 4 or 5, who watch very adult videos . . . and you're horrified at some of the things that they've seen. I just wonder about this blurring . . . I wonder whether . . . as we are so used to seeing real violence on television. I think I used to know that Cowboys and Indians weren't real. (Male rural school headteacher)

The blurring of realities in products aimed at the young is as topical an issue as it has ever been. A central thread of this book is that the manufacturers of screen-based products are, on the one hand, selling their wares directly to the very young and on the other attempting to close the gap between what we, the audience, experience in the flesh and what we experience through technological media. Thus they aim to realize their much vaunted ambition of producing 'virtual reality'. Video is a key product in the moral debate concerning censorship. It is also a medium around which questions of realism and its effects, revolve.

The Emergence of Video Technology in Schools

It has taken twenty years for video to make its **full** impact as a mass medium which is distinctly different from its two nearest relations: television broadcasting and the cinema. Video is unlike television and film in that there is now a degree of control and interactivity over the medium that you have not got with its precursors and hence the media experience is different — to a greater or lesser extent. It differs also in its form. Video technology records dynamic events on magnetic tape; rather than celluloid as in film. The quality of the images are dependent on electronic processes. The tape used is economic in size, scale and portability. This progress in design and technology is paralleled in the developing miniaturization and ease of use of the hardware. Also, in terms of its utility in the home environment, the success and acceptability of video is due in a large part to its reliability and accessibility.

It is instructive to follow the growth and development of video technology and its applications in educational establishments. One of the researchers recalls the introduction of a cumbersome, yet effective, reel-to-reel machine in a London FE

College in 1970. Other teachers will have memories of their first encounter with VCRs in schools, which usually meant that it was their first encounter with VCRs, full stop. If they had had prior domestic experience of the equipment, their initial attitudes towards it, and their experiences with it, may well have been more adventurous and imaginative — and less daunting. Although teachers could recall brief induction sessions in the early days with the LEA (local education authority) video camera (once certificated they were allowed to use the equipment), few remembered any formal training in the use of the VCR. One of the great assets of VCR technology, the ability to shift time so that the recordings of television programmes may be viewed at other times, has still not been exploited in schools to any great degree. Neither has its potential in staff training.

All the schools visited had at least one video cassette recorder as an available resource for use by teacher and class. The equipment may be held and stored in a variety of ways. The VCR and TV may be fixed to a trolley (or rover) which can be pushed from room to room as required. Sometimes the mobility of this system is utilized solely to pull the machine out of the security of its storage cupboard into the classroom or hall where the viewing takes place. On these occasions, it is the teacher and class who are expected to be mobile. Making the school hall the place for video viewing does enable more than one class to view at the same time. The following interview took place with the headteacher of a first school: on role, approximately 225 pupils. Her comments were not untypical of what we found elsewhere.

R:	Does each room have a television?
Headteacher:	No, no. We have two televisions in the school. One that's based at **that** end . . . because there are some steps.
R:	Is it on a trolley with a VCR?
Headteacher:	Yes.
R:	Do you do any video recording in the school?
Headteacher:	No, we would like to have a video, because there are so many occasions when we feel we should have video so that we could record things.
R:	To record television programmes?
Headteacher:	No, to record. I'm talking about a camcorder.
R:	I was talking about recording programmes.
Headteacher:	Oh, yes, we record programmes.
R:	Here on site? Rather than at home and bring them in?
Headteacher:	We have a classroom assistant who's responsible for doing that — so she does that and sometimes she'll do it at home.
R:	One person responsible for the whole school or for each class?
Headteacher:	The classes work together; so a year group will watch television together . . . so that cuts it down to four year groups. They don't watch much television; there might only be one programme per year group a week . . . so she's given notice if it will follow on.

R:	And these tend to be schools programmes?
Headteacher:	They tend to be, but members of staff also record programmes in the evening or at weekends, if they think it will be of interest. And they bring it in. You know, occasionally there might be a good programme about volcanoes and they record it.

When the TV/VCR system is used, it appears to be perceived solely as a teaching aid; there were no examples of pupils using it as a learning aid. There are of course sound safety, economic and resource reasons for this, but pupils in most of the schools we visited did have interactive access to audio equipment. As in the first school:

Teacher:	We use video in the first two terms which is a storyline . . . which is a serial they follow linking phonics with grammar. We also use a music video so they have experience of learning through video.
R:	Do they use the video themselves?
Headteacher:	Oh, no! It's only used as a television programme.

The interchangeability of some terms in teachers' (and parents') vocabularies — 'video' for 'camcorder'; 'television' for 'monitor'; 'television' for 'video recording' — was common to all schools in the research. This ambiguous usage of the terminology by teachers may indicate the low priority given to this technology (lower even than that given to IT by some) and it may also be due to the fact that many teachers appeared not to spend a lot of their time at home watching either television or videos. Not being a priority in their personal lives — unlike those of their pupils — they tended not to see its fuller potential in their school lives. It was noticeable how few teachers or headteachers referred to any form of video camera. Every school will either have its own camera, or will have access, formally or informally, to one. It may be used for the recording of a music or drama production or it may feature on sports day or on a school trip but it was never referred to as either an actual or potential resource for teaching or learning. The researchers were not made aware of any child or group of children who had access to a camcorder.

The Pre-eminence of Print

The irrefutable evidence to be witnessed in every classroom in every school, points to the dominant role that the printed word and image still play in educational resources. Teachers have been educated and trained in a print culture with which they are familiar and comfortable. The introduction of a new medium, *albeit* one which their children use and consume regularly, is challenging. Despite the fact that video facilities have been in some educational institutions for twenty-five years now, the technology and the rich range of its possible applications still do not appear to have entered the professional consciousness of the majority of educators.

Paper rules, as shown by this conversation with the headteacher of an urban middle school:

Headteacher:	I don't watch television either. So in the spare time I have I read books!
R:	Are you addicted to books?
Headteacher:	Yes. Funnily enough I can always remember talking to my son, he was always desperate for a computer and we wouldn't have one . . . wouldn't have one. And I can remember arguing about the reasons I didn't want one. And I can remember saying things like 'It isolates you. It takes you away from your peers'. All these social things . . . and I suddenly thought, 'That's what reading does too. You do go and hide and read. You're reacting with a way words work . . . but seeing pictures.'

Our observations seemed to show that the accepted teaching convention of reading aloud from a book, discussing a written story or using a verbal narrative as a focus for class discussion, did not generally apply to media forms such as photographs and moving images. There seemed to be no incentive on the part of teachers to explore the meanings of, say, visual representations, with either individual pupils or the group as a whole. There were no resource banks of photographs, although of course there were photographs with the accompanying writing (which helps to close their meanings down) in books, on posters, on charts, etc.

R:	What are the resources that are found in most classrooms?
Headteacher:	Well, there would be a lot of books.

The importance of print-on-paper is also reflected in its predominance as one of the less permanent resources.

> There would be plenty of implements for the children to write and draw with and they can usually choose. There'll be a variety of paper and if they're doing some technology, or art and craft, there'll be a variety of card or paper to cut, stick or glue. There'll be maths games and language games. (Headteacher urban middle school)

The games, here referred to, are board games, not computer games; although educational games for IT hardware can be found in many classrooms. An intriguing aspect of this apparent reluctance by teachers to fully acknowledge the part to be played by the video cassette recorder in the classroom, is the way in which the equivalent audio technology has been not only accepted but also integrated. It would be instructive to know to what extent the audio cassette machine is a part of a teacher's domestic life: in the car, in the sound system, in the bedside alarm.

Headteacher:	There'll be a Listening Centre that children can plug into. Four or five children can listen to usually a story being read to them, or music.

| R: | Would that be on a pre-recorded cassette? |
| *Headteacher*: | Yes. So they could sit there listening. Either listening to the stories, poetry, music or whatever — or sit in groups or on their own. |

The apparent lack of enthusiasm for TV and video in several schools may be the result of cultural, class-based, financial or organizational concerns. Those schools which **have** addressed this new technology have learnt how to integrate videos as a school library resource.

R:	Is the television used in the classroom at all?
Headteacher:	We didn't use it enough to make it worthwhile, but we do. We watch one or two programmes which go on for about ten weeks which is excellent.
R:	And the video?
Headteacher:	Well, we do video it. We don't watch it live. I want to see the programme before we see it ... before we do it. We might want to stop halfway through. We watch one consistently. And occasionally, if we're doing a history or geography project, we'll use one. Some of them are very high quality, but then again there are so many good things available that you could spend all your day watching television and doing nothing else. Whereas I think you need to watch television as an aid. For example, you can't go to Egypt, but you can watch a video of it.

Whatever the school's priority, teachers are fully aware of their children's wholehearted acceptance of the medium in the domestic context, not to mention their familiarity and confidence with video tape recorders.

Headteacher:	Well, I know that they have no problems with actually working a video. So I would guess that the majority of them would have a video at home.
R:	When you say that they have the experience of using video technology, would that include recording, setting timers ... or just playing?
Headteacher:	I would guess so. I mean young children certainly have no problem with putting the video in, starting it off, rewinding, fast forwarding and all that ... and I would guess as they progress they would also be able to put it on the timer. It would be interesting to ask them. I just know that when I am faced with a new video recorder, if there's a class there, I'll say to the class, 'Does anyone know how this works?' and they usually do.

Watching Video in School

Teachers can be very aware of the sophisticated ways in which children, at least, may be using video technology at home, whilst in school the utilization, on the whole, appears to be much more basic. From the perception of young viewers, it doesn't automatically follow that because they watch moving images at home, the watching experience for them is similar at school. The **mode** of viewing is dramatically different. For instance, children at home may be on their own or with a few members of their family or friends, sprawled on chairs or floor and capable of many shifts of position and vantage points. At school, it is usual for First School and some Middle School children to be sitting on the floor in a large group. The probable physical discomfort for some, if not all, of them does not appear to be appreciated by the teachers.

R:	Do you watch television at school?
Boy (6 years):	Sometimes if . . . like 'Words and Pictures'.
R:	Do you like that?
Boy:	Yeh . . . but I get neck . . . my neck gets hurt sore 'cos I keep on like that. It keeps . . .
R:	You have to look up?
Boy:	Yeh . . . yes, 'cos it's like that.
R:	High off the ground?
Boy:	Yeh.

His teacher's preoccupations are different:

R:	How attentive are the children when they're watching that?
Teacher:	Very glued.
R:	Very glued?
Teacher:	Yes.

The attitude to discomfort of middle school pupils perhaps differs from that of many first school children in that they are bigger and **do** mind sitting in uncomfortable positions:

R:	How does it feel watching video or television at school, compared with watching at home?
Boy (6 years):	It's much more like hush-hush at school; but it isn't at home.
R:	Do you pay as much attention?
Boy:	Yeh . . . you have to pay more attention.
R:	You have to pay more attention at school than you do at home?
Boy:	Yeh . . . at school, yeh.
R:	You enjoy it more at school?
Boy:	Ummm . . . no.

R:	Why not?
Boy:	'Cos it's not like . . . 'cos it's history instead of what you want, like a programme.
R:	Does it make it interesting?
Boy:	Yeh.
R:	Why?
Boy:	'Cos that's what we're doing and it's interesting what we're doing . . . Anglo-Saxons as a topic . . . so it's interesting.

This seems an extremely important point made several times by pupils of different ages. The different focus given to a video or TV programme by their teacher in an educational context can make the subject of the text more interesting. Even if they've seen the programme previously at home (when it hasn't been explored and discussed with them, by an adult or older sibling).

R:	And do you feel comfortable when you're watching at school?
Boy:	Er . . . yeh. Yeh . . . yeh, I'd prefer if it was at home though . . . but I do feel comfortable.
R:	Would you watch these programmes at home if they were on television?
Boy:	Um . . . no.
R:	When you've watched it, does your teacher then discuss it with you?
Boy:	Yes.
R:	Does the teacher stop the video to discuss bits?
Boy:	Yes.
R:	How often?
Boy:	About three times in the programme.
R:	And the programme would last roughly how long?
Boy:	Half an hour.
R:	Do you get a chance to discuss it with the teachers?
Boy:	Yes . . . yes.
R:	Do you do that in small groups, or in the class as a whole?
Boy:	In the class as a whole.

Teachers are aware of the importance of verbal literacy, but may be unable or uncertain of their ability to explore the concept of literacy more widely. By giving a major emphasis to the words in an audio-visual message (as with one teacher who equated watching television with listening to a teacher) images and non-verbal sounds may become marginalized.

It would appear that some educators regard these media as teaching machines: that the TV and VCR are interchangeable with human presenters. Such notions may have been favoured in the mid-1960s when the white-heat of technology was promising a machine-led educational revolution: today the role of an empathic, skilled (both socially and professionally), knowledgeable human being is hard to gainsay.

In attempts to raise the profile of media education in schools generally, most teachers readily see the benefits and attractiveness of using media artefacts as classroom resources. They might see the importance of, say, a TV documentary as an end in itself. The fact that the programme makers responsible had a large number of choices and decisions to make before arriving at the finished documentary is rarely addressed. If it were to be perceived as just one of several valid interpretations of the subject matter, the pupils might acquire useful learning and research skills. The analysis of media texts as primary sources is encouraged by a few, but many teachers appear to lack confidence in the wider realm of media education. Considerable time and effort is spent in schools teaching and learning the reading and writing of words: compared to that devoted to those aspects of media literacy that lie outside the traditional notions of verbal literacy.

Teaching and Children's Video Experience

From an early age, children learn how to read images. Their ability is dependent on a number of factors including the environment, encouragement, and the experiences they have had themselves. When they start school, attention will be given to their verbal skills, but less attention appears to be paid to their visual (and, by extension, media) literacy. To gain valuable insights from viewing moving images, it would seem essential that the observer has a good understanding of the codes and conventions of the relevant visual languages. There is no reason why these, too, cannot be taught in first schools, rather than offering visual imagery as a passive adjunct to classroom life:

> *R*: When they watch television are they watching a broadcast programme or a videotape?
>
> *Teacher*: It's always videoed because of having to fit into time slots. Yes.
>
> *R*: Could you give me some examples of what they might have been watching?
>
> *Teacher*: We watch *You and Me* on a weekly basis because it's got quite a lot of the social skills we need. We watch *Story Time* and, for science, we watch *Come Outside*. And they are weekly broadcasts and we watch them the following week.
>
> *R*: When children watch videotapes — I know it's difficult to generalize — are they as attentive as they might be if they were watching one of their favourite programmes at home?
>
> *Teacher*: I think their attention is excellent. It's one of the things that I think I notice more than anything . . . it's that they **do** see, they're very watchful . . . er . . . concentration is excellent. Mainly, I . . . I mean . . . whether that comes from children, but I do insist when it's television that we don't interrupt and that we do watch and it's one of the early skills that I do teach. It's that if something's on then we are watchful. (City first school)

One of the problems for the outsider researcher is how to unpick fact from fiction; reality from fantasy. The difficulty is compounded by society's apparent desire to focus upon (often through the channels of the mass media themselves) the unacceptable media experiences of young people. Whether teachers were well versed in popular culture or not, their children were, either through first-hand experience or their sub-cultures. Handling the issues of screen-based experience in the young was not straightforward for teachers, particularly as their own knowledge of these experiences was usually quite minimal:

R:	Has any concern been expressed by members of your staff about material that the pupils may have come into contact with?
Headteacher:	Yes. We are aware that children tell us about videos that sound unsuitable for young children.
R:	How do you know that they've seen them and they're not just talking about what older children might have talked about?
Headteacher:	Well, they've said, 'I was watching this video last night.'
R:	Right . . . and normally you can tell when they're telling the truth, can't you?
Headteacher:	Sometimes you can't. It's the same dilemma when there's a problem on the playground. Sometimes, you believe a child and it turns out the child is a very competent liar.
R:	So age really has nothing to do with it? You can't say that because they're younger, they're more likely to tell the truth?
Headteacher:	Yes. The younger children are more difficult, because they'll say what they think you want them to say and that clouds issues too. And older children say things for a variety of reasons, because it sounds big or to get out of a problem or whatever.
R:	OK. So in a way it's hearsay.
Headteacher:	It is very difficult. I mean, on the whole, we believe the children, whatever they tell us. We believe them because without any other evidence it's often dangerous not to believe them. Because you can dismiss things.
R:	Well, coming back to the video material, you have reason to believe that some of the children have said that they've come into contact with material which is probably meant for adults. Do any titles of films or videos spring to mind?
Headteacher:	Well, I haven't been here so long . . . but it's interesting what happened at another school. I mean I can remember one child who was only Year 1 at the time. So, 5 to 6. And it turned out that the film he'd been watching was 'The Living Dead' because he was absolutely terrified of dying. He was preoccupied with dying, and wanted to know what happened when people were buried and whether the skeletons could move and what things would get out of the grave and so on.
R:	Do you know the context in which he saw the film? Was it with parents?

> *Headteacher*:   The parents denied that he'd seen it.
> *R*:   The parents were challenged . . . questioned . . . asked?
> *Headteacher*:   Yes . . . well, because he was so upset about death and dying.
> At the time, it was outside school and it was opposite the
> Methodist Chapel. And there was a funeral going on one day
> . . . and he started sobbing terribly . . . and it came out, he was
> worried about dying and death and so on . . . and um . . . I then
> spoke to the parents and they said 'No, he hasn't seen it'. I
> said, 'Well, he said he has.' 'It must have been when we were
> out; with his brother or cousin. Must have been when he was
> round his cousin's.' They denied it had happened. Not in the
> home. (City First School)

As can be seen from the above conversation, people working in schools are often
not only aware of, but also find themselves involved in, the repercussions which
can occur when a young child is exposed to stimuli aimed at an older audience.
Teachers might also feel strongly about what they regard as the unacceptable content of many of the programmes available to young people, within normal viewing
hours on television:

> I go to my father's quite often and he watches it a lot . . . and I cannot
> believe what I am seeing. The sexual innuendo at 5 o'clock in the after-
> noon. I don't think that children's television should be about marriages
> breaking up and people going to prison and lesbians and homosexuals and
> all the rest of it . . . But what is the watershed really? You talk to some
> of these kids and ask them what they've seen the night before and your
> hair stands on end. Some of them have been up until half ten . . . eleven
> o'clock. (Headteacher, City First School)

We found a great many teachers who were willing to make judgments about children's viewing habits, such as the suggestion below that children might watch more
video than television, without any corroborative evidence.

> *R*:   Do the children talk at all about the kinds of things they watch on
> television or watch on videotapes? Just generally . . .
> *Teacher*:   Yes, about videos they do . . . not television so much. I think a
> lot of them do have videos and perhaps watch those more than
> television.

The same urban school teacher, a year earlier admitted, for example:

> I just don't encourage that kind of talk; there's too much violence on
> television. But it is a useful medium for discussion.

There is a tie up here with the project's findings concerning teachers' attitudes to
computer games and their apparent refusal to allow much discussion about such

activities in the classroom. Sometimes the child's needs overrode this reluctance to have popular culture in the classroom, leaving a powerful imprint in the memory of the teacher. The following conversation represents a typical example of this effect — but also highlights how dramatic events serve to confirm a mindset, based on very striking, singular events. All the survey's teachers could remember such dramatic events in their teaching biographies — but most were not recent. On this project, there were few examples given by teachers of children's inappropriate viewing.

R: Have you ever perceived any problems that children have had because they've had access to adult material and video? At this school . . . or generally?

Teacher: Yes. Yes. Yes . . . I have. Not necessarily adult material, but **inappropriate** . . . things like 'Jaws' a few years back. A child was very . . . **severely** traumatized by having seen that and it dominated her conversation for quite a long time.

R: How old was she?

Teacher: Five. With two older brothers . . . and she was really quite disturbed by it. That lasted quite a long time. But that's the most specific incident I can think of.

R: Was the school involved in developing any strategies for helping her to come out of, or cope with, this trauma?

Teacher: The whole family were being supported by the school and social services and everything, so . . . it's a big issue. (Middle school)

Children seem to have a fascination with stories which explore the worlds of monsters and the occult. Many branches of the entertainment media produce artefacts, in genres such as 'Horror' and 'Sword and Sorcery', which can intrigue and frighten the younger members of the public. More specifically, many books especially written for children explore these themes in a variety of ways. The careful control of books, and other texts, which find their way into the classroom illustrates the paradox whereby the traditions of the literary medium allows ghosts, death and witchcraft to enter the classroom, when they would be forbidden in their more technological forms. They also happen to be very popular. Examples of books in a not untypical classroom of 6-year-olds, observed by a researcher, were:

Monica's Monster Sheila Lavelle
Where the Wild Things Are Maurice Sendak
Winnie the Witch Korky Paul and Valerie Thomas
What's the Time, Rory Wolf? Gillian McClare
Dr Xargle's Book of Earthhounds Jeanne Willis and Tony Ross
When the Dinosaurs Lived Jonathan Shelly and Julie Park
Meg's Castle Helen Nicoll and Jan Pienkowski
A Diplodocus in the Garden Sarah Hobhouse and David Mackay
The Wizard's Cat Colin and Jacqui Hawkes

On the walls of this classroom were displays of the children's work, including a series of paintings. Not all the pictures were captioned but most were; and all the captions had been word processed by the individual artists themselves. Children's preoccupations with death are evident in many of them:

> The sheep bashed in the telly. (Girl)

> Once upon a time there was a butterfly and that was very good. The butterfly liked that he was good said his mummy one afternoon the butterfly crashed into the tree. (Girl)

> once upon a time there was a cat and the cat wanted a mouse. So one day he called all his mates and they looked everywhere even in witch cafe. But they still couldn't find it, so they went into the mouse barn and they found one. They took it home and ate it. the end. (Girl)

> the princess and the queen lived in a castle the prince went out. a hunter came and killed the king and queen and princess. (Boy)

> one day there was a dragon and a dog and the dragon ate the dog and the dragon ate the cat and the dragon ate the snake and the dragon ate a piece of his self. (Boy)

The class teacher explained the background to this work. It was the first piece of creative writing that the children had done for her. She hadn't wanted to restrict them by a detailed briefing, so she had given them a focus and had talked simply about a basic narrative structure (i.e., beginning/middle/end). The children could write about whatever they wanted as subject matter. Whether all the children concerned chose a violent theme, or whether they originated in the imagination of an individual child, who passed it on orally, is difficult to tell. But, whatever the source, it was embraced by many of the children. The work was handwritten through its initial stages, with the opportunity to discuss it with the teacher. When approved, it was word processed; the amount that was word processed depended on what they had time to do. The re-occurrence of events including the fantastic, the horrible and the terminal do not seem to be untypical of children's work at this age. In that sense, children may often seek to recount the same experiences of fear, repugnance and excitement from a range of media and utilize these experiences in their output.

In another school the headteacher pointed out the work of a boy who was a keen *Dr Who* fan: 'His drawings are very much spooky and witches, and last week he started to draw a laboratory.' In a third (Rural First) school, the headteacher reflected on his own childhood before describing the activities and imaginations of his pupils:

> When I grew up I had lots of toy soldiers and we played a number of violent games, like Cowboys and Indians . . . although I can honestly say

that I am not a violent person. What worries me is the desensitizing of some of these experiences. I don't know what to think of TV and video games, it's very difficult. And the other thing is the violent imagery. We certainly have an awful lot of violent imagery in terms of speech and drawing and early writing . . . and I seem to notice that.

. . . We were trying to get across real management of plot, and this child started with children sitting on the beach and mum goes to buy an ice-cream . . . and everybody was following this. It seemed quite logical, and next minute there was a chainsaw massacre going on, and the mother was being sliced up. Now . . . the children were discussing this, and generally concluding that this was too much . . . what with a bomb going off, etc. But I was thinking to myself, 'Where does that come from?'

It is not possible to list the influences on a child's imaginative processes, nor can they be quantified or weighted. From the evidence available, it is reasonable to assume that one child is going to retain different information and impressions to that retained by another child (even an identical twin) from the same stimuli, given the unique composition of each individual. Educators may be aware of many of the influences present in the formal school day but they can only surmise at the wealth of other influences on a child's mind. An examination of the statements of children and parents in the domestic context may assist in giving a fuller picture.

Before leaving the school environment, here are some observations about the other kinds of effects that TV or video watching might have on young people, beginning with the physical effects.

R: In your experience are there children who you know are spending a lot of their non-school time, possibly at their own home or at other people's homes, watching television or videos and it's obviously having a detrimental effect on their health?

Headteacher: No.

R: So . . . no children coming in tired or . . . ?

Headteacher: Children . . . some children do come in tired, but at the moment I . . . don't know for any one particular child I can say that's because they spend the night watching television. I know children stay up late, and they do watch television, but I wouldn't say it was detrimental . . . not too tired.

R: You wouldn't see it as a problem in this school?

Headteacher: Not a particular problem, no. I'm sure it does happen, and it happens on occasions . . . I know families, for example, who will go and visit . . . um . . . friends during the weekend; rather than have a baby-sitter, they'll take the kids with them. And what they'll do is put all the kids together in one bedroom perhaps and they can watch a video and go to sleep when they want. So bedtime that night might be too late. Now perhaps that isn't desirable and the next morning if the kids are tired, then perhaps they should have left it to Saturday, but I can also see it from the parents' point of view. So that does happen.

R: And it's not happening night after night?

Headteacher: It doesn't happen every single night of the week. Perhaps occasionally. (Middle School)

Whereas the experience of this Middle School headteacher differs considerably:

You tend to notice the negative things, don't you? The thing that worries me most . . . is the 4- and 5-year-olds. The things I notice are incredible tiredness . . . so that children come to school first thing in the morning physically tired. I'm not saying it is television but when you talk to them socially as you do over lunch, and you draw the conversation, subtly, to what happened the night before, you have 6-year-old children saying they stayed up watching this and that until ten or eleven o'clock. So I feel that there are children coming here to school physically unprepared.

What about any social and psychological effects? Read this conversation with the headteacher of an urban middle school:

R: How do you perceive entertainment in the lives of the children? If they spend a lot of time watching television; if they enjoy films and videos; if they enjoy playing computer games, how does that rest next to the work that they do at school?

Headteacher: It's interesting, that one, because I think we spend more of our time encouraging children to work together with other children, either in pairs or in groups or the whole class. Then there are times when they work as individuals. But when they're watching television, they get a lot of time, a lot of them are playing on a computer by themselves. I know that some of these you can play with friends; and the hand-held ones are for individuals that the others are watching, but I am aware that sometimes children can become very insular and isolated when they are with technology which contrasts with a lot of the work that goes on in the school: cooperation, working differently.

And from another perspective comes this opinion from a headteacher at a rural primary school, which emphasized how biography casts its shadow over current perceptions:

Headteacher: My main thing about television is that it has broken up social life because people don't go out and socialize like they used to. When I was brought up in the 1950s, people had television, but it wasn't on for such a long period in the day. People used to talk more as families. I can remember playing cards and board games as a child which doesn't seem to happen these days. I used to teach nursery children and lots of children have trouble with eye-to-eye contact, because of talking a lot of the time and screaming.

R: A teacher in this school said that over the last few years it is far more difficult. Kids are far noisier and it is far more difficult for some to sit still and concentrate. Would you go along with it?

Headteacher: Yes; and also to keep their attention. They're used to seeing high quality graphics. Whizz! Bang! Crash!

R: Do you think that television is the cause?

Headteacher: Where else? Why else? I think it's cause and effect. I think the television works . . . helps because they don't talk to people eye-to-eye. There are so many people who watch videos, before coming to school, and Breakfast Television. They get home at three o'clock and it's back on again. When my children came home from school, I used to let them watch it until 6 o'clock and then that would be it for the night.

A final view:

I would say that just generally, as a teacher, that children are more difficult to handle now, don't listen as well . . . and don't concentrate as much. I don't know the reasons for that. But I do think that conversation with children when they are younger, and reading with them, has been replaced with putting a video on . . . and then that goes on to video games or whatever where children are just looking at them flickering. They don't have to relate to them. I'm sure that is having an effect. I mean that the National Curriculum has brought in specific Speaking and Listening Skills under a heading. And certainly since being here, I've had four classes, and each year they have not been as good as the previous year. They should be better at it because we're focusing on it strongly. (Teacher, middle school)

Currently, there are understandable concerns being raised in schools surrounding the relationship of education and screen-based entertainment technology; and the consequences for the National Curriculum. The debate tends to be based on hearsay evidence and is influenced by teachers' perceptions of what is good for children, their nostalgia for their own childhoods and their own lack of affinity for much of popular culture. It would seem appropriate, within this debate, also, to question the under utilization of the media technologies which already exist in schools; and perhaps, the urgent need to address an expanded notion of literacy.

Children are educated to be critical readers of books from the moment that they're first introduced to books, but there is no equal emphasis on, say, critical video or television reading. They are not formally taught about the usage of the technology, the amount of creative flexibility offered by the medium's interactivity or the complexity of the reading processes. The 9-year-old daughter of one of the researchers has watched the video of the BBC's 'Pride and Prejudice' at least fifty times over a two month period. Why? What is she getting out of it? What needs does the video satisfy? How (if at all) can these needs be met through the education system?

As things remain, and the evidence of our research in schools seems to confirm it, teachers rely upon an anecdotal and somewhat fabricated view of what children are doing with video technology. Isolated instances of children being seriously affected by what they have seen become compounded into a school-wide view. Teachers may, on the whole, remain so far outside the orbit of popular culture, that they are left to develop instinctive theories, from the bits and pieces of evidence that come their way during the daily round of teaching. There is some evidence that this is not true of some inner-city schools in mass conurbations but, at the same time, there often do exist unwritten codes reaching the level of taboo, concerning what is acceptable to schools, in terms of children's experience. Very often, screen-based entertainment lies within the boundaries of the unacceptable.

The following chapter seeks to illuminate exactly what those experiences might be.

Chapter 6

Vexed Whys and Videotape:
The Use of Video in the Home

Oh, 'Curse of the Mummy' is it? I said to her if they put it on that late there must be a reason why. But, yes, I'll let her watch things. I tend to watch as I'm taping so if we find it's a bit too gory, we just tell her that we forgot to tape it. I know that she is a little girl but she's really into blood and guts — her father will sit there watching it but I have to turn the sound down if it gets really bad . . . but this one'll just sit there watching everything. (Mother of 6-year-old)

Video Technology in Family Life

When it came to identifying children who could participate in the video part of this research project, the sole requirement was that the home of each child contained a video cassette recorder. The number, and sitings, of the VTR (or indeed VTRs) varied from home to home. Its usual positioning was in one of the communal rooms in the house, where it could be used, to a greater or lesser extent, by all the members of the family. It was often the case that middle school pupils were in homes that were better resourced in terms of entertainment technology than were the first school pupils' homes. The assumption might be that as the child grows older, then technology is both demanded but also proves more useful in keeping the child occupied, or 'prisoner' as is suggested by research into how children's freedom outside the home and school has become limited owing to parental fears about their safety. Some children were very well catered for:

R: Where is the video kept?

Boy (9 years): One in my room and in my mum's room and one downstairs. We've got four TVs — one downstairs, then there's one in my mum's bedroom, one in mine and also the monitor for the computer. I've also got cable in my room.

Many of the older children, and some of the younger ones had televisions in their bedrooms:

Girl (8 years): Well, we used to have two, 'cos one used to be mine, but my mum had to sell it because it was the biggest telly in the house.

113

| R: | Do you miss having your own? |
| Girl: | Yeah. |

Some children had the benefit of resources in two homes as they spent some of their week with one parent and some with the other.

R:	How many video players have you got access to?
Boy (8 years):	In which house?
R:	Well, tell me about your week.
Boy:	Okay. We've got two. Um . . . one in my dad's house that's very ancient Panasonic [he also had a Panasonic Super Drive].
R:	What's so special about the Panasonic Super Drive?
Boy:	Well . . . um . . . it's got really good sound qualities. You can record very well and it's really hi-tec and we've got a big video . . . er television.

Several children were conscious of the quality of the equipment that was available to them. This was a constant theme across all technologies in the home and school. Children have become very knowledgeable about quality and design. Brand names and technical capabilities run through much of their conversation, as does deprecation when things don't work:

R:	Do you have a video?
Girl (8 years):	Yes, but it's a bit knackered.
R:	What's wrong with it?
Girl:	I don't know but it's just chewed up all my videos.

It was apparent (also supported by national statistics) that parents felt it important to have particular hardware in the house for the use of the children. Indeed, it was felt by the team that in most homes normal interaction could not occur unless there was a background of screen-based image and sound. Many of the researchers' initial observations when visiting a child's home contained notes to the effect that the television was on and usually remained on throughout the visit — irrespective of whether or not anyone was watching it.

T is sitting on floor in the sitting room when I arrive. He has a friend with him. The TV is on — it is Children's TV. The volume is quite high. No-one turns it down when I come in. H is sitting on the floor watching and younger brother R is sitting in a big armchair watching. Mum takes me into the sitting room where the children are and we sit down but the TV is left on and the volume is not turned down. (Researcher's field notes)

Visits to homes also led to researchers realizing that, despite the investment in video technology, it was mostly its most basic function that was used — that of play back. It did not automatically follow that, because the machine was in a shared space, children had limitless (or indeed any) access to video. Even in a communal part of the house, its use was usually controlled by one or both parents:

R: Do you video things from the telly?

Boy (9 years): Not really. My mum and dad do sometimes. I asked for the footie to be videoed, but she wouldn't let me. mum doesn't like football.

If a parent can't be persuaded to record programmes or films, then there may be others who will:

R: Do you ever ask your mum to video anything that's on late — that you can't stay up for?

Girl (7 years): It's my nanna up in Newcastle who tapes everything for me. (*She giggles*)

At times family members did not seem to be aware that the VTR could be utilized to solve conflicts over what to view, with a seeming preference being given to the exercise of parental power over who chooses what is on the screen:

Girl (7 years): We don't record things. We just watch videos but I don't watch videos very much.

R: Why?

Girl: There's normally good things on telly. And other times I've just got to do some reading or play on my computer or something else. Mum always wants to watch something totally different. I like watching the news sometimes as well. Mum watches the news all the time so I just watch it.

There were parents in the survey who were aware that televisions without aerials could be used as monitors for videos. This could afford them some control over viewing habits by denying access to television programmes:

R: Does A watch television up here?

Mother: Not on her own. I don't think that's right, but my husband rigged it so that she can just watch videos up here. I don't mind her watching a video on her own ... obviously, I know what it's about. (Mother of 6-year-old)

There was also plenty of evidence that families tended not to build up libraries of video material for viewing again. Most families seemed to have a policy of wiping a tape once the contents had been viewed, although some tapes might be kept for a while if they had impressed on first viewing. Where taping of programmes did take place, it appeared to be the custom that the man, if there was one in the household, was the recorder of programmes, especially if the timer needed to be involved. Most women expressed their lack of ease with the technology, which could prove poor role models for their daughters and result in sexual stereotyping by their sons. There were extreme examples, mentioned elsewhere in the book, of women staying up beyond normal bedtimes in order to record programmes because they couldn't pre-programme the video recorder.

R:	Do you know how to programme the video?
Daughter (8 years):	No . . . I watch my mum sometimes. I think I could do it if my mum was here.
(Interruption)	
Daughter:	Once we were watching *Cinderella* and I pressed record instead of rewind, so I wiped some of it off.
R:	Did it take a while to learn how to programme the video, Mrs S, or do you find that kind of thing quite easy?
Mother:	I'm afraid I have to get the book out every time.

Within households which did record programmes from television, there was a range of activity, some of it highly limited. For example, in one the only things to be recorded (by the father) were 'football and some documentaries'; another family taped Hyacinth Bucket and *Pride and Prejudice* and then watched it on Tuesday evenings — 'it's too late on Sundays'. They were watching the drama series and reading the novel at the same time. This description, by the mother of a 4-year-old girl, of taping procedures was a more familiar one:

I sometimes tape *Play Days* if I know we are going to miss it and I occasionally tape a schools programme . . . but they tend to be forgotten about and we never get round to watching them. Sometimes I'll record a Disney film from the TV — like *Cinderella*. Over Christmas there's a lot of animated films on the telly and we tape them to watch later. We keep things like that — we don't tend to wipe them.

This woman's daughter demonstrated her collection of audio tapes, putting them in her audio cassette player by herself. The family often listened to them at breakfast. She wasn't allowed to use the hi-fi in the sitting-room. She could load the VCR, but always had to ask first. Her mother again:

There is a child lock on the video machine. We got the video before we had the children, but I'm so glad that we've got the lock . . . it's the best thing we could have got.

However, the more typical responses to whether women were using video for recording are shown in this conversation with mother of an 8-year-old girl:

R:	So you never record anything from the TV?
Mother:	No, not really.

R: Do you know how to?
Mother: Yes, I think so. (*Dubiously*)

Here are another mother and daughter (8 years old):

R: Do you get your mummy to tape things from the telly for you?
Daughter: I can do it myself. I just get the box and take the tape out and put
            it in over there and press the button.
Mother: She doesn't know how to actually record anything.
R: Do you ever video anything for N?
Mother: No. We watch anything we want straight from the telly ... like
            Sesame Street.
R: What about for you?
Mother: No. I never really video anything from the telly.

Censorship and Education

If access to the technology varied from household to household and use of the
machine to record programmes proved limited, what about access to the videotapes,
themselves: both those in the children's domain and those containing more adult
material? In most homes, videotapes were freely accessible, though parents tended
to feel that their children wouldn't watch what wasn't suitable. Our speculation,
inferred from our experiences rather than directly being informed, is that many
parents take the packaging of products as an indication or guarantee of suitability
— and think that it is the same for their children. That is, that their children will
not watch tapes that don't have cartoon or bright, child-oriented covers.

R: Do you have those tapes in the house?
Mother of 5-year-old: Yes.
R: But you have no worries at all that they have easy
                         access to these tapes?
Mother: No.
R: And they have no inclination to watch that kind of
                         material?
Mother: No, I don't think so.

One way in which a parent can ensure that a child only sees appropriate video
material is to vet it beforehand. In other words, to look beneath the cover. It
appeared that only a minority of the parents we interviewed went to such lengths:

The only time they sit and watch on their own is if H is very tired, say,
and I'll let her have a video on while I'm getting tea ready ... but I know
exactly what's on each video, because I've seen them all so often. (Mother
of 7-year-old boy)

> The children have some pre-recorded tapes — they are all Disney cartoons
> — which they have had as presents. (Mother of 7- and 9-year-old boys)

Disney-style cartoon characters and similar graphics on the box covers seemed to influence parents in procuring tapes, judging by what we discovered in children's collections, whether from the shops or from second-hand sources. 'We get them from car boot sales . . . like *Basil, the Great Mouse Detective*'; and 'There is also a Turtles video that O [5-year-old boy] bought at a car boot sale.' Apart from one or two examples, as portrayed in the first chapter, children did not seem to possess adult-oriented products. However, this does not mean that they did not have access to them and view them. Tapes have followed the same route as books and can be bought, rented or borrowed, new or second hand, from a variety of sources:

R: Do you ever rent videos?
Mother: Not often. They like watching all the old videos like *Bambi*, *The Rescuers* — things like that.

In our survey, the evidence for renting seemed to suggest a decrease in interest, at least as far as children are concerned. Pre-recorded videos as presents dominated. Thus, children swapped tapes and borrowed quite frequently. Most of this activity seemed to involve products marketed for their age group. Given that pre-recorded video titles have recently outstripped novels in sales, it is not surprising that ownership of them follows similar patterns. There were those children who jealously guarded their tapes and watched them over and over, and those who dumped them in the drawer with the rest of the family artefacts. The younger the child, the less important the issue of ownership of the individual videotapes seemed to be; although this did depend on the dynamics, size and ethos of the particular household.

Girl (8 years): Well, my [5-year-old] sister, she watches *Grease 1* and *Grease 2* over and over again.
R: What have you got?
Girl: *Beauty and the Beast*, *The Little Mermaid*, *Mary Poppins*, *Snow White and the Seven Dwarfs*, *Aladdin*.

Ownership of videotapes is also an issue over which child and parent may not have the same perceptions, the parent imagining that they are for the whole family or just themselves whilst the children have contradictory views. On some occasions, it was felt that the parent (or parents) claimed that their offspring liked a particular video, or video toy — especially if it appeared to have an educational purpose, when, in fact, the child didn't. The desire of parents to 'improve their child's minds' by buying them technological aids, could be very strong and was a central reason for their acquisition of computer technology. However, the child's attitude towards such enterprise might indicate fatigue at these attempts to foist unwelcome products upon them. A researcher in one home situation was invited by the mother of a 4-year-old girl to watch a demonstration of *TV Teddy* — an educational toy — which involves the Teddy talking to the presenter on the television, through pre-programmed tapes:

Mother: Show her *TV Teddy*.
(*A brings the Teddy back while mum gets out the video*)
Daughter: (*Points to a box of videos*) I hate the *Mr Men*.
Mother: (*Coming back into the room*) What does she say she hates?
R: The *Mr Men*.
Mother: Oh, you don't. A. She loves the *Mr Men*.
Daughter: I don't, I hate them.
Mother: You do like them. I bought you one the other day because you crazed for it.
Daughter: I don't.
(*They talk about which video to load to operate with TV Teddy*)
Daughter: TV Teddy can sit here between us. You can hold his hand.
R: What does he do?
Daughter: He talks to you.
R: What does he say?
Daughter: You have to wait.
Mother: I've got loads of tapes here of A when she was a baby.
(*A turns the switch on Teddy*)
Mother: My mum bought that for her last Christmas: she's an only child. She thought she gets lonely. It was £40 and the tapes are £10 each.

(*TV Teddy starts to sing 'I'm TV Teddy — it's time to start the show. I hope you're ready. 1, 2, 3, 4 . . . Go!'. The Teddy talks to the TV presenter, and suggests ways of tidying the room on the video by shapes. A watches but does not seem to be particularly engaged. She then starts talking to the researcher about her dress, ignoring the video. We agree to stop the TV Teddy video. A's mum offers to show me a video of A as a baby. She tries to find the one she wants to show me — no 4.*)

Viewing Habits

In discussing their video viewing habits with children and their parents, it was impossible to keep the conversations away from the related topics of television and film. In some ways parents were more wary of television than of video. This seemed largely because content could not be controlled, as it can in a pre-recorded videotape. Also, as will be reiterated elsewhere in this book, very few parents had any listings for what was on television, adding to its unpredictability. Only those parents who had a strong sense of their ideal of childhood, seemed to go the lengths of pre-planning and vetting viewing habits with regard to television. Otherwise it seemed to be a matter of channel hopping and memory. This might have been a contributory factor to the low level of off-air video recording that seemed to be the general rule, as with this mother of an 8-year-old girl:

R: Do you have the *Radio Times* or *TV Times*?
Mother: No.
R: So how do you know what's on?
Mother: We get the pullout bit from the *People* on Sunday . . . or failing that the *Sun* does it on Saturday.
R: Do you plan ahead what you are going to watch?
Daughter: Well, yesterday there was *Halfway Across the Galaxy*, I just switched on and it was on. I didn't have anything else to do. It was quite good about these people that come from another planet.
Mother: You never sit down and look at the paper and decide what you want to watch for the rest of the week, do you? We just do it on a daily basis really, don't we?

This description of an evening was a familiar one for several of the children interviewed:

Boy (5 years): In summer, when I get home from school, I just watch TV — that's all I do and then have supper. Then I stay up 'til 10 o'clock. No, 9 o'clock.
R: And then what?
Boy: Well, I just go to bed, don't I?
R: What do you do up to bedtime?
Boy: Watch telly. Sometimes mum lets me stay up a few minutes more to finish watching something. I like *The Bill*, *London's Burning*, *The Brittas Empire*.

Children's viewing habits were subject to a wide range of family controls. These controls were rarely consistent and often broke down, anyway, when children stayed at friends' houses for the night. Often they seemed to be dependent upon whichever parent was sitting with them. Quite a few households had satellite or cable television. The content of some programmes labelled as children's programmes, did cause some parents some concern, as this conversation with a mother of 6-year-old boy shows:

R: Don't children come into contact with violent imagery through films and television?
Mother: I try to . . . um . . . limit that.
R: How do you limit it?
Mother: Um . . . I try to keep track of what they're watching . . . um . . . and we have a ban on *Power Rangers* and *X-Men*.
R: Who's we?
Mother: Um . . . my husband and I.
R: And how do the children respond to that?
Mother: They have accepted that.

R: Do they understand the reasoning behind it?

Mother: Mmmm . . . yes.

R: You're not sure?

Mother: I think so. (*Pause*) I don't know whether they understand the full reasoning. I mean I was trying to explain to them that it isn't just violence, it's also mindless violence, and I mean in the case of *Power Rangers* you have this authority that will tell the *Power Rangers* that . . . er . . . to go out and fight and they just go out and nuke everyone they've been told to destroy . . . um . . . and nobody ever gets an explanation of why these are the baddies and I think they did understand that. But we have also got . . . um . . . sometimes both films and games and I said, 'Oh! Those are horrible!' and I changed my mind eventually . . . I said, 'OK!'.

There is a general awareness of the existence of a television watershed on British terrestrial television at 9 o'clock in the evening. But in all the talk with parents about their children, the media and bedtimes, they made very little mention of the word 'watershed'. The term seemed to be one used mostly by teachers. It would appear that parents have differing notions as to their responsibilities, and those of the broadcasters. For example:

> Goes to bed about 7 pm but sometimes comes down again if she can't get to sleep. Sometimes comes down in the middle of *Casualty*. Mum is a bit worried about her seeing this because it is so gory. Her husband wouldn't approve: he thinks it's too gory, but if he's not there mum lets her sit with her and watch it. (Researcher's field notes)

Children we talked to were allowed to go to bed at wildly differing times. Some stayed up as late as their parents while others were in bed by early evening. Many of the older boys in the survey seemed to have fairly relaxed arrangements about both access to television and a bedtime. Typical was this 9-year-old boy:

R: What time do you go to bed?

Boy: Usually about 12.00 pm, but it's different on weekdays. I go up about 9.30 pm but I don't go to sleep.

R: Do you watch ordinary programmes on BBC and ITV?

Boy: No, I only watch *Strange but True* . . . that's my favourite.

R: Do you have to ask your Mum if you want to watch TV?

Boy: No, I can watch what I like. She stops me playing computers late, but I can watch TV for as long as I like.

Parental Interest

By focusing on the watershed, it was possible to ask some key questions about parents' responsibilities for their children's viewing behaviour. There were some who did have clear ideas:

> R: Do they watch television programmes after 9 o'clock?
> Mother: NO!
> R: You say that quite vehemently.
> Mother: But they are only 6 and 9. No, I couldn't countenance that.
> R: So, if they said that somebody at school had seen a programme that started at 9.30 pm?
> Mother: Yes ... they do tell me that, and I say, 'Well, that may be so. But not in this household'.

This mother again, later:

> I'm trying to tread a very fine line between protecting them and exposing them to what's going on. Um ... I mean the 9 o'clock threshold I think is a very hypothetical thing because at 6 o'clock the whole detail of the Rosemary West trial on BBC 1, at a time when all the children are at home and quite likely watching TV, so you have to keep an eye on what's going on and ... um ... my strategy with for instance something like the Rosemary West trial is ... is not to ignore it completely but I wouldn't let them watch the full investigation but I'm trying to explain to them what happens then. Um ... I'd rather they heard it from me.

This mother was very unusual in the survey in that she exemplified a role which seemed to be largely missing in most children's lives — that of the mediating adult, helping children to make sense of their experiences. With parents reneging, generally, on this role and teachers rejecting popular culture, children were very often adrift, with no support from a significant adult. The subject of 'unsuitable' viewing material, whether on late night TV, early evening or on video was referred to earlier in this chapter. It often arose in interviews with very little prompting.

> Mother: I don't ... with the videos that I've allowed them to watch that are over their age, I've vetted first anyway. And I had a nonsense scenario once when I allowed them to watch ... um ... *When Harry Met Sally* and I wouldn't let them watch the scene where she was faking an orgasm in the cafe.
> R: Why?
> Mother: Because I didn't want them to see that scene.
> R: Why?
> Mother: Because it was very explicit, and I didn't want them to be asking detailed questions about that.
> R: Don't your children know about orgasms?
> Mother: Well they do now ... because they were ... because I wiped that scene out ... and fast-forwarded it, the next time they watched the video, they pestered and pestered and pestered to watch the scene and I'd made more of an issue about it by not allowing them to. And they didn't really understand what the big deal was about.

Another common referent in these discussions was the popular children's film. A film can be viewed at the cinema, on television, or as a video recording (either off-air or pre-recorded). Again it was difficult to ascertain when talking about this subject, especially with children, to know exactly which format was being discussed. Whichever, the phrase 'a popular children's film' was usually a trigger for the conversation to include a reference to a product of the Disney Corporation. Disney products (and not just the films on video, but other merchandise as well) were constantly being mentioned by children. For example, in a conversation by an 8-year-old girl:

R: What do you watch if you do have the telly on?
Girl: Mostly Walt Disney.
R: Do you have Sky?
Girl: Yes.

and an 8-year-old boy:

Boy: We sometimes act out *Aladdin*. We turn the sound down on the video.

and a 9-year-old girl:

R: What kinds of things does she video?
Girl: Well . . . things like *Pinocchio* she's recorded . . . like mostly Disney films and things that have been on . . . (*Later in the same interview*) . . . I've got *The Lion King* . . . I got it for my birthday and it was nice because I had some of my friends and we watched it and it was like being at the cinema. (*Laughs*)

Parents, too, often talked about Disney films and other products, usually without critical comment:

She role plays from *Beauty and the Beast*, *Aladdin* and *Cinderella*. She used the videos, but added in her own imagination. We've got the books and the audio tapes as well . . . and, in fact, we use them a lot more than the videos. She sees the videos in the supermarket or the Disney Store. (Mother of 4-year-old girl)

Another interviewee — mother of 4-year-old girl:

Mother: Just after Christmas we're going to Disneyland, aren't we darling? For your birthday. And we'll probably get the new computer when we come back.
R: Do you like Disney films, A?
Daughter: (*Long pause*) Mickey Mouse, I like.

In her appraisal of Disney films and the necessity of having a critical purchase on content, the following parent was an exception:

> *R:* Do your children have many Disney films?
>
> *Mother:* A fair amount, yes ...
>
> *R:* And yet you were expressing some reservations about the Disney Corporation's approach to mythological stories?
>
> *Mother:* Yes, but I have also come to see that ... er ... they have such a strong role in ... in the market for children's entertainment, there is absolutely no way I can, sort of, go around them. So I might as well choose those Disney films that I think are OK.
>
> *R:* How do you feel about your children coming into contact time and time again with American culture when you're so well-versed in Austrian, German and English culture?
>
> *Mother:* I would prefer it not to be quite so uniform, but on the other hand I think you cannot eradicate indigenous cultures, so although there is a globalizing aspect to it, I ... I can see this very clearly, there are also quite stubborn elements that are distinctive to a particular nation and ... er ... you can see in the BBC — they pull out a lot of rubbish to fill the time ...

To return to children's use of videos, something which was picked up on early in the project and was confirmed through repeated questioning, was the apparent need that children had to view their videos from the beginning. Even if they'd watched the first half-hour earlier that day; on returning to it, they tended to want to see it again from the start.

> *R:* If you're watching something like *Pinocchio* ... you've already watched it once ... when you watch it again, do you always watch from the beginning or do you go to a particular bit that you really like?
>
> *Girl (9 years):* Mmm ... no. I'd watch it from the beginning.

Another example from a mother and her 8-year-old daughter:

> *R:* Do you watch that kind of video right from the beginning or do you just watch your favourite bits?
>
> *Daughter:* Right from the beginning. I know some of them off by heart.
>
> *Mother:* We taped *Short Circuit* from the telly and she was word perfect on that.
>
> *Daughter:* I kept repeating that in bed and that.

A father described in clear detail the way in which his 7-year-old son (E) acquired certain language skills from his favourite videotapes. E has severe learning difficulties — his cognitive age is much lower than 7.

Father: My youngest son memorizes — he's got an amazingly retentive memory so that at the level he's at (*Postman Pat, Fireman Sam, Spot* — all those sort of commercial videos) he often gets sat in front
      * of one . . . He can be very difficult to handle and his grandparents are quite elderly . . . but if they're having to look after him they . . . they naturally have to recourse to something that will keep him occupied. But . . . certainly there are times when . . . having absorbed whole stories, he can repeat whole stories.

R: How many viewings will he have had?

Father: Quite a few . . . probably . . . but he learns very fast.

(*Later*)

Father: He wouldn't be able to do it. His language is very limited in terms of interactive speech . . . and often not clear. His words are not clear if he's saying something to you that he's generated himself. It's **remarkably** clear . . . you know, **startlingly** clear when he's lifting a prepared phrase from something he's absorbed from video.

R: This is a very loose question: How much understanding does he have of the content of the phrase that he's repeating parrot-fashion?

Father: Oh . . . There's a very loose answer! I mean, it's the full range. Sometimes he'll repeat things and I suspect he hasn't a clue what he means. Other times there is an appropriateness, a relevance to the way he is using a phrase. I'll give you a for instance. Fresh in my mind from yesterday . . . um . . . 'No, thank you. Not today.' . . . I'd asked him if he needed to go to the toilet, so it was inappropriate in a sense, but it was clear that he'd lifted that from somewhere else where 'Not today' was (*laughs*) appropriate in order to say 'No'. So he sort of had a half understanding of the appropriateness of it. He had to go to the loo 'some time today', you see what I mean?

Children as Viewers

Children were used to viewing on their own, with siblings, with one or more adults in the communal part of the house. Other activities may or may not be going on at the same time: eating, drawing, game-playing, talking, arguing, much of the cut and thrust of domestic life. When they were watching TV or videos in their bedroom, it follows logically that it was much more likely to be a lone activity. Whatever the mode, an end result was their ability to use their knowledge and understanding of the video 'stories' in their play:

R: And when you do that sort of game, do you act out things that you've seen like — oh, I don't know — *Beauty and the Beast* — have you seen that?

Girl (6 years): Yes, but no, we just pretend to be ordinary people but sometimes after I've watched a video — like I've watched one a few days ago — then I like to be one of the special characters on the video. I used to have this special blanket and I've got the video of *Robin Hood* when I was quite young and I used to pretend to be — they were sort of animals — and I used to pretend to be the fox — Maid Marian. I used to put this blanket over my head and pretend it was my baby because that's what she does and, mm, I like . . . I still like to pretend to be characters off films.

The imagination of a child can be open to any and all stimuli. It's impossible to predict what cause might produce what effect: although we do know that there is some content in films, TV programmes and videotapes which might have quite an effect on children's minds.

R:	Have you seen any other scary films?
Boy (7 years):	(*Pause*) No. I can't remember. I do remember one, but I don't remember what it was called. (*Pause*) Oh! Now I do . . . It's *Never Ending Story*. That's a little bit scary.
R:	Which bit was scary?
Boy:	Forgotten. Where the black thing . . . black wolf bites the boy.
R:	But the boy was all right was he?
Boy:	Yeh . . . he was all right and he meets a live wall — a cliff that's alive. That's . . . that's a bit . . . that's a . . . that's a funny bit.
R:	Yeah.
Boy:	(*Laughs*) 'Cos he meets a wall, a big, big cliff that's alive.

Later on in the interview, the same boy expands on the subject of what makes him scared:

R:	What does it . . . When you see something scary, what does it feel like?
Boy:	It feels like you're doing it **here**.
R:	You get upset?
Boy:	No . . . don't get upset. Makes me scared and I think it's fun.
R:	Why? How can it be fun if you're scared?
Boy:	It . . . it m . . . it ma . . . It **scares** you in a different sort of way of being scared . . . in a different sort of way of being scared of **something**. Because you don't actually . . . like . . . you don't really . . . (*sigh*) . . . you don't really do very many . . . um . . . you don't actually really **cry** or **yell** 'cos . . . um . . . when you . . . when you're scared and you think it's funny, you always . . . well, it always makes you feel funny. (*Pause*) Don't know why it makes me feel funny, it just does.
R:	Is there a difference between scared really — something really scares

you — and being scared by something that you're watching on television or the pictures?

Boy: I'm not scared of television 'cos all it is a screen ... but some things
on television that ... um ... people really have to fight are really scary
that makes me scared as in 'scared of something horrible'.

There was quite a deal of evidence in the survey to suggest that children could
differentiate between fiction and fact — providing the content was properly cued.
Where they were particularly undermined was in documentary programmes about
ghosts, hospitals or catastrophes and, sometimes, news stories. As far as the young
were concerned, programmes and videos could still precipitate activity, as shown
in this conversation with a mother of a 3-year-old girl and a 6-year-old boy:

Mother: Oh, yeah, yeah. What can you do?
R: Does she like them?
Mother: She seems to.
R: Do the children ever act out what they have seen on the TV?
Mother: T does. Yes, definitely. You get *Power Rangers* on and then for half
an hour afterwards he's kicking round the room. It drives me mad.
The programmes are very violent. It's awful.
R: What about adult programmes? Does T stay up to watch any of
those?
Mother: Oh, yeah, yeah.
R: What sort of things does he like?
Mother: *Heartbeat, You've Been Framed* — he's crazy on that. Really, he'll
watch whatever's on of an evening. Films he loves.

Now, for comparison, the mother of an 8-year-old girl talks about realism and its
effects:

R: What sort of programme do you really not like?
Daughter: (*Long pause*) I can't think of anything really.
R: Do you watch any programmes that are really meant for grown
ups?
Daughter: *Casualty*.
Mother: Oh yes, you love that.
Daughter: *999* I like too.
Mother: Very bloodthirsty, my daughter. (*She laughs when she says this*)
Daughter: I don't really like blood when it's real. I just back off then but
when it's on *Casualty* I watch it. *Jimmys* is a bit different — if
it's really bad on there I have to hide my eyes behind a cushion.
R: What about bad language on TV?
Mother: Well, I don't know really.
Daughter: *Casualty's* got a lot of swearing in it.
Mother: Oh, I don't know. I just think that that's a way of life. If you

shield them from it they're going to think — well — I don't know — well, I mean, we swear — not bad words, you know. I think because they've been brought up with it, they don't use it — they tend to accept it a lot more.

A final exchange between the same mother and daughter which involves children's knowingness of what they mustn't see:

> *R*: What other films do you like?
> *Daughter*: I don't know. I haven't seen *Terminator*.
> *Mother*: No, and I don't want you to either.
> *R*: Why is that?
> *Mother*: Well it's just terrible isn't it?
> *R*: Why do you want to see it, H?
> *Daughter*: Well, I just know about it.

In the research project, the researchers tried to cross-reference the perceptions of individuals via interviews with the child, those at home and in school. Each interview/observation session is informally structured, but care has to be taken to ensure that all the issues are addressed. It may be inconvenient to return later because of a missed point or a forgotten question. At the same time, the researcher can discover whole areas of experience that did not immediately present themselves at initial interviews. Here is just such an example. After a long interview with a 6-year-old pupil (and also with his teacher) the researcher felt that he had a reasonable overview of the child.

> *R*: Do you have videos at home?
> *Boy*: Yeh — got lots and lots of videos. So many that you can't actually fit them all on a shelf.
> *R*: How many of them are yours? How many do you have? Do you have a lot?
> *Boy*: Yeh. My brother has more of them.
> *R*: What kind of things do you have on your video tapes?
> *Boy*: I've got . . . I've only got stories and . . .
> *R*: Like what?
> *Boy*: I've got . . . lots of different stories. I can't remember any of their names. I've got so many.
> *R*: On video?
> *Boy*: Yeah.

Within minutes of arriving in the home, new facts emerged. Here the researcher is speaking to the same child's mother:

> *R*: I was thrown. I've spoken to L in the classroom, and when I arrived you spoke to him in German and he responded which threw me

because that was not on our agenda at all when I spoke to him at school. So already, I've discovered something about him that I had no idea about. You are German?

Mother: I am Austrian, but my native language is German of course. And I try and speak as much German with them as possible . . . [L has a brother who is three years older] . . . but from the age of when they start school, I find it harder to keep up a continuous stream of German. Cos once the children start school they enter a completely new world and they make whole leaps in the subject matter and the articulateness and it's not possible for me as a one-person subject island (*laugh*) to reciprocate that. And so, I wouldn't call him bilingual but he understands a fair amount of German.

The researcher questions her about the number and content of videotapes:

Mother: Only ones that have been bought. Because my brother tapes German Children's TV and sends us . . . which hasn't been bought.

R: OK. So first of all then: films that have been sold through the shops — like the Disney films — and so on?

Mother: Maybe twenty.

R: How many videos are there of German television material?

Mother: About ten.

As can be seen in this chapter, there is much diversity apparent, when entering children's homes. And, as homes, themselves, differ from each other, so do they differ from schools. Parental attitudes to video, their content, when they can be watched and at what age vary and vacillate. The child today, has to pick a route through the minefield of countervailing adult attitudes, finding acceptance here and disapproval there, often about the same subject matter.

From the child's own point of view, there seems generally to be a strong ability to differentiate media fiction from media reality, although there will always be children for whom this is more difficult, particularly those children who are already disturbed as a result of their upbringing. The power of the peer group was always apparent in this regard, often persuading children that they should watch something, despite their better judgment. Given that parents seem to believe that they knew what their children are doing, without particularly checking, there seemed to be occasions where the researchers felt that children were seeing more than their parents were aware of. Or were seeing material, deemed unsuitable, in other households.

As contentious, perhaps, was the overwhelming approbation for Disney products which had an almost universal appeal. The place of Disney within culture needs a separate study but it was a surprise to all of the team to discover how much Disney affects the daily lives of children, with products in every conceivable room of the house.

Finally, the theme of planning and controlling the use of technology was at the fore with video recorders. Only a few of our families spent any time in pre-planning. Few used the *Radio Times* or equivalent, one or two used the daily paper, but most seemed to operate from within the moment, or from knowledge based on habit. Then there were strong gender issues concerning adults' feeling for technology, and the role models they were projecting on their children, which will be explored in more detail in the next chapter. Against this background, as with other screen-based technologies, children tended to be forced to move in a space that was unguarded, no matter how much parents felt and said otherwise.

Chapter 7

His and Hers: Screen-based Technology and Gender Issues

Girl: Let me play now. It was me that switched it on. You were doing something. You wouldn't have thought about it if I hadn't started.
Boy: I'm just going to finish this go.
Girl: You always say that. It's not fair.
Boy: Shove off.

One aspect of children's interaction with screen technology that has attracted debate is the question of gender. Interest has largely centred so far on two aspects of the gender question: whether girls and boys behave differently in their interactions with screen technology, and; whether the content and promotion of screen technology products reflect and foster gender stereotyping.

What Research Tells Us

Research studies into gender differences have been notoriously difficult to conduct and interpret. Reviews of the literature suggest that there is some evidence for difference between the sexes in certain of their physical attributes, personality characteristics and abilities (e.g., Maccoby and Jacklin, 1974). Most of the reported differences are, however, fairly modest in size and there is some evidence (e.g., Hyde and Linn, 1986) to suggest that verbal, visual, spatial and mathematical ability differences are becoming even smaller. What seems to be most applicable to this study is that boys and girls play in rather different ways and show preferences for different toys and activities. Sex-typed toy preferences can appear as early as at 18 months of age (Caldera, Huston and O'Brien, 1989) and differentiated play activities seem to continue with age. Even very young children have opinions as to what constitutes appropriate play for boys and girls (Carvalho, Smith, Hunter and Costabile 1990). At most ages it has been shown that boys have a higher level of physical activity and engage more in rough-and-tumble play than girls (DiPietro, 1981) and that girls tend to show greater timidity and caution than boys in unfamiliar situations. Research so far conducted into video game playing suggests that boys and girls are equally attracted up until the age of ten but that from then on the aggressive themes of much of the game software has the effect of deterring girls from computers in general.

During the course of our study, we made a number of observations which suggested differential behaviour between the sexes in their interaction with video and computer technology, although it was beyond the scope of our research project to investigate causal factors. One noticeable difference related to the interest shown in the hardware. Boys, on the whole, although there were some exceptions, were more knowledgeable about their computer games consoles or PCs in terms of their memories and technical capacities and were also more likely to compare their machines with others available on the market or with those of their friends. Even quite young boys showed a level of awareness we rarely encountered in the girls:

Knowledge of Technology in Families

My daddy has a laptop. It's got a keyboard not like my special children's computer — that's not the same thing as a PC at all. It's just really simple — not like a proper one. I think it's for babies really because I know easily how to use the keyboard. Daddy's has got a mouse as well. Well, he's got two actually. One of them he keeps in the pocket — you know — the case for the laptop. You can plug that in. But mostly he uses the one that's built into the keyboard. You just have to press a rolling button built into the keyboard. I know how to use it. I can get into Windows on my daddy's computer — that's if I want to write something. That's called word processing and then I can print it out. (Boy, 4-year-old)

This boy came from a home where the father frequently worked on his computer and he showed enormous understanding and practical aptitude for such a young child. Girls, on the other hand, were often more unsure about the equipment they had in the home, as shown in this conversation with a 9-year-old girl:

R:　You told me that your daddy has just got a new computer at home. Do you know what type it is?

Girl:　Mm. Well it's probably an Apple Mac. I think so. The last one was. This is better, I think. It's probably just a better Apple Mac.

Or, an 8-year-old girl, whose father works in the computer industry:

R:　What sort of computer do you have at home?

Girl:　Well, my father had a CD-rom. He had three computers actually, but the first one he had he put into his work because he didn't like it. I don't know why. Then he had another one and then another one and he went to China and Japan for work. It was something to do with PCs.

R:　Do you know what he does at work?

Girl:　Mm. No not really. I'm not really interested in all that.

This lack of interest in and knowledge about the equipment often extended to the mothers of the children as well.

R: Do you ever have a go on the boys' Mega Drive?

Mother: No. It all seems so strange to me. Years ago we bought the older boys a little Spectrum, you know, but I just couldn't get the hang of it. It doesn't appeal to me at all, I'm afraid.

R: Have you ever had a go on a PC?

Mother: Well, I'm doing some now as part of a nursery nursing course that I'm doing at the college. Unfortunately that's a part of it. I did try a couple of years ago as well. I went to evening classes but it didn't work out. Many years ago I was a secretary so I would have thought it was a good idea but now I just can't take to it . . . I'm quite frightened by it really. I suppose I think there must be something wrong with me not knowing how to . . . well, not being able to . . .

R: Do you mean that you're worried about looking foolish or are you afraid that you might do something wrong?

Mother: It's partly that. I think I would be happier if I had one at home to play around on — you know, make my own mistakes.

This lack of mastery in the face of technology was also evident, to a slightly lesser extent, with video use. As indicated in the last chapter, many of the mothers were able to make instant video recordings from the television but were unable to pre-programme the VCR to record later programmes. An extreme example was encountered in a mother living alone with her 8-year-old son. She was interviewed during the 1994 World Cup season and we had the following conversation.

Mother: He loves the footie. He's been watching most of the games.

R: Some of them are on quite late. Does he stay up to watch or do you record them for him?

Mother: Well, like tonight, he wants to watch the Nigeria game tonight. That player, you know, who plays for Norwich — he's Nigerian so A's got to see it. It doesn't start 'til after midnight.

R: So, will you video that for him?

Mother: Yes, I'll just have to stay up. Then it doesn't finish 'til about 3 in the morning. I hope I can stay awake. I might drop off. I usually go to bed quite early.

R: Why don't you programme it to record instead of staying up?

Mother: (*Long pause*) Well, I don't know how to do that.

R: Have you still got the instructions for the video?

Mother: They're somewhere I expect. I don't need them. I hardly ever use the video.

R: Isn't it worth trying to find out how to do it so that you don't have to stay up until midnight?

Mother: Well, I'll have to stay up until 3am to turn it off as well.

R: Won't it stop when the tape runs out?

Mother: I don't really know. I don't want to leave it running all night.

R: Don't you mind going to all that trouble?

Mother: Well, it's only for the World Cup. He really wants to see the games.

Further conversation with this mother revealed that she had no idea of all the facilities available on her VCR. She knew as much as she felt that she needed to know, could load a pre-recorded video and record programmes simultaneously from the television (she had been shown this by the man who had installed the machine). However, she had never consulted the instruction booklet: 'I can't be bothered with them things. I never understand them.'

Male and Female Teachers and Parents as Role Models

Although it is fair to say that the majority of mothers encountered in the study were somewhat ill at ease with technology, this was not universally the case and a few mothers were extremely competent, both with video recording and computing. It was noticeable that it was frequently single mothers who showed the most confidence. In two-parent families, we often found that the man took charge of the technology, as shown in this conversation with this father of a 5-year-old girl and a 7-year-old boy:

> *Father*:　You see, I don't like things if I don't know how they work. I know the satellite and the telly and the videos and everything. How to set the timers which I do.
>
> *R*:　Does your wife do those things too?
>
> *Father*:　No, no, it's just me. She asks me to record things. If a thing's there and you got all these facilities and gadgets you've got and you don't know how to use them, well I think you should do.

There was one interesting observation of a recently divorced mother with two children, aged 1 and 5 years, who made use of the stereotypic image of female helplessness as a means of controlling her son's use of computer games. She was happy for her young son to watch videos of *Dr Who* even though she had to conceal the video cases from him because he found the images depicted on them so frightening. However, she objected to what she saw as the gratuitous violence and aggressive imagery of computer games. She tackled this problem, not by exercising control over the type of games played, but by removing the child's Nintendo and putting it away in a cupboard. She explained the removal to her son by telling him that it was only his daddy who was able to work the machine. This relates strongly to the realization by the team that children have a great deal of power when negotiating with their parents. Rather than negotiate, this mother opted for evasion of conflict.

　　Another example of a mother feigning incompetence to conceal disapproval was revealed in a conversation with a 9-year-old girl:

> *Girl*:　My mum hates games. We beg her to play with us when we're on our own with our mum.
>
> *R*:　Why do you think she hates games?
>
> *Girl*:　'Cos her eyes start going all blurry and everything.

R: Is she any good at them?

Girl: No, 'cos she says she's not really good at them but she really is sometimes.

Parents and teachers are obviously important and influential figures in a child's life and they offer powerful role models. Children in our study frequently perceived their mothers and their female teachers to be less competent with technology than their male counterparts and, sometimes, as in the above examples, adults appeared deliberately to perpetuate these stereotypes. We came across many examples of children seeking advice from male friends, teachers or relatives. For example, a conversation with a group of 8-year-old girls:

Girl 1:   Um, if I can't do anything, I just get my stepdad, I say, 'Can you do this because I just get fed up with it'.

Girl 2:   Yeah, I always call my uncle when he's there.

Girl 1:   And I always have to say, 'John, could you just do that bit for me,' and then he carries on and finishes the game.

Girl 3:   I always have to call my uncle when I'm in the middle of the cave bit 'cos there's this really long bit where you have to jump over and I can't do that. So I call my uncle and he comes up and he jumps over and then I can't do the rest 'cos it's really hard after that bit.

However, where mothers were confident and familiar with technology, children readily accepted this and were surprised to find that the same level of competence did not apply universally outside the family. The following conversation was recorded between a researcher and the mother of a 7-year-old girl and 5-year-old boy. This particular mother had trained as a computer programmer and was currently working part-time in a computer support role for a local company:

R: Do the children know what sort of things you do at work?

Mother: My children find it really funny when I say that I've been helping this lady today who got stuck on her computer. They can't understand that adults don't know computers as well as they do.

Similarly, we encountered some examples of female teachers enjoying the challenge of the new technologies, although this was hardly widespread:

I did a course at the Inset Centre — 24 hours. I had lots of hands-on experience. I like machines. I don't like being beaten by machines. (Teacher, first school)

Another first school teacher, we interviewed, who had become aware of gender stereotypes, actually made a point of positively discriminating in favour of girls:

R: Do you notice any gender differences?

Teacher: To be honest, I do make the computer female-friendly. If I demonstrate, I do choose a girl, and with first gos I will usually get a girl to show a boy. I do positively discriminate. With last year's group, if I said, 'It's the word processing disk,' it was the girls who would demonstrate enthusiasm for it, but if it was a games disk I left out, it would be the boys who would show the most interest. But in relation to confidence and problem-solving, I would say there was little difference between boys and girls — but big differences in the way they were drawn to it.

Dominance by Boys

In our observations of children interacting with screen technology, boys and girls, on the whole, seemed equally competent at loading machines and dealing with difficulties as they arose. However, in mixed groups there was a marked tendency for boys to take over. Girls with brothers also frequently complained that they scarcely got a turn and that their brothers would try to interfere when they did actually get to play.

Girl (8 years):	Let me play now. It was me that switched it on. You were doing something. You wouldn't have thought about it if I hadn't started.
Boy (10 years):	I'm just going to finish this go.
Girl:	You always say that. It's not fair.
Boy:	Shove off.

Similar sentiments were expressed by some 9-year-old girls in a conversation with one of the researchers:

Girl 1:	Yeah, when my cousins came to stay it was very annoying — all they wanted to do was to play on the computer.
R:	What did you want to do?
Girl:	Well, we was playing this game, me and my sister, and then they came up and all they wanted to do was play on the computer and when we were at their house all they wanted to do was to play on the computer as well.
Girl 2:	Yeah, when my brother's cousins come up, my step-brother puts the Sega on and they won't even let me have a go.
R:	Are these boy or girl cousins?
Girl 2:	One boy and one girl.
Girl 3:	I've got a cousin and he's a boy and he comes on my computer and he goes, 'I'll finish in a minute and I'll let you have a go,' and about an hours gone and I say, 'I thought you said you'd finish in a minute,' and he says 'I'll finish in a minute,' and about two hours gone and he's on the computer still.

Girl 4: I used to do that to my brother 'cause I just had a normal Nintendo and he had a Supernintendo and whenever he was out, I'd go and play on it and never tell him. My mum would let me and I'd, like, complete the game loads of times and get millions of points and I'd have to turn it off when he came in.

Even allowing for obvious exaggeration, it was clear that the girls' perception was that they were being edged out by the boys.

A study carried out in Denmark in 1989, in which teenage children were observed while making a video, demonstrated that boys and girls both began with the preconception that video is a technical medium and, therefore, the province of the male. There was an automatic assumption that boys would take charge of the lighting, props and camera-work even though one of the participating girls was taking an electronics course at school. We encountered similar trends during the course of our observations of the younger age group in our study, where boys were often seen to take on the mantle of 'technology expert' even when this was not particularly appropriate. For example, a group of 9-year-old girls and boys were observed working on the computers in a middle school library. The group consisted of six children who had been asked to word process some material for their project work. They were unsupervised by a teacher although they had ready access to a nearby classroom if they encountered difficulties. One of the boys had designated himself the group 'expert' and was offering advice to the other children. The boys ignored him and got on with their task but the girls seemed to be influenced by his suggestions. One of the girls wanted to change the font size and the 'expert' told her which button she needed to press. The suggested procedure did not lead to the desired effect and the boy offered a few more possibilities, the last of which wiped the text from the screen. The boy then got quite angry and said to the girl, 'You're just stupid. Look what you've done, now. I'm not helping you any more.' The girl seemed quite distressed but neither of them mentioned the fact that it was the boy who had engineered the blank screen in the first place and the girl seemed ready to accept that her 'stupidity' had been the causal factor. Girls were not always observed to be quite so subservient in the face of male bullying but they did often tend to deal with difficulties differently. The following conversation was recorded in a class of 7-year-olds where four children (two boys and two girls) were trying to print out a piece of work on which they had been collaborating:

Boy 1: Look. (*He points to the screen and reads slowly*) It says: small, medium or large.
(*All 4 children call out their choice but one of the boys shouts loudly:*)
Boy 2: No, I want it LARGE.
Girl: No, 'cos then we won't fit it all in.
Boy 2: (*Pause*) Oh, yes. OK, medium then.
Boy 1: No, small.
Boy 2: NO, medium. (*Moves cursor to medium*)
Boy 1: NO, small. (*Moves cursor to small*)

Girl 2: Oh, just press PRINT now.

Boy 1: (*Moves the cursor to medium again and presses PRINT by jabbing his finger a couple of times on the key*) Look, it's printing now. It's OK now.

Boy 2: Oh, no, stupid, you pressed it two times. Oh, no. It's gonna type two times now.

Girl: Oh, it doesn't matter. You can just take one home.

Boy 1: Let's pull it out now. (*He pulls the paper from the printer before it's finished printing*)

Girl: Don't rip it. Don't pull it. No. Stop it. I'm going to get Miss P [the teacher].

Boy 1: Let's press PRINT again.

Girl: Don't be stupid. We don't want to print again. Let's get Miss P. We don't know what to do now.

Boy 2: Just press ESCAPE. That's what you always do.

This seemed a significant exchange because, whereas both boys and girls seemed confident about operating the computer, the boys were more impulsive and assertive and the girls rather more pragmatic and less confrontational. The girls also seemed to be more concerned about doing the 'right thing' and were more inclined to call in the teacher when difficulties arose. This tendency of girls to refer more readily to the teacher was noticed quite frequently. Boys were generally more likely to seek their own solutions to problems as they arose and did not seem to worry about 'doing something wrong' on the computer. Girls were more inclined to seek immediate assistance from the teacher and were usually less likely to try to find their own solutions. We also observed a number of instances of teachers 'helping' girls by telling them precisely what key to press or strategy to apply but challenging boys to find their own solutions by thinking about the various options open to them. This observation is in line with previous research which suggests that teachers interact differently with boys and girls in maths classes where it has been noted that boys are often allowed to dominate class time by interacting more with the teachers and, as a result, are given more attention, both positive and negative (Eccles, 1989).

One area where we encountered an interesting difference between boys and girls was in the use of control pads and joy sticks. We observed boys who became totally absorbed in game play, the joy stick gripped with both hands and manoeuvred with incredible speed and dexterity. Girls often seemed more tentative and were happier than boys to use a mouse or to use the keyboard. Some girls complained about the discomfort of using a control pad. For example, a conversation with a group of 9-year-old girls:

Girl 1: I hate controls because they always make your hands sweat and your fingers go all numb because of going like that (*She mimes the gestures*).

Girl 2: Yeah, and in the end you go 'I'm not playing this any more'.

Computer Games and Gender Stereotyping

A number of commentators have noted that the content of computer games seems to perpetuate gender stereotypes. Provenzo (1992), for example, looked at a range of Nintendo games and found that women, if they were included in the games at all, were usually portrayed as passive recipients of action rather than as initiators of action in their own right. He feels strongly that the stereotypic content of video games conditions children of both sexes to see females as dependent and males as dominant. He describes the content of a popular game *Double Dragon 2* as follows:

> The hero Billy Lee and his former rival Jimmy Lee try to save Billy's girl-friend Marian, who has been kidnapped by the Black Shadow Warriors. The cover of the game box shows Marian clutching Billy as he supports her with his hand wrapped around the small of her back. His other arm is entwined with a whip that he is wresting out of the hands of a woman who has enormous breasts and a punk 'rooster crest' hairdo. Marian in high heels, wears a torn mini-dress that reveals curvaceous thighs and buttocks; her tank top is ripped, allowing a glimpse of her midriff and breasts pressed against Billy's chest. With her blonde hair cascading behind her, Marian's face radiates confidence as she is held in the arms of her saviour/hero Billy. (Provenzo, 1992, p. 31)

Provenzo describes the images portrayed in this and similar games and makes the interesting point that, while such crass stereotyping is relatively common in video games, it is no longer generally tolerated in children's literature. He suggests that the explanation for this lies partly in the fact that parents and teachers are largely ignorant of the precise content of video games, regarding them as part of an 'invisible' child culture to which they have no access.

This was borne out in the group work we did with parents and headteachers. We gave them computer games magazines to read. All the adults evinced surprise when working their way through the pages. What was obvious was that they would buy these or similar magazines for their children but, even in the cases of parents who had strong views about gender issues or violence, remain quite ignorant of content. This tended to confirm our observational findings in the children's homes, where the technology helped them to insulate themselves in their own private worlds. Children sometimes played on this ignorance for their own ends, even to the extent of trying to persuade parents that they should buy magazines which were unsuitable for their machines, but which they'd set their sights on.

Certainly, we found evidence in our study of many parents and teachers having vague concerns about the content of video games, but far fewer examples of adults having detailed knowledge. Those parents who talked in any detail about the games were people who also enjoyed playing them. This group of parents were, on the whole, not bothered about the unsuitability of images contained within the games. They simply enjoyed the buzz of playing. Where anxiety was expressed about content, comments were focused almost exclusively on violence and aggression. Gender stereotyping did not seem to be an issue for most parents, and yet children often made reference to examples when they were talking to us. Usually, these references were unintentional — the children merely demonstrating their unconscious absorption of the image presented to them. For example, from 9-year-old boy:

> Yeah, there's this boxing game I've got on my computer and it's ... er, me and my friend play it and he doesn't want to fight the person so he says he'll be the manager, 'cos there's a manager, and I'll be the fighter so I be the fighter and he's got like a Porsche and everything and they go into different rooms and he's got like a secretary and she gives you all these pieces of paper and it tells you what fight and you can press buttons where you want to go in the draw and if you want the secretary to come in and give you something ...

Sometimes the children were more aware of the gender-specific content but boys, in particular, were generally scathing about games designed especially for girls, as shown in this conversation between a researcher and four 9-year-old boys seated round a table in a school setting:

> *Boy 1*: Most of the games have just got boys, it's true, most of them are boys.
> *Boy 2*: Yeah, except for *Barbie* games, there's a *Barbie* game that no people get.
> *Boy 3*: Is there?
> *Boy 2*: It's a bit rubbish though.
> *Boy 4*: On *Mortal Kombat* they've got two or one girls.
> *Boy 2*: Two girls.
> *Boy 3*: Yeah, there's two girls.
> *Boy 1*: I saw this *Barbie* game in 'er, the window when I was shopping and it was just like a story reading to you.
> *Boy 2*: ... like a sort of pink thing.
> *Boy 1*: And you see her walking around and saying 'Hi' to the boys and everything ... it was just like walking around.

Some of the girls we interviewed showed more awareness of the gender bias and seemed keen to change the emphasis, for example, in this conversation with some 9-year-old girls:

> *Girl 1*: There was one like, there was one game that they made where a girl had to save a boy and the boy was trapped by the mean witch or something and it was like really good because like the girl ... well, like the boy was like really scared and he was like 'Aarrrgh' and the girl went and saved him. It was good because she was like — 'Oh, stop being a wimp.'

Girl 2: That's good because it shouldn't be always . . .

Girl 1: Yeah, and he was like 'Oh, help me.'

Girl 2: I like it . . . I think it's good when it's girls saving boys 'cos it shouldn't always be boys saving girls. I think it's good when it turns round a bit.

Occasionally, we came across a parent who was concerned about the gender bias, but this was fairly rare:

On this game (*Toejam and Earl*) you notice that boys are harder to kill than girls. The girls just go all stupid and keel over. And, then, you can make one of the characters fall in love and that's supposed to be a way of making them lose control. It seems to be a pretty strange message to put across to children. But then again, some of the messages are good. Like the idea that you get on better in the game if you work cooperatively with the other person than on your own. (Mother of 8-year-old girl)

Violence in Games

The aspect of game content that was more frequently mentioned by teachers and parents was violence and aggression. As suggested at the beginning of this chapter, past research findings indicate that boys and girls differ both in their levels of aggression and ways of manifesting it. However, research into the effects of violent computer games on levels of aggression in players has so far been fairly sparse and inconclusive. There has been a much longer history of research into the effects of violence on television and there are probably enough parallels between the two types of medium to draw similar conclusions. Many researchers would claim that there is a link between aggression on television and aggressive behaviour and attitudes in children but establishing the precise nature of that link is difficult. Even if a link is established, the mechanism by which children are affected has certainly not yet been determined. One influential theory (Bandura and Walters, 1963) has suggested that aggressive behaviour is acquired through a process of social learning. In other words, the child becomes sex-typed through behavioural reinforcement and imitation of appropriate models. However, it would seem likely that this is only one possible process and that different factors operate depending on the circumstances. More recently, social cognition theory, which has focused on the processes by which knowledge about the social world is acquired, has been put forward by Serbin and Sprafkin (1986) as an explanation for sex-typing. Other suggestions have included attitude change whereby children become so used to television violence that they come to see aggression as less unacceptable and are, therefore, more likely to engage in aggressive behaviour themselves (e.g., Drabman and Thomas, 1974). Zillmann (1982) has suggested that viewing increases arousal levels in children which, in turn, increases their likelihood of engaging in aggressive behaviour.

Given the more interactive functions of computer game playing, this may be accentuated in this activity.

Links have also been demonstrated between amount of time spent playing on computer games and levels of aggression. However, as with all correlational studies, some caution needs to be exercised in the interpretation of the data. It could simply be that more aggressive children are drawn to video game playing and not that game playing actually causes the aggression in the first place. Interestingly, some of the children in our study suggested that the causal link operated in this way:

Girl (9 years):	I think *Mortal Kombat* is the most violent game we've got. I don't think it's the most violent game.
R:	Don't you like it that much?
Girl:	I like it. It's fun but it's a bit complicated.
R:	Do you know any other violent games?
Girl:	Yeah, um, *Streetfighter 2*, well *Superstreetfighter 2*, that's the one I've got. It's really violent but you don't see the blood or anything.
R:	What do you think makes violent games popular?
Girl:	Because a lot of people like playing them.
R:	What is it do you think that they like about them?
Girl:	I don't know. J definitely likes playing with them and he's a bit violent himself.
R:	So, do you think that violent games make you violent if you play with them?
Girl:	No. They play violent games because they are violent already.

Fling *et al.* (1992) also sought to demonstrate a relationship between low level of self-esteem and amount of play but they did not find a significant correlation. They were rather surprised by this failure to find a correlation since Dominick (1984) had demonstrated just such a relationship in boys. However, Fling *et al.* (1992) suggested that low self-esteem might well lead to more frequent play which would in turn lead to more mastery and therefore higher self-esteem. This would be an interesting hypothesis to investigate further. Certainly, in our study, we came across several examples, particularly among boys, of children with apparently low levels of self-esteem and confidence enjoying game playing for the sense of mastery and control that it endowed. One 5-year-old boy, for example, who was observed after two terms at first school, was described by a class teacher as having changed from being extremely shy and anxious at the start of the academic year to being self-assured and confident by the end of the first term. This was attributed to his familiarity with computers which allowed him to operate as an 'expert' in the classroom and thus gain respect from teachers and other pupils. His mother also noticed the change in him since he had started school: 'Yes, J can help the other children. It's been good for him. He used to be very shy and withdrawn, but, being able to show other children has helped his confidence.'

Competition and Cooperation

It does seem to be clear that girls and boys often want different things from computer games. Boys, on the whole, prefer games which are competitive, have strict rules and require the player to demonstrate supremacy. Girls, on the other hand, prefer purposeful games that involve practical, real-world problem-solving and give a sense of completion. Boys seem to enjoy competition and gaining high scores while girls often say that video games are a waste of time. We found evidence to lend support to this distinction:

Boy (8 years):	I get fed up with the racing games 'cos you've only got to drive on roads and turn round and things. It gets really boring.
R:	What sort of games do you prefer?
Boy:	Well, I like fast games, you know, zapping things, monsters, you know, getting on to high levels.

And in this conversation with a 7-year-old boy and his 10-year-old brother:

R:	Do you play games together?
Boy (7 years):	Well, sometimes. I like it but he doesn't usually let me.
Boy (10 years):	I play *Goal* with him. That's good.
R:	Why don't you mind playing that together?
Boy (10):	'Cos I always win. (*He laughs*)
Boy (7):	We play *Batman* together as well.
R:	How does that work with two players? Do you both have a joystick?
Boy (7):	No, we have to take turns. I watch first and then I do the next level. He's much better than me. When I play with him it means we get on to really high levels.

In conversation with a 9-year-old boy:

R:	Do you usually play on your own?
Boy:	I prefer it on my own usually but *Mortal Kombat 2*, that's better with two people. Against the computer you can never win. I play that with my friend L so I can win.

In conversation with 8-year-old girl:

R:	Do you keep on playing a game until you've completed all the levels?
Girl:	Not really. It just gets silly. You get stuck on a level and then you've got to go back to the start. I get fed up with it. I can't see the point.

In conversation with 8-year-old girl:

> R: Do you enjoy playing computer games?
> *Girl*:   Well, they don't really get you anywhere do they? I've played at a friend's house but it's a bit boring — I keep getting drowned or killed. You just go across streams and things — this is for the Sega — and you fall in so you're dead and then you just have to go back to the beginning and start all over again. I mean, it's just a waste of time.

Finally, in conversation with 9-year-old girl:

> I get a bit bored with playing sometimes. It's just the same thing over and over.

Most manufacturers tend to produce games that appeal to boys. This is partly because software designers have traditionally been male but partly, too, because the manufacturers have failed to recognize the famale market potential. There was an attempt by Nintendo to launch a female version of Game Boy called 'Game Girl' but this was not a commercial success. This is not altogether surprising since the predominant view of the whole computer game and arcade game scene is that it is a male-dominated culture. All the researchers engaged on this project spent considerable periods of time in arcades and games shops and the clientele was always predominantly and, sometimes exclusively, male. It is probably more important to concentrate on the content of the actual games rather than on the packaging of the console. Several girls in our study expressed a wish that games should be designed to reflect their particular interests. For example, a 9-year-old girl:

> They should make a *Farthing Wood* computer game or a *My Little Pony*. Well, I don't know about *My Little Pony* but they definitely should make a *Farthing Wood* one 'cos then you could get all the bad guys in it so you could play as one of the animals — vole, rabbit, toad . . . There was this game called *Mr Nuts* and I want to play it but no-one lets me. They don't let me buy it, but I've seen it on TV and it looks really good.

This difference in attitude towards content was also evident when we asked children in our study to design their own games. We approached this by sitting with groups of 8–9 year old children in a school setting and talking to them about the things they looked for in a good game. We then gave them large sheets of paper and pencils and asked them to design their ideal game. We told them that they could do it as a group or on their own. Perhaps surprisingly, most of the children opted to produce an individual design, although there was much general chatter and comparison of notes during the course of the exercise.

There were clear gender differences in the way that the children tackled this exercise. The girls seemed to concentrate on first building up a narrative structure and then provided detailed elements of the game. Nearly all the girls had a clear objective in mind which would signal completion of the game. The boys, on the

Figure 7.1: 'You have to kill a monster.'

other hand, went into considerably less detail and concentrated more on action, mostly in the form of killing and 'splatting'. The object of the game for most of them, although they were less explicit than the girls in stating goals, was to kill as many creatures as possible. Some examples of their outlines are shown in Figures 7.1, 7.2, 7.3 and 7.4.

Heidi Danglemaier (as reported in Koch, 1994), a computer-game designer based in New York, has been committed to raising the awareness of games manufacturers about gender bias in their games and also of trying to encourage girls to be interested in computer interaction. Manufacturers are just beginning to recognize what girls want from games. Two games recently released in the States on CD-rom, *Hawaii High* and *Madeline*, feature strong, central, female characters engaged in challenging problem-solving tasks. Maria Klawe, director of computer science at the University of British Columbia, has a particular interest in the issue of gender and computers. She believes that games are the best introduction for children into the world of computers. She is reported as saying: 'Currently it is the boys' culture that is addressed in computer games. It is important to include girls' culture as well. Computer games can be intellectual activities that help children learn by making learning more attractive to them.'

It is not only the games manufacturers that could help to attract girls to the world of computing. Magazines and comics, long criticized for perpetuating gender stereotypes, could be influential in changing girls' perceptions if there was the editorial will. The cartoon strip *Joy Stick* featured weekly in the *Sunday Times* comic for children makes a valiant attempt to overturn the image of the helpless female. However, it does it by turning the eponymous 'heroine' into a rather unpleasant, obsessive child (see Figure 7.5).

There is much research suggesting that males play more frequently on video games than females. Fisher (1990) has demonstrated a similar gender difference in

Figure 7.2: 'The Lamp'

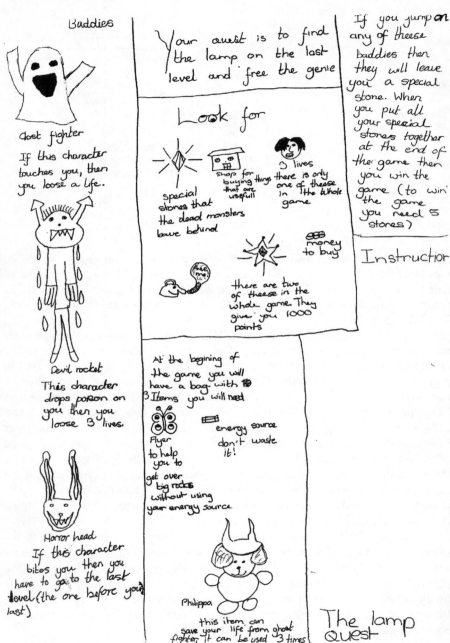

Baddies

Ghost fighter

If this character touches you, then you loose a life.

Devil rocket

This character drops poison on you then you loose 3 lives.

Horror head

If this character bites you then you have to go to the last level (the one before your last)

Your quest is to find the lamp on the last level and free the genie

Look for

special stones that the dead monsters leave behind

shop for buying things that are usefull

3 lives there is only one of theese in the whole game

money to buy

there are two of theese in the whole game. They give you 1000 points

At the begining of the game you will have a bag with 3 Items you will need

Flyer to help you to get over big rocks without using your energy source

energy source don't waste it!

Philippa

this item can save your life from ghost fighter; it can be used 3 times

If you jump on any of theese baddies then they will leave you a special stone. When you put all your special stones together at the end of the game then you win the game (to win the game you need 5 stones)

Instruction

The lamp Quest

Figure 7.3: 'Robocop and Terminator'

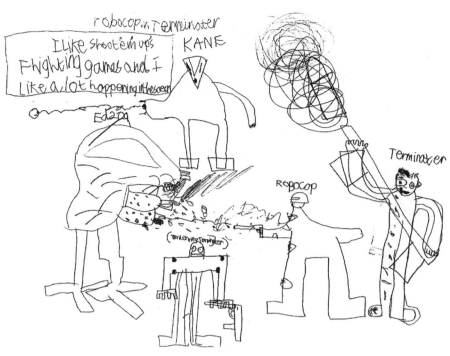

fruit machine playing. Exactly why this is the case has not yet been adequately explained. One possible explanation is in terms of the content of the games which, as discussed above, is aimed more at boys than at girls. Another factor that has been considered is the finding that boys, on average, perform better than girls at tasks requiring visuo-spatial skills. Such skills are essential for successful computer game playing where the player has to demonstrate high levels of hand–eye coordination and the ability to make rapid judgments about spatial relationships. Keisler, Sproull and Eccles (1983) has suggested that these superior skills would enable boys to score higher on games than girls and that girls' average lower scores could be a discouraging factor in their motivation to spend time playing.

While the differences we have observed between boys and girls are interesting, some readers might feel that they are of little general importance. However, there could be serious long-term consequences if these differences are not better understood and addressed. For example, there seems to be evidence of dwindling numbers of women taking up information technology as a career. In 1993, Staffordshire University set up a three-year action research project to disseminate information to girls about the career opportunities in IT. The industry expected increasing numbers of women to apply for jobs as the technology became more widespread. In fact, the reverse seemed to be the case and there is evidence of a considerable decrease of female applicants to university computer science courses. Applications from

147

Figure 7.4: 'Maze Adventure'

Figure 7.5: Joy Stick (source: the Sunday Times)

females have fallen from a figure of 25 per cent of the total number in 1975 to 11 per cent in 1995.

It is not yet entirely clear why this has happened but Christine Whitehouse (1995), a lecturer at Stafford University, has put forward an interesting suggestion. Originally, the only method for transmitting coded information between humans was by word of mouth. The first 'technological' product used for the exchange of information between individuals was papyrus. Computers are simply the latest in a long line of tools devised by humans for the efficient handling of information. However, whereas the earlier communication tools were essentially seen as a means to an end, Whitehouse suggests that computers have become, for some people at least, more important than the material they handle, in other words, the computer has come to be seen as an end in itself. She believes that girls have traditionally been keen to work on information handling tasks — particularly those involving problem analysis, communication and team work — and that they are still being attracted onto business courses where these skills are important. However, they do not seem to recognize that very similar skills are needed by the computing industry. Whitehouse (1995) believes that girls are under a misapprehension about the nature of the computer industry, thinking, erroneously, that it requires knowledge and understanding of the hardware. Girls, according to this suggestion, do not want to know how the computer works, nor do they wish to work in what they see as a predominantly male culture.

The action research project based at Staffordshire University is seeking to change girls' perceptions of computing and to make them aware of the exciting career possibilities. Part of the awareness programme involves parents, teachers and local education authority careers personnel as well. It is estimated that by the year 2000, over 80 per cent of all jobs will involve familiarity with information technology. Since it is likely that by the year 2000 a sizeable proportion of all wage earners will be women, it is important for industry and for schools to be addressing the question of how best to prepare children for this. Materials need to be developed in schools which will affect girls' attitudes to see computing as an attractive and appropriate career choice. Boys, too, need to be correctly prepared and advised so that it is not only the male technophiles who are attracted to the jobs but the analytical problem-solvers as well.

It is not entirely clear how the interest and efficacy of girls in the computing culture can be increased. If the cultural perceptions of 'male superiority' in the computing world arose from innate aptitude differences, there would be little that could be done to counteract them. It seems, however, much more likely that the differences arise mainly from early socialization. It is an irony that the first computer programmers were women taken on by the US Navy during World War II to work out shell trajectories using mechanical calculators. These tasks were deemed to be of relatively low importance and were assigned to women precisely because of this. It was only as the status of the computing profession grew that women were relegated to a back seat. Given that the key to computer literacy is really procedural thinking rather than technical wizardry, there is no reason to assume that girls are any less proficient than males.

One step towards changing the 'masculine' image would seem to be ensuring that pre-school children aged 3–4 years have the opportunity in nursery settings to interact with computers. Research in the US (Williams and Ogletree, 1992) has shown that girls of this age have not yet acquired the stereotype of the computer as masculine although the idea that computers are more appropriate for males than females grows rapidly as children get older (e.g., Johnson and Swoope, 1987). It is therefore important to expose children to the technology in a non-sexist setting before the stereotypes have a chance to take hold. It also seems likely that very young children are less inclined to be inhibited by the preconceived ideas about the 'threat' of computer technology that are often firmly entrenched in older people. One highly computer-literate, professional mother in our study made the following comments:

> I mean the young children take to it so quickly. J [5-year-old son] picked it up so easily. [She had introduced him to a PC when he was about 2 years old] They haven't even got any idea of wiping things out or breaking something — they just get stuck in. Like, remember the other day, D (*turns to daughter, 7 years*) when Mrs J [class teacher] said that she was going to show E [classmate] how to print something out and, by the time she'd turned round E had already done it on her own. (Mother)

It may also be that children should be divided into same-sex groups when engaged in computer-based activities. While this may seem intuitively wrong to primary school teachers, there is some empirical evidence to suggest that older children working in same-sex computer groups lend one another a degree of support that is not evident in mixed-sex groups. Teachers should also beware of allowing boys to dominate and take on the role of 'expert' in computing contexts. It is important for girls to have strong role models and to understand the enormously wide ranging applications of computer technology. Elizabeth Emmanuel, for example, the fashion designer, featured in an article in the *Times* where she admitted to her conversion to computer-aided design.

Judith Church, Labour MP for Dagenham sees legislation as a way of tackling the gender imbalance and has recently tabled a Bill aimed at promoting the role of women in the UK IT industry. She believes that the competitiveness of the UK industry will suffer if women's skills are not exploited. She has noted that women account for only 23 per cent of IT staff in the UK. This compares unfavourably to other countries such as Singapore where the figure is 55 per cent and in the US where it is 45 per cent. Women account for 9 per cent of managers in the UK generally but for only 4 per cent in the IT industry. It seems, too, that the Internet is almost exclusively the preserve of young men. Surveys suggest the 95 per cent of Internet users are male and that 80 per cent of all users are under the age of 35.

What future is there for the information revolution in the UK if women fail to be as enthusiastic about the prospect as men?

Chapter 8

The Enchanted World: Screen-based Entertainment Technology and Visions of Childhood

I also feel that childhood seems to me like a special time when the mind should be able to look at things very imaginatively or very openly — very freely — and I feel that contemporary children almost have a kind of weight of history and politics and appalling things they're hearing about all the time and, in some sense — it may just be romanticism — but I feel like it is almost ageing them and creating a sort of great weight of our concerns on them. A lot of material that is going out on adult television and on the news is materials and issues which adults feel disturbed by and is being presented without often exploring what constructive responses there might be to it. I feel in a way that this is burdening children and it seems to me that, as an inevitable consequence, we are limiting them in terms of their ability to dream dreams. (Father of 9-year-old girl)

Background Research on Childhood in Families

There are many variations between and within cultures as to what constitutes 'childhood' and as to the best child-rearing practice. The study of the history of childhood in Western Europe is relatively recent and the picture it paints is by no means clear. However, it seems likely that the view of childhood as an intrinsically valuable period of life, is comparatively recent and associated with the rise of the affluent household in the sixteenth and seventeenth centuries. Since then the fashion in child rearing has veered from the 'spare the rod and spoil the child' philosophy to a complete child-centred approach, with all possible variations in between. In this century, particularly during the 1950s and 1960s, the work of psychologists such as John Bowlby proved extremely influential with its emphasis on the importance of the first five years of life. Bowlby's views on the importance of the mother figure were instrumental in shaping government policy at the end of World War II which encouraged women to stay at home with their children. His statements such as 'Mother love in infancy and childhood is as important for mental health as are vitamins and proteins for physical health' (1951) led many women to feel guilty if they went out to work and were instrumental in creating the idealized picture of family life that emerged. Social and economic changes have produced a very different picture for the 1990s. This extract was taken from an article in the *Guardian* (1994):

> Approximately a fifth of all five to ten year olds are now left alone after school or in the holidays because both parents are at work. That is some 800,000 children and, unless action on child care is taken rapidly, the figure will only get worse.

So, many children are being left to their own devices, unsupervised at home and 'looked after' frequently by those electronic child minders, the television, VCR and games machines. Yet, at the same time that more mothers are out at work, parents seem to be becoming more anxious about allowing their children the freedom outside the home that, even as recently as the early 1970s, was commonplace. A survey by the Policy Studies Unit (PSI) looked at five places in England and compared them to similar locations in Germany and also with the same English towns that had been surveyed in 1971. Results showed that, whereas in 1972, 80 per cent of English 7- and 8-year-olds were allowed to travel backwards and forwards to school on their own or with other children, by 1990 this figure had dropped to under 10 per cent. Clearly, parents have decided that children can no longer be given that sort of freedom. The PSI survey found that, for parents with primary school aged children, the danger of traffic was cited as the most feared phenomenon (43 per cent). Twenty-one per cent of the sample said their greatest fear was abduction and a similar number of parents believed that their children were simply too unreliable to be allowed out on their own. It is difficult to assess accurately the reality of these fears but there are now only half as many children killed in road accidents (approximately 4 per 100,000 children) as there were in 1922. As far as abduction is concerned, Home Office statistics put the figure at about 275 cases per year but this includes incidences of children being abducted by an estranged parent.

However, it is possible that parents who are protecting their children by taking them to school by car are simply creating new and different problems for them. Mary Ann Sieghart, in a recent issue of the *Times* (5 August 1995), suggests that parental escorting has a number of knock-on effects. She says that children are now three and a half times more likely to be driven to school in the 1990s than in 1971 and that the PSI report estimates that these escorting services take up 900 million hours a year and cost up to £20 billion in lost earnings and road congestion costs to other road users. And this is not the only price to be paid. The incidence of child asthma has almost doubled during the last twenty years and it is thought that the increase in traffic fumes is a considerable causal factor. There has also been concern expressed recently about the decline in children's fitness and the loss of exercise entailed in being transported everywhere must contribute to this. Low levels of fitness can lead to health problems in later life: 460 people a day die of coronary heart disease.

One of the other consequences of adult fears about child safety is that children's opportunities for free, unsupervised, adventurous play are severely curtailed. Many children, prevented from straying outside the home without adult supervision, find that their need for privacy and independent play can only be met in the enclosed world of their bedroom. Their companion is often the television or the games console. The harsh realities of the outside world from which many parents seek to protect their children beam in instead from the set in the corner.

There can, then, be little doubt that the environment in which a child grows up is a highly influential factor in the developmental process. However, 'the environment' is not easily defined for a child living at the end of the twentieth century because of the many and various factors that can exert an influence on his or her life, particularly in relation to exposure to new technologies. The extent to which children are made familiar with and influenced by IT is likely to depend on many factors such as the attitudes of parents, siblings, teachers, peers, the school environment, the relationship between school and home, the policies of local education authorities and, in a much wider context, the political will of national government. However, many parents in our study and some teachers still seem to see childhood as a kind of enclosed and enchanted world which is somehow immune to these outside influences.

Technology and Play

Parents and teachers often seemed to view computer games as a completely alien form of entertainment for children with none of the charm, innocence or 'educational' value they associate with traditional playthings. A typical comment was the following from a mother of an 8-year-old daughter:

> I think computers are a good thing but the Mega Drive is the worrying one. It's so addictive. It's almost like a drug.

We encountered the idea of addiction many times with children and adults although it was not always expressed in those terms. It was more usual to be told:

> You just get carried away. It's so easy to lose track of time. (Mother of 8-year-old boy)

Or a conversation between a researcher and the parents of a 9-year-old boy and 5-year-old girl:

> *Father*: I play occasionally, yeah, I have to admit that.
> *Mother*: Occasionally! You must be joking. Every night, most like.
> *Father*: Well, OK, yeah, I suppose most nights — for a bit.
> *Mother*: (*Turning to researcher*) I have to go to bed and leave him to it — he just doesn't want to stop.

Or a conversation with an 8-year-old girl and a researcher:

> *R*:   How long do you play for?
> *Girl*: I never want to stop when I've started. My mum yells up the stairs to me to stop.'L, you've been on that thing for ages. Turn it off and do something else.'

The manufactures are almost certainly aware of the way in which players can lose track of time and become virtually mesmerized. Some of them seem set to capitalize on this aspect of game playing in an effort to boost sales. A recent article in the *Sunday Times* (8 October 1995) reported on a new game released by Time Warner Interactive in the US called *Endorfun*. This is supposed to send subliminal messages to the brain to produce 'feelgood' sensations. This technique is banned on television and radio under the terms of the 1990 Broadcasting Act but computer games currently fall outside this legislation. Up to a hundred audio messages are embedded in a rhythmic soundtrack and offer such statements as 'I expect pleasure and satisfaction', 'I can do anything' and 'It's OK for me to have everything that I want'.

The game itself has been designed by the same team that produced the hugely successful *Tetris* and is aimed by the manufacturers at teenagers. They defend the game by saying that the messages are all positive and can, therefore, only be beneficial for the player's self-esteem. However, if this trend in games design is allowed to continue without controls, it raises ethical issues and blurs the definition of entertainment. David Shaw, Conservative MP for Dover and a member of the parliamentary Information and Technology Committee was reported as saying that he intended to take up the issue and call for a code of conduct to be drawn up. This kind of development is bound to fuel the concern and anxieties already surrounding the issue of uncensored games content and seems to make it even more imperative that parents make an effort to become aware of what their children are actually doing when they 'plug in' to their computers.

Stephen Heppell, in an article written for the *Sunday Times* in 1995, has suggested that parents should sit down and play with their children in order to appreciate the complexity of the games and to understand the skill required to play them well. Many parents we talked to had neither the time nor the inclination to do this so they continued to feel isolated from their children's activities and uneasy about the potential effects. This fear that computer games can somehow undermine childhood innocence and lead children into a closed world of unhealthy absorption and addiction seemed to arise most often among adults who had little or no hands-on experience with the games and felt excluded by their ignorance from their own children. Some parents who fell into this category simply refused to allow their children to play games but others, while expressing overt disapproval, bought games consoles and supplied the means to acquire new games. They offered comments such as: 'I don't like the games but what can you do?' This fairly typical remark from a mother of four boys represents a view that parents are powerless in the face of a relentless onslaught of demands from their children. It is supported by this conversation with a mother of two boys:

Mother: I played on a game once but I just got killed straight off. I hated it. I can't see what they see in them. I don't understand what's going on. I aren't interested. All that noise is terrible. I stop them playing on it for too long.

R: How long have they had their games machine?

Mother: I don't know. I lose track.

R: Do you know what the games machine is called?

Mother: Well, I think they play on the new one — that Nintendo. They used to have another one but they don't play on that no more. That's gone out a bit now, hasn't it? That Master System, I think it's called.

R: How many games have they got?

Mother: I don't know. I aren't interested.

R: Who buys the games?

Mother: They get them — I just pay.

This was a significant and representative exchange between a researcher and a mother who purported to have anxieties about the games and their potential effects, and yet who colluded in the children's desire to play and acquire more games. She seemed unaware that her own lack of interest and involvement allowed the children 'carte blanche' to do as they wished.

Another example of a parent expressing overt disapproval and yet, in reality, allowing her child to set the agenda came from a mother of an 8-year-old boy. On this occasion the context was television viewing rather than computer game playing:

R: Do you mind A watching television every day?

Mother: No, not really. I mean some of the programmes are really good. They're educational, aren't they?

R: Do you ever stop him from watching anything?

Mother: Yes, I don't like him watching *The Bill*. I don't think it's good for him.

R: Why's that?

Mother: Well — it's horrible isn't it? — very violent.

R: Do you watch it?

Mother: Only when it's on.

R: Why do you have it on? [It is only the mother and her son who live in the home.]

Mother: (*Long pause*) Well, A sometimes turns it on. I mean all the children watch it at school so I can't really stop him.

Parental Control

We encountered a number of similar situations where parents talked about the unsuitability of certain programmes and maintained that their children were not allowed to watch them. On investigation, though, it often transpired that this embargo only operated with respect to the main television set in the family living area. Once the child was ensconced in his or her own bedroom, viewing was largely uncensored.

Children in our study sometimes delighted in telling us ways in which they eluded attempts at parental control. This frequently occurred in connection with video and television viewing rather than with computer games. Often this involved collusion with grandparents, as the following conversations reveal:

- Conversation with 8-year-old girl:

    R: Does your mum ever tape anything for you that's on too late for you to watch?

    Girl: Mm, not really. (*She giggles*) It's my nanna who tapes everything for me.

    R: She taped *Jurassic Park* for me and *The Addams Family*. She buys me tapes as well.

- Conversation with 7-year-old girl:

    R: Do you ever watch television in the morning?

    Girl: No, I'm not allowed. My mum won't let me.

    R: So, you've never seen Breakfast TV or watched videos in the morning?

    Girl: Well, if I'm round my nanny's. She lets me do anything.

- Conversation with 8-year-old boy:

    R: Do you have a video recorder at home?

    Boy: No, my mum and dad won't have one in the house and I hate their guts for it.

    R: Do they know you feel so strongly about it?

    Boy: Yes and they don't care. It's not fair but I just go round my nanny's. She videos things from the telly for me and I watch them at hers. (*He laughs*)

- Another 8-year-old boy:

    R: Do you ever play in the morning before you go to school?

    Boy: I'm not allowed to.

    R: So, you never play before school?

    Boy: Well —

    R: It sounds as if you sometimes manage it.

    Boy: Well, like if I've been playing in my room and it gets late, right, and my mum says I've got to go to bed. Well, sometimes I've got to a really good bit — like the other night I got really far on *Jungle Book*. I've never got that far before. Then my mum goes 'You've got to stop, it's late.' When she came up, I turned off the computer but I didn't really. I know how to turn off the screen but you don't lose the game, right. There's just this little red light on. She doesn't know about the light so she thought it was off. I left it on like that all night then I turned the screen on in the morning and I could start again where I'd got to — at the same level. (*He laughs*) My mum still doesn't know I do that sometimes. She'd be mad if she knew. (*He laughs again*)

While this lack of parental knowledge — particularly on the part of women — and control was widespread in our study, we did encounter some examples of strict supervision and intervention. One father, for example, did not allow his 9-year-old daughter to watch television at all, preferring to video material himself that he deemed suitable and then making the recorded tapes available to her. He bought the *Radio Times* on a regular basis and sat down for about 15 minutes every week with his copy and made a note of any programme which he thought would be worth taping. He considered the whole range of material and did not simply look at programmes designated for children's viewing. In fact, he had a rather jaundiced opinion of those particular programmes:

I've got a sort of bias against children's television as a sort of . . . You know, while there seem to be some individual programmes that seem to be good, some of the ethos . . . I mean, there is a kind of condescension in a lot of contemporary broadcasting which says that, you know, it's a bit like when you go somewhere and they are doing catering for children and they start from the premise that modern kids aren't going to relate to this at all unless we give them burgers and chips and coke, or at least unless we have a lot of these things around. They actually are in a sense programming children not to expect or aspire to anything else other than that. I find a lot of the sort of presentation and the presenters are very much that style. Even programmes like *Blue Peter* are likely to have a lot of pop culture references. You can take two views of it: you can say that somehow this is the kids' own culture, which is a view that some people put forward, or . . . I actually feel that it is a culture that is largely being created by the interest of manufacturers and industry and so on. What seems to be happening as a result of that saturation through television is that things have come down the age scale so pop music and pop stars which, in the past, might have been an early teenage phenomenon have now got down so that you have 4- and 5-year-olds relating to Madonna.

An indication of the 'pseudo-sophistication' of young children mentioned by this parent, was found by all the researchers, particularly in the bedrooms where we often encountered a strange juxtaposition of images and artefacts. One 4-year-old girl's bedroom was a classic example (see Figures 8.1 and 8.2).

This child had a huge collection of soft toys and dolls which were arranged on the bed and on shelves around the room. There was also a television set and

Figure 8.1: *Photograph of a corner of a 4-year-old girl's bedroom*

Figure 8.2: Photograph of posters on the opposite wall of the same child's bedroom

video recorder on a pull-out shelf overhanging the end of the bed. One wall was covered in an eclectic mix of posters ranging from *Superted* through *Barbie* to *The Gladiators*.

In a later part of the conversation with the father quoted above, he went on to give his views on the exposure of children to news programmes:

R: Do you let J watch the news?

Father: No, I avoid that completely.

R: Why?

Father: I suppose two things. Again, I feel it reflects the kind of preoccupations of adults.

R: What about something like *Newsround* which is aimed at children?

Father: No, again I feel unhappy with the news agenda. I also feel that it's quite a manipulative situation in a way. We have a situation where news is not just focusing on what's going on but on what's going wrong, where's the row, you know, focusing on negativity, disputes — it lacks any kind of constructive sense. I can't really think of any good examples except the classic one — which I think Martin Lewis quoted — where the Toxteth riots received so much coverage that there has been an improvement in the crime and social statistics in the Toxteth area — a lot of good things have happened since then and haven't received coverage. I feel very unhappy about that kind of media news agenda and I just feel it's something to avoid. I also feel that childhood seems to me like a special time when the mind should be able to look at things very imaginatively or very openly — very freely — and I feel that contemporary children almost have a kind of weight of history and politics and appalling things they're hearing about all the time and, in some sense — it may just be romanticism — but I feel like it is almost ageing them and creating a sort of great weight of our concerns on them. A lot of material that is going out on adult television and on the news is material and issues which adults feel disturbed by and is being presented without often exploring what constructive responses there might be to it. I feel in a way that this is burdening children and it seems to me that, as an inevitable consequence, we are limiting them in terms of their ability to dream dreams.

The idea that children's television viewing needs to be censored in some way was encountered frequently, particularly amongst parents with professional backgrounds. However, even those parents who strictly enforced the rule that their children could only watch Children's TV, often made assumptions that programmes designated for children would by definition, be suitable. *Blue Peter* and *Newsround* were programmes frequently cited as completely acceptable, even though many of the parents were simply remembering them from their own childhood and were not currently monitoring them. It was rare to find parents, like the father quoted above, who were sitting down to watch with their children, discussing the content with them and actively censoring material. Some parents were quite openly admitting that they felt unable to curb their children's viewing and games playing habits almost as though they had passed over the responsibility for it to the broadcasting authorities and the games manufacturers. This powerlessness in the face of pervasive external influences is reflected in the current debate about the use of the 'V'chip, a device designed in the United States to allow parents to block transmission of unsuitable material on the television. There is a similar device available for computer games consoles but it is expensive at approximately £80 (Griffiths, 1993). These gadgets offer an effective way of barring access to material deemed unsuitable for children but they do not address the problem of how to establish what is unsuitable in the first place. Parents are still going to have to take the trouble to find out exactly what their children are up to and they simply cannot rely on some external aid to do this for them.

In an increasingly stressful world, it can be tempting to shift the burden of responsibility to outside agencies. An article in the *Sunday Times* (12 November 1995) reported on the alarming rise in the use of the anti-depressant drug Prozac to control attentional and conduct disorders in children. The number of prescriptions mentioning Prozac for 5–10-year-olds rose from 61,000 in 1992 to 220,000 two years later. While there is obviously a place for such treatments for certain children, Breggin, a child psychologist, is quoted in the article as saying that the real problem lies not in some chemical defect in the children themselves but in the attitudes of the adults who care for them: 'The scientific-medical approach may temporarily assuage guilt, but it cannot be taken without undermining the most fundamental family value of all — that adults are responsible for the lives of their children.'

Supporting the Technology

This is not to say that the parents in our study were shirking their responsibilities or failing to provide what they saw as the best possible environment for their children. Parents in most of the families we visited wanted only the best for their children and sought to deliver this in ways that they perceived to be appropriate. Many parents who lavished toys and equipment on their children felt that they were providing their families with opportunities that had been denied them in their own childhood. Typical of this view were the remarks of the mother of a 4-year-old daughter — an only child. This child had a vast array of toys and play equipment including her own television and VCR. In addition to her bedroom, which was full of toys and games, she had another upstairs room, 'her playroom', which contained large items such as dolls' houses and miniature kitchen ranges. Out in the back garden, a whole shed was devoted to her 'outside toys'. Shortly after the conversation with the researcher, the parents were taking her on a holiday to Disneyland in Florida:

> I suppose it looks as though she's got lots of things but I can't resist buying things for her. I never had anything when I was a child. We couldn't afford lots of toys and things but, all the while I can do it, I want her to have everything she needs. I didn't have it myself, you see. I expect that's why it's so important to me. (Mother)

This mother, like many other parents in the study, was keen to stress the educational value of the toys she had provided for her child:

> (*She points to a large plastic miniature kitchen toy*) We're going to get rid of that because we've bought her the new, bigger version for Christmas. She doesn't know yet but she'll love it because she plays with this one all the time. And, look, this is a till from the Early Learning Centre. It's got all the right money, see. You know £5, £10 and £20 notes — all the right colours. So it's all learning for her. And you ought to see the food she does in her kitchen — she loves it. It's the thing she plays most with and, as I say, she's learning from it.

Parents we interviewed often said that they had bought items for their children because they would be 'educational'. It was not always entirely clear what they meant by this term and in almost all cases the parents seemed to feel that they had acquitted themselves of their responsibilities simply by providing them: there was little evidence of active parental involvement in some of these 'educational' pursuits. One example of this kind of purchase was the large collections of magazines

Figure 8.3: A typical collection of part magazines neatly arranged in an 8-year-old boy's bedroom

published in weekly or fortnightly parts which were often to be found stacked neatly on shelves in bedrooms (see Figure 8.3).

These part works are not inexpensive and the cost gradually mounts up as the collection is built over time. The collection illustrated in Figure 8.3 consists of forty-six editions of *My Body Works* at £2.99 each and fifty copies of *Farthing Wood* at £1.20 each. In addition, this particular child also showed us his set of fifty-eight *Dinosaur* magazines which had been acquired at a cost of £1.50 per issue. This adds up to a considerable sum (£275) and the parts are still being collected.

It was interesting to note that many parents who balked at the expense of acquiring a PC would nevertheless make considerable outlays of cash on material such as this. They sometimes seemed surprised themselves at how much they had spent. It was only in conversation with the researchers that many of them had stopped to think about the amount of money involved. The gradual process of acquiring magazines has lessened the impact of the cost. It is also fair to say that many of them had been bought for children by people other than their parents — most often by grandparents. We were interested in the motivation for the acquisition of these large and costly collections, not least because the children themselves often had rather mixed reactions:

R: Do you look forward to getting this magazine every fortnight?

Boy (8 years): Yeah, mum gets it and it's there when I get back from school.

R:	So, do you sit down straight away and read it?
Boy:	Well, I look at the pictures.
R:	When do you read it?
Boy:	(*Long pause*) Well, I don't really read it.
R:	Why's that?
Boy:	Well, (*long pause*) it's hard really. It's not always that good.
R:	What do you do with them?
Boy:	I keep them upstairs in my bedroom.
R:	Do you look at them again later?
Boy:	Yes, well, no, not really, not usually.

We often had the impression when talking to children about these collections that they derived more pleasure from the actual process of acquisition than from the magazines themselves, particularly when the choice of magazine seemed to be that of the parents rather than the children, as shown by the following conversation with the parents of a 7-year-old boy and an 8-year-old girl.

R:	Do you have comics, C?
Mother:	He gets *Treasures of the Earth*. It's an educational one. He's got a whole collection of those. J gets *Fox and the Hound* comics, you know the Disney ones. Go and get some of those magazines, C.

(*The boy returns a few moments later with some magazines and dumps them on the researcher's lap*)

R:	These look interesting, C. [One of them has a tray of minerals attached] Do you know what any of these minerals are called?
Son:	No, it's too difficult.
R:	What made you want to get these magazines, C?
Son:	(*Long pause*) I don't know.
Father:	It was advertised on TV. Every time it was on telly, he kept on about it.
R:	Do you look for interesting stones and things when you go out for walks, C?
Son:	No.
Father:	Oh, come on, we did once. Don't you remember — we were walking along and you kept picking up stones and putting them in your pocket. Your trousers kept falling down, they were so heavy. He picks up stones all the while.
Mother:	And then, when they grow up, that kind of thing will be handy for the big school.
Father:	'Cos they **are** educational and they'll last a long time.

It would seem that parents are expecting their children to absorb the 'education' from such publications almost by a process of osmosis: simply being exposed to them will ensure that information is assimilated and understood. The children in our study certainly did not seem to be reading these magazines — at most they liked to look at the pictures. This is not to say that children are no longer reading. We found many examples of children gaining tremendous pleasure from reading story books or having them read to them. They often mentioned classic children's books and it usually transpired that these had been bought or taken out from the library by parents, as shown by the following extracts:

• Conversation with 9-year-old girl:

> I especially liked *The Hobbit* because it was all magic — all the characters were different — not human. I like *Pride and Prejudice*, too. My mum is reading that too because it's a bit difficult. We are keeping up with it on the television. [This conversation took place during the Autumn of 1995 when *Pride and Prejudice* was being screened on BBC television.]

• And from another 9-year-old girl:

> I like things like *Anne of Green Gables*, *The Borrowers* and *Swallows and Amazons*.

• Conversation with an 8-year-old girl:

> *R*:   What is your favourite book?
> *Girl*: It's called *The Faraway Tree*. I forgot who writ it but it's about these people who live in a magic tree and then they — well, there's these children who don't live in the tree who go up into the forest for adventures. Actually they go up a ladder and through the clouds and into a land of fairy tales.

• And from an 8-year-old boy:

> I read in bed most nights. I like adventures. Roald Dahl is my best.

A number of the children were regularly reading comics, but we rarely encountered children who were regularly reading computer magazines. The older boys were very aware of them, however, from window shopping, street talk and elder siblings:

> *R*:   Do you like reading?
> *Boy (8 years)*: Yeah, comics mainly. *Dandy* and *Beano*. They're really funny.

And in conversation with the mother of four boys:

> *R*:   Do they read much?
> *Mother*: They have *Dandy* and *Beano* every week. They've got millions all over their bedroom. I get them when I go shopping on Wednesday and that's the first thing they want to look at when they come home that day.

Figure 8.4: Symbols on the Internet that cross language barriers

:-)	(:-)	:-)>	:-')
Smiley	**Bald**	**Bearded**	**Has a cold**

Although we found evidence of children continuing to read for pleasure, we also found that children dislike reading instructions for computer games and tend to ignore written directions that come up on the screen. Children like visual images and many of them told us that they only liked books with pictures. The publishing industry is rapidly responding to technological change. Dorling Kindersley, the family run British book publisher founded in 1974, has launched several titles on the CD-rom including an encyclopaedia of the human body which can be assembled and taken apart using the computer mouse. All parts of the body are revealed on the screen in colourful detail and lively animations show how each part of the body works. Peter Kindersley, the chairman of the group, is reported in the *Sunday Times* (22 May 1994) as saying, 'Within three years, I doubt if we will be publishing anything in printed form'. He used an old Chinese proverb to sum up his enthusiasm for publishing on multi-media CD-rom: 'I hear and I forget; I see and I remember; I do and I understand.'

This kind of development heightens fears of parents and teachers that the printed word is in danger of becoming obsolete. There is an anxiety that children will move away from traditional forms of communication and develop an alien, computer-based jargon which is inaccessible to adults. Already on the Internet a spontaneous set of symbols has been generated that crosses traditional language barriers. These symbols are made up of key strikes which can be 'read' horizontally as a head turned on its side. They are called 'smileys' after the first one to be devised, and which is supposed to indicate that the user is feeling happy (see Figure 8.4). It seems unlikely that the printed word will disappear completely. Literacy will retain its importance for the foreseeable future, but societies are changing. The labour market is undergoing a huge transformation and the number of traditionally low-skilled jobs in manufacturing will dramatically decline. The use of information technology in the workplace will probably mean that higher standards of literacy will be required from a larger proportion of the workforce. There could be a new meritocracy based on IT and the 'haves' will leave the 'have-nots' behind. It is time for adults to work **with** their children to prepare for the next century.

Chapter 9

To Boldly Go:
Issues and Consequences

In the preceding chapters, we have discussed our experiences of entering homes and schools and observing children and adults, listening to their conversations and asking them directly about their experiences of screen-based entertainment technology. In this chapter, we will summarize the issues that have arisen from these experiences and seek to suggest reforms in educational policy, as a consequence of them.

First, it must be said, there is an undoubted change taking place in homes, which, even though it is accelerating and pervasive, is having effects upon people of all ages and which are very difficult to pin down. Screen-based technologies are rapidly increasing. They fill up people's time. They offer sublimation for so many experiences. The commercial imperative behind them means that they are moving inexorably towards their ideal goal of virtual experience and maximum emotional, psychological and, even, physical impact upon the user. In their largely unregulated activities, content and processes, they contain within them the inevitability of both beneficial and detrimental effects upon the maturing learner.

Screen-based entertainment technology, whether video related or computer based, comprises a major part of domestic interaction with popular culture. Much of this book explores the variety of ways in which adults and children negotiate the use, abuse or rejection of various elements of popular culture via new technologies within the home. The suggestion here is that parents and guardians who take a really active role in helping children to navigate screen-based experience are uncommon and that this lack of support is compounded when children go to school to discover how little contact teachers have with this same culture. The result seems to be that most children lead a rather unmediated existence within the theatre of the screen. They are not being educated and supported to develop a critical awareness of their experiences, to explore quality issues relating to them or to understand their role as consumers and users, in the face of powerful commercial forces. The ignorance of adults, regarding children's activities involving computers, computer games, the Internet and videos means that issues involving, for example, gender, emotional impact, aggression, IT skills development, alienation, reading and writing, the interface between reality and fantasy and a whole host of other interrelated themes, documented in this research, are not being raised within educational settings.

Drawing together these issues and summarizing them, we will begin with gender, as this has proven to be a truly major theme within the research. As pointed out in Chapter 7, before the age of four, children appear to have no gendered response to interaction with this kind of technology. After this, it appeals more and more to boys. Even worse, the lack of knowledge among teachers and parents about what is educational and developmental in these technologies, leaves us with a consuming public which is vulnerable to manufacturers' claims. A consequence seems to be that it is mainly boys who end up playing shootemups and beatemups on dedicated games machines, which have a rapid product cycle and may perpetuate the monochrome virtues of macho behaviour. This activity is part of a constellation of environments and products such as commercial shops, arcades and magazines which are becoming increasingly male preserves. Attempts to differentiate these activities from those that might be regarded by educationalists as having more value, educationally, are not consonant with how children see them. In a boy's world, they *are* computers and are inextricably linked with everything computing. This can give boys an advantage over girls in terms of an initial affinity for IT. It is significant that, as pointed out in Chapter 7, research has shown a growing female unease concerning IT hardware, itself.

Where we observed computer usage involving boys and girls together, there was evidence of boys' dominance and of boys having different values regarding the content of programs and machine functions. The rough demarcation seemed to be that boys preferred direct competition and physical action motifs, and girls tended towards more complex themes such as adventure narratives or puzzle-solving. Also, boys were far more physical in their interaction with the technology, itself, particularly joysticks, pads and mouse. This did not mean that we couldn't find girls who enjoyed beatemups. We did. But the majority of games enabled the boys to enter into simulated versions of worlds where they are normally marginalized spectators; sports and games with a fighting content. There was evidence, too, that within such simulated environments, boys, particularly, could take on older siblings and fathers and beat them in macho activities.

At the end of the day we felt that there was a great deal of social conditioning at large and schools will need to make enormous efforts to counteract this. But, as is being reiterated, teachers need the experience and knowledge of popular culture, technology and interpreting the media to be able to intervene in this process. The practice of positive discrimination, which one or two schools observed involving girls-only computer days, for example, hardly changes the underlying problem, at all.

The research team's overwhelming impression was that not just computers but *most* technology is male dominated. Female adults, whether, teachers or parents, were, in general, poor role models to the young, whatever machinery they were using. There was, however, some substance to the notion that where one-parent families were headed by women, particularly from the middle classes, these individuals made more effort to assert themselves over the technology. This being said, many children never saw a confident woman handle a video recorder, games machine or PC. The lack of training and confidence among female teachers that we encountered, led to unappealing activities including inappropriate use of technology, relegation of it to the fringes of the curriculum (and the physical space of the classroom), repeated failures to handle its problems and quirks, 'quack consultants' drawn from supposed child experts, frustration and apathy. Whilst at home many women — particularly those from non-professional backgrounds — refused to touch machines or software, had little or a very rudimentary knowledge of them in terms of their operating functions and, generally, confirmed the worst of female stereotypes. All this was in the face of the fact that computers, for example, are changing rapidly and fit the home and school context more easily than they once did in that they are: more powerful than ever before; able to process and store more information; are much easier to use; are miniaturized and portable so that they need no longer be locked away in corners of classrooms or take up too much domestic space; and they are cheaper. And, on top of all this, it will be through the computer that all other forms of communication and entertainment will flow into homes and schools.

Moving from gender to the more specific issue of computer games and video products, the research confirmed previous findings that significant adults in children's lives were unable to discern what elements of technology might be productive in children's learning. For some children it is obvious that there are real educational advantages to playing games like *Theme Park, Sim City* and even adventure games which incorporate text and image or *Tetris*-type games which encourage the development of spatial awareness. There was also evidence that computer games gave children the experience of success and completion, often denied them in the classroom context. They did not see the use of short cuts or cheats as undermining this sense of victory. These were merely different routes to the same end. However, for most teachers, such software and its integral structures was effectively rejected as being part of the general mass of corrupting influences of the commercial scene. This fitted the pattern, elaborated within the research, of primary school teachers having little time for most products of the popular media.

Since parents tended to regard these forms of technology as being the province of the young and to have been invented 'since their time' or formative years, there was a strong tendency towards *laissez faire* parenting. Assumptions were made that if the products of this technology were advertised as being for children, then they were covered by regulatory structures and wouldn't do harm. They tended not to be as knowledgeable about age categories for computer games as their offspring. In their turn, children tended to feel that age restrictions and taboos concerning games and videos were always for children younger than themselves.

There were also parental assumptions that computer games playing was a good first step into computing itself and would make a child better at it. Again, many parents could not discriminate between dedicated games machines and PCs. Parents might have a sceptical view of the content value of some games, believing them to be too violent or superficial, but would often not invoke their beliefs in front of the children. This was often because their children gained status among their peers for having the hardware and software.

When the research team introduced headteachers to some of the commercial software that children were using, they were astonished at the quality of graphics, the skills that were being demanded and the heady nature of the experience. They were able to define educational benefits in even the more action-oriented software, notwithstanding reservations about implicit gender bias or concerns about violence.

Because we are living in a time of rapid technological change, we are faced with a major issue which spans all areas of knowledge and human activity. This involves the complex strategies we must devise to educate the young in a free market economy, where the capacity of technological products to thrill, entice, frighten, educate, proselytize, isolate or alienate is growing rapidly. Somewhere down the line there must be adult mediation — which is at the very heart of education. Otherwise, and this research threw up many examples of it, the young can become unreconstructed, raw consumers of manufacturing hype with their parents either complicit partners or nonplussed bystanders. The hype can be as sophisticated as that used to sell cars. It involves cross-over products between film, television, comics, cartoons and computer games. Very often there is little allowance made for the consumer being at a vulnerable age. The publicity often talks up elements of the experience in very adult terms, concentrating upon gore and the thrill of violence or aspects of fear. It is a dangerous practice to allow direct selling of conceptual worlds to children, with little regulation and no attempt at educating them to deal with it. The chapters concerned with computer games, videos and computer magazines emphasize what little influence many children receive from significant adults in their lives. They do spend much time in their private worlds, the contents of which are largely the creative output of non-educationalist adults whose conceptions of what is a turn-on, a thrill or an addiction, can help fashion the play of the young.

The wider issue in the education of the young concerns how best to develop critical thinking skills. The researchers had to work extremely hard, and often subtly, to reach beyond conditioned or superficial responses to questions. Children were not used to exploring their own experiences of these media, or taking a meta-view or talking propositionally. Of course, in the very young this is not particularly expected but, as we found over time, even the very young can begin to place themselves in context and describe their experiences in a language more complex than 'cool', 'ok' or 'boring'.

The mediation of children's complex experience of screen-based activity requires teachers and parents to engage with children, on a regular basis, to help them handle critically the resulting emotional, physical and intellectual consequences. In its most prosaic form, it was obvious that often neither children nor parents were able to use instructions. Pre-programming and exploring videos, entering computer games and exploiting the full range of experiences on offer, exploring the range of functions on a PC were activities quite beyond many parents and teachers. It could be argued that being able to read and follow instructions requires the individual to begin to develop a meta-view over the environment. Indeed, many households did not even possess the means to make decisions about which TV programmes to watch, having neither daily papers nor TV and radio magazines. Consequently, they made choices from a mixture of channel hopping and memory of stock programme fare.

Enabling the young to become critical consumers in the face of adult apathy, indifference or antipathy, and to develop control over the technology and authorship within it should be at the heart of education. It doesn't appear to be. Technology is often the last point of call in the curriculum. Given the potential of screen-based technologies in the classroom, in every facet of work across subjects, as information source, interactive teacher, improver of communications, mathematical tool, text manipulator and so on, the sad finding of the research was that its major use was still as a bolt-on to the curriculum. There was very little evidence of teachers trying to keep pace with the drift from print, in young people's daily lives. The technology provides for most children in classrooms, a bit of history here, a bit of maths there and a great deal of fair copying of existing work to go on classroom walls.

In schools, the technology itself varied from ancient BBCs to CD-roms. The prevailing attitudes of the majority of teaching staff towards technology, whether it be video recorders or computers, often ranged from the disdainful to the fearful. The high moral ground to which schools retreated, concerning the commercial end of the IT revolution: the dedicated machines, the games and the videos, created obvious puzzlement for their pupils. The very lack of children's work and conversation concerning their experiences of screen-based technologies, whilst at school, spoke volumes for the way that schools could create a taboo about children's activity. The crude and simplistic attempts on the parts of some teachers to differentiate technology into what might be educational and what might be for leisure, added to children's difficulties. Children lump them together as computers or videos. The technology tends to be intrinsically enthralling to them — but not the use to which it is put. Whilst videotape could be used to educate, utilizing the same techniques found in, say, story reading, it was trundled out mainly to show schools broadcasts. The content of much computer software was dated and bore little relation to the impressive changes that have taken place in games software.

To move between home cultures and those of schools leaves the researcher with a strong sense of paradox. Schools, which ought to be the progenitors of future society, via the education of the young, appear to spend more time, effort and resource in conserving the past. The primary school emphasis upon reading, writing and mathematics is, of course, essential but now excludes so much else in the curriculum. It is driven by the National Curriculum, Ofsted inspection and government-inspired league tables and is an emphasis which excludes much that is central to children's lives. This, together with a paucity of wide-scale training and updating in the use of technology for teachers has led to the situation where many schools appear to be not fulfilling the obligation to begin preparing the next generation's adults for a technology dominated work and leisure society. The opening account of the technologized Orgill primary school in Chapter 2 points in a direction few schools are even contemplating. The central theme of this final chapter is that the young are generally being denied a vital link in the chain of their development. This may be summed up as 'the capacity to utilize technology for a personal, educational and working future'. It includes not only being able to manage PCs, games machines, the Internet and video recorders, but also being able to manage this technology as critical consumers, comprehending the way that information is generated and used, how images seduce and how fictions need to be separated from facts.

If schools are unable to offer media education to the young and help them develop their critical awareness and capacity to exploit technology rather than be exploited by it, as has been inferred already, parents are unlikely to undertake this role, either. Research led us to place families along a spectrum, from proactive and controlling parents or guardians, to reactive and *laissez faire*. There was a polarization into the following responses to screen-based technologies. At one extreme, and the vast majority clustered at this end of the spectrum, families exerted very little control over what appeared on screens, whether bought, rented or beamed into their living rooms and bedrooms. In many cases, finance appeared to represent the only limitation on children's experiences. Parents often could not discriminate between a PC and a games machine, therefore often providing their children with a limited learning horizon, but from the best possible intentions. Parents (and grandparents) were unwilling to say no to their offspring and at best negotiated over the length of time they spent in front of the screen rather than what appeared on it. In such settings children seemed to be growing up as relatively uncritical, subordinated consumers. At the other extreme, there were one or two families who exerted massive control, had very idealized and somewhat nostalgic views of childhood and who denied their children much of the range of new technological experience. For them childhood meant *Swallows and Amazons*, no television and protection against society's ills and dangers. Between these polar opposites, we found only a small number of examples of parents engaging in serious debate with their children over what they were experiencing or had experienced on screens, either in their own homes or in those of their friends. Thus the everyday child can move from a home environment, enriched with whatever the family can afford, but with few real restrictions on usage, to a school environment rich with prohibitions and taboos but little technological quality and expertise.

Other research, noted in this book, has shown that, increasingly, children are being kept indoors because parents fear what will happen to them if they are allowed unsupervised play outside. If the tendency of fearful parents is to lock away their daughters and sons and give them the screen to keep them quiet, they would be constraining children's social development with consequences we cannot yet foresee. Much of what we have witnessed in the research suggests that children still prefer, in the main, to socialize rather than act alone, whether in front of a screen, in the home generally or in the playground or park. And that they often prefer to act physically rather than seek vicarious sublimation. Hence the seasonal nature of many of their activities. Parents and teachers, for example, feel they are safer in daylight and allow them more freedom in the summer months.

There were many cases of children enjoying the company of peers, siblings or parents in front of the screen, whether by associating with characters in a video by turning down the sound and acting out the parts or whether by competing at soccer or kick boxing or by joint problem-solving activities in platform games or complex simulation games. In schools, where we observed children using newish problem-solving technology, such as, for example, a game based upon archaeology and the artefacts one might find in a stone age settlement, it was noticeable how quickly the activity drew other children in. Once there, lively discussion ensued. On the other hand, there were a few cases where solitary children became very absorbed in games play or repeated viewings of videos and these experiences seemed to further their separateness from their peers. What happens to children who are allowed an unrelieved diet of a narrow range of media products, without recourse to discussion of content and emotional effects, remains an area for further research.

If anyone was in doubt about the place of screen-based technology among the ghouls, phantoms and other horrors of popular demonology, he or she should look at the way the press has raised it as a spectre whenever a motive needs to be found for the apparently motiveless crime. Newspapers found video the evil culprit behind the horror of the James Bulger death and a popular mind-set had set in despite later evidence to the contrary. Television, film, video and computer games are accessible suspects whenever the elastic boundaries of moral conduct are stretched too far. The awful tragedy of the Dunblane massacre of young lives led to a *Daily Express* editorial blaming 'celluloid sewage'. It may be because video, television and computer games' monitors involve the viewer in vicarious interaction and each of us is aware of the degree of frisson raised by being actively engaged in events which, in real life, would be regarded as socially unacceptable. Screen media can play the dual role of rupturing moral codes and simultaneously satisfying the desire for escapism. Sublimation through moving images has become so commonplace that, for many, life's experiences must be proven to have happened, by video recording. Camcorders are found focusing on all the more meaningful events in our lives. Births, marriages, anniversaries, holidays and festivities are duly captured on tape. As, more recently, are funerals. A bizarre event recounted by one child in this survey, for example, involved a recording made in a pub, in which the child's grandfather is seen to die from a heart attack.

The darker side of this can be seen in the increasing number of cases of photography and video being used by hostage takers, to prove their violent capability, or by perpetrators of obscene crimes as part of the obsessional pathology of both relishing and then advertising the act. Where once the impact of such crimes was mediated and inevitably blurred by texts in newspaper reports, so that, eventually, the reader could, emotionally, find a way to handle it, the new medium of instant replay, allows no such acclimatization.

The technology of moving images thus becomes guilty, in popular consciousness, by association. The consequences seem to be that a mind-set is developed whereby even otherwise informed individuals, such as teachers, become jaundiced about the possible benefits of such media. Given many teachers' lack of interest in and moral distrust of popular media, it is no surprise that they have no way of being able to verify, one way or another, whether such media are affecting, unduly, children in their care. The only teachers we talked to, who had evidence of such an effect, cited examples from some years previously. But, as has been noted, singular dramatic events can go a long way towards creating the attitude of an entire professional body. Many teachers, for example, spoke of tired pupils in class during morning sessions and put this down to children staying up all hours. Initial views that this was because of their involvement with screen events in their bedrooms dissolved under questioning. Teachers didn't know why. They had no real evidence to support their beliefs. As has been shown, our research suggests that children may indeed be up late and entirely with the blessing of and often within the company of parents. On the other hand, teachers were alarmed by stylized fighting in the playground and the use of violent language in games and, in other research, put this down to the powerful effects of computer games and videos. Our research tended to confirm the view that children, like other members of society, develop language and forms of physical expression within specific contexts. This is an essential element of play. Therefore, descriptive terms within games play such as 'kill', 'splat' and 'die' are dislocated from their everyday meanings. They do not indicate, necessarily, increasingly violent dispositions.

Thus, in our research, we found very little evidence thus far, that children were being particularly affected by the fictions of computer games or videos. The evidence was that, apart from a few individuals, whose life histories already contained evidence of emotional disturbance and who found expression or catharsis through screen entertainment, children were able to differentiate between fact and fiction. Even in the earliest years they had a sense of the difference between cartoon, computer game, video, documentary and, say, the news. This discrimination became increasingly sophisticated as they grew older. There was some evidence that real life events portrayed in the news and documentaries were the ones that affected them most dramatically. There was also some evidence that very realistic screen fiction could disturb them and that they were left undermined if they weren't helped to rationalize their experiences by a significant adult in their lives. In the main, however, the traditional view of children knowingly acting out in response to their screen-based experiences or willingly suspending their disbelief whilst engaged in them, seemed to hold good. But it would be complacent for anyone to assume that this scenario will hold good indefinitely. The power of the media to stimulate, entertain, persuade and affect us is growing, almost daily.

******

Summing up the issues raised in the research is one thing. Suggesting forms of educational and family-based response to the issues is quite another. Within a society where deregulation and market force ideology is so strong, it is difficult to envisage a wholesale response to any perceived need, on the part of a whole generation of children. This is particularly so when the emphasis in primary education is upon a very narrow conception of what should constitute the curriculum.

Everything is changing except schools, one might say. Even the dubious notion of schooling being a vehicle for socialization is being exposed in the current climate. Socialization is increasingly taking place outside school and through machines which provide vicarious experiences so that within institutions the divisions are growing between the expected behaviours and outlooks of children and those that children are experiencing elsewhere. These are unlikely to narrow as access to the Internet increases; as children's homes become repositories of proliferating and cheaper interactive technologies; and governments seek cheaper ways of delivering education and training, perhaps requiring families to take on more and more responsibility in this area. Providing better resources is not the answer on its own.

The revolution in micro-technology in the 1980s led to a government policy of providing computers to all schools. Just as television was introduced into schools two decades before. Neither really changed the teaching practices and learning processes of the majority of classrooms. Without extensive and continuous training, how are teachers going to help children to benefit from the vast potential of screen-based technology? And, equally, how are they going to help them to avoid the hazards? Without teaching interest and training in dissecting the content and production of the products of entertainment technologies, how are children going to be educated in handling the media and continuing to be able to differentiate between fact and fiction? And in homes, are we going to follow the American route and develop a new meritocracy, where families who can resource their children with the latest PCs, help them gain the fewer high salaried jobs that become available, because equality of opportunity no longer exists in this domain in schools? And will games playing become the new opiate of the masses — or the underclasses?

There have also been increased concerns, for example, over direct exploitation of the young in this country on the Internet, with the citing of pornography to the fore, and general concern over the unregulated freedom of the Net. Perhaps we are reiterating the issue too much, but it does seem as though education is abandoning the young to technologies which can be both purveyors of fantasy, as well as catalysts for fantasy building. If we allow these circumstances to continue, we may arrive at the time when fantasy precedes reality: that is, where experience is accumulated through simulation and sublimation to become, subsequently, the foundation upon which individuals make decisions about people and events in life. As a society we may be preparing ourselves for this to happen. As we have inferred in this book, moral panics about the effects of video, computer games, television, comics and magazines rear up whenever extreme human behaviour shocks the nation. We are, it could be argued, living through a period where we are helping to construct a causal link between immersion in entertainment media and human behaviour. As technology becomes more realistic and virtual, as the subliminal features of it become more complex and subtle and it becomes an inseparable feature of all waking life, the basis for believing in such causality may become better founded. Whether such media will continue merely to entertain and, at their extreme, provide us with acceptable surrogate experiences, or whether they propel us into forms of behaviour which we might not otherwise have found palatable, remains to be seen. Meanwhile, social change and the place of the child as virtual prisoner in the home, mean that the diet of the young is being constituted more and more by entertainment technology.

We suggest, at the end of the book, that you return to the early chapter, 'The Land of H', and re-read the transcript. So many of the issues in this book can be found in either explicit or implicit forms in the dialogue between the child and the researcher.

Chapter 10

The Crystal Maze:
How the Research was Done

This final chapter must be prefaced with a statement regarding our gratitude and respect for the schools which collaborated with us on the British Library/British Film Institute project. We were always astonished at the commitment of staff, their teaching quality and the way they tried to integrate our work with theirs. There are chapters in this book which are critical of educational policy on new technologies and its implementation. But, in many ways, teachers are victims of the whole social unease about new technology and the policies to implement education and training to handle them. They still suffer from the early days of IT-led education, rather than, as it should have been, education-led IT. Staff's and parents' behaviours, including their views and attitudes, are documented to show how we, as researchers, interpret the current place of screen-based technology in the home and school and the consequences for children's learning and maturation.

We begin this chapter with three descriptions from the researchers, regarding their feelings when entering 'the field'. The pressures upon them to adjust to the school and home settings are very evident.

As a lecturer spending most of my time with the 16+ age group, the first challenge was to find a means of communicating with the young children in our study without alienating them or making them feel ill at ease. Teachers will probably all recognize the sinking feeling they experience when their whole class erupts into guffaws of laughter at an unintentional gaffe when, for example, they use a phrase in all innocence that turns out to have a new and unlikely connotation because of a cult sitcom or whatever. The way round this for me has been to try to keep up with the current trends — a task that has been enormously (not to say unavoidably) helped by having two teenage sons. This 'youth cult' knowledge, however, has been acquired at the expense of keeping abreast of the influences on the habits and language of younger children. At the beginning of the project, I made a real effort to turn back my 'parental clock' and try to attune myself to pre-teen activities. I was often to be found lurking in local toy stores, bookshops and computer games shops noting (covertly, I hope) the kinds of things which appeared to attract the younger children. I also rediscovered some of the pain and pleasure of watching children's television programmes. Having acquired some small insight into the leisure activities of 4–9-year-olds, it also seemed important to find the appropriate tone and level for my conversations with children. It would clearly have been insulting and patronizing to 'talk down' to the children but equally unhelpful to try to engage them at too abstract a level. Misunderstandings would have arisen on both sides and the resulting data would have had little value. The best approach seemed to be to spend time in schools observing and talking to children and teachers before I tackled the research project proper. This was really helpful to me in terms of familiarizing myself with current classroom practice and in finding a comfortable way of engaging with the children. It had the added advantage that the children became used to me being around and were very ready to talk openly when I began focusing on the area of entertainment technology. (Roger Whittaker)

I was always extremely conscious that I was a guest in schools where enormous workloads and impending Ofsted inspections were placing heavy burdens on teaching and ancillary staff. I tried to make myself as unobtrusive as possible but, it was clear on occasions, that harassed teachers had no time to talk to me. Sometimes, I played an active part in the classroom listening to children read and helping them to correct pieces of written work. On one occasion early in the project, a crisis arose which the class teacher had to deal with and he left me in charge of a classroom of 7-year-olds 'just for a minute' which turned out to be 15. My admiration for teachers in the primary sector increased tremendously as a result of this somewhat unnerving experience. This was obviously an isolated incident and had occurred only in response to a fairly major emergency, but it did make me feel very uncomfortable. I had sought to differentiate myself from the teachers so that the children would not see me as an 'authority' figure and this experience was not helpful. I had, at my request, been introduced to the children by my Christian name and talked to them about things that they were unused to discussing with adults in school so this sudden role change into 'teacher-in-charge' was as difficult for the children as it was for me.

The question of IT competence and delivery is a prickly subject for many teachers and I was anxious not to seem critical or disapproving. As a practising teacher myself, albeit in a different type of institution, I know the difficulties and constraints that operate in simply delivering the curriculum without having to pay due deference to IT provision as well. I was conscious at times that my sense of fellow-feeling with the teachers clouded some of the objectivity required of an interview. However, this same lack of objectivity probably prompted more honest responses from teachers than would have been elicited from a more formal approach.

This anxiety was also with me when I sought access to family homes. We followed up the parents' reply to our letter either with a phone call or by personal contact at the school gates to arrange a home visit. Many parents were understandably wary at first — suspicious of our motives and worried about exposing themselves and their homes to criticism. I tried always to keep in mind my own likely feelings and reactions to being asked to open my home to an unknown researcher. Again, I sacrificed some object-ivity by sharing with them a few details about my own home and family in an attempt to reassure them that I was in no position to be critical. Probably as a result of this 'chatty' approach, I sometimes found myself on the receiving end of personal anecdotes and confidences which had very little direct connection with the research project. Sometimes these confidences related to difficult relationships that parents experienced with their children, marital problems and, on occasion, pretty explicit criticisms of schools and teachers. This was quite difficult to handle, both in terms of responding at the time and respecting the confidentiality when later dis-cussing interview data with other members of the research team. Parents also sometimes saw me as some kind of 'expert' who could advise on assorted aspects of child-rearing problems but this was clearly not part of my remit nor within my professional expertise and I had to make this clear to them. The most I could do in those circumstances was to refer them to appropriate sources of assistance where I thought that could be helpful. As with the teachers, however, I feel grateful to the many parents who allowed me into their homes and who were generally so warm and welcoming. (Jane Willson)

On my first visit to a home I was greeted by the mother and father (who had taken a half-day to be there). The sitting room had been arranged so that the three of us were sitting in a circle and I found the whole thing a rather unsettling experience, so much so that I didn't have the confidence to ask whether I could tape the interview or video the child playing on the computer. The second interview I had in a home was much more relaxing, but it was with the infamous Ashley's parents and the revelation that he had been telling me a pack of lies was also an eye-opener. Virtually all the interviews in the home were of a different nature, some being quite formal with most of the family present, and some far less so with a virtual freedom to roam the house. There was one occasion when the mother had forgotten I was coming and I had to interview her from across the room because she had invited an elderly friend into her home, who was sitting in her chair, in the middle of the room. The son was also in on the interview which limited the opportunity to probe in any depth. On another occasion a grandfather arrived and on being informed by his daughter that I had once played cricket for Wales proceeded to talk, in great lengths about his cricket career. It transpired that his cousin was the Test cricket umpire, David Constant. I had a tape-recorded interview full of the cricketing merits of Ian Botham, but little relating to entertainment technology. Generally I did not at any time feel threatened in any home, but I always felt some apprehension before each visit, although I was usually fairly well briefed by the schoolteachers prior to the visit. That being said, however, the visits did generate some excellent data although I cannot say that I would be desperately keen to repeat the exercise.

Likewise the visits to the schools were also very different, although generally they were well supported by the staff. In some schools I was given freedom to roam, whereas in others it was more structured. In a couple of instances the communication between the head and some of the teachers left a lot to be desired, and led to certain amount of hostility. One elderly teacher, with two very difficult year groups found the experience extremely unsettling, and, as often happens, the children spotted the weakness and some created havoc. This was also a very uncomfortable experience for myself, as they were constantly coming over to fiddle with the tape recorder and the video camera, to the point that eventually I had to stop filming, and placed the tape in a less obtrusive spot, which did not lend itself to quality recording. I felt extremely sorry for the teacher, who was also, as she admitted, a bit of an IT luddite and found it very difficult to control the children. I find it much easier to interview adults than some of the younger children. It was sometimes difficult to grasp whether these children really understood some of the questions, and likewise difficult to frame the questions. (Bryn Davies)

As is evident, there are pressures upon researchers entering unknown territory, working with comparative strangers and becoming witnesses to the vagaries of human relationships. Social life is not amenable to easy analysis and does not afford cut and dried data.

Warning

This book is based on evidence. Around a hundred children have been observed closely in their homes and at school, individually and in small groups. They have been interviewed along with their friends and teachers. The research has led the team to explore new ways of reaching into children's thoughts, by-passing some of the glib responses which may have been given to researchers in the past. The insights of the research are scattered through the book but are also gathered together in the final chapter. But what cannot be said, is that evidence of the social behaviour we have witnessed may, therefore, be generalized to the entire population. There will be other children in other settings who will behave differently. However, elements of what we have found will be found elsewhere and lessons from the research may be pertinent to a whole range of other settings. Case-study research allows us to gain a feel for what is happening out there in society. Whilst individual children are unique and idiosyncratic, an intensive study involving about a hundred of them from differing backgrounds gives a great many pointers to social change.

Introduction

When this project was first voiced to the British Library and the British Film Institute, what may have attracted them was the notion that here was a project which would employ qualitative research methods to unveil some of the activities which were occurring in the homes of young children. Instead of relying upon conventional interview or survey-based research, the promise was that researchers would enter domestic rooms and classrooms, following up to a hundred children in their hitherto hidden activities. By doing so, light ought could be cast upon what is happening when teachers and parents are not looking. How are children handling entertainment media — essentially video and computer-based technology — What are they getting out of it? What are the consequences for their maturation?

Choosing Children

Choosing the children presented us with the first set of problems. Whilst case-study research does not require the researcher to seek representativeness, in the way that a traditional statistical sample would require, nevertheless, we wanted a spread of life-styles and environments within the study, urban and rural, differing family profiles and age ranges, in order to enrich the enquiry. As it turned out, differences in, say, class and gender proved significant features of our study. Nevertheless, what must be appreciated is that what might be lost in providing a so-called representative sample in the traditional sense, may be gained by the sheer detail and subtlety of in-depth study. There are very few studies which give close-up descriptions of children in domestic environments and which give indications of the variety of ways in which they live their lives on a daily basis; how they organize their rooms; play; interact with their families over technology; and how parenting affects their development. This was how we articulated our choice of case studies in the early days of the research:

> The choice of pupils for the study presented the team with an intriguing challenge. Qualitative research does not necessarily require rigorous sampling because the in-depth nature of the case-study approach compensates for undoubted lack of representativeness of the population in a statistical sense, with the detailed illumination of the complexity of particular cases. This process can throw up issues, which, when investigated, cast light on social behaviour and change. What we decided to do was to try for some midway position and, within the 100 case-study sample, provide a spread of cases which fitted the most recent demographic profile for families in Britain. However, built into this sample was a desire to include a spread of socio-economic backgrounds and an equal gender split — even though most

Table 10.1: Sample of case studies based on national demographic family profiles (1992) (assuming a 50/50 gender split in the hundred cases)

Married couple with one child	Married couple with 2+children	Single Mother with one child	Single Mother with 2+children	Single Father with 1+children	Other
17 case studies	60 case studies	5 case studies	12 case studies	1 case study	5 case studies
selection factors	selection factors	selection factors	selection factors	selection factors	selection factors
Age range, locality and ability	Age range, ability income and locality	Age range and income	Age range, income and locality	Any example	Any examples (e.g. with disability, or behavioural problems etc)
					Further cases developed by a BFI MA student: on ethnic groups

previous research points to computer and video game activity being dominated by boys. By doing so we hoped to focus on gender-based responses to the hardware and software on offer, as well as the use of video-taped material, whether personally recorded or pre-recorded.

By including 9-year-olds in our range, we gave ourselves opportunities of following some pupils through transition from First Schools to Middle Schools with their different curriculum emphasis. It also allowed for the inclusion of male teachers within the pupils' school context.

This sample (see Table 10.1) would allow us fast access to field research because any immediately forthcoming pupil cases would fit somewhere on our schema. Difficulties might arise later when we start looking for particular cases to complete our sample range.

Teachers were very helpful in their first trawl of likely pupils, in that a family profile was an ingredient in the descriptions they provided in their lists. The teachers used a variety of means in bringing to our attention likely case studies. Potential pupils were tracked through their response to simple picture-based surveys suggested by ourselves, teachers' own detailed knowledge, drawings done by children on the theme of the study and occasional requests from parents or teachers from initial and new schools, asking us to follow up unusual cases.

The notion of a demographic sample, as depicted in Table 10.1, had to fray a little at the edges, once we became heavily embroiled in the research. At the end of the day, there were more single parent families in our survey. However, the overall profile at the end of the research was sufficiently like the original, for us to feel that our sample covered the range of family profiles. There were not one hundred case studies, explored in the detail we would have liked, by the end of the research. Some studies took longer and were in far greater depth. In one or two cases, the studies were aborted because of family difficulties, or because children simply moved away. On the other hand, the researchers worked with a number of small groups of children, both at school and at home, so that the total number of children interviewed and observed was closer to 150.

Parents were asked if they were willing to work with the project. From that point, all negotiation took place between the research team members and individual households. A letter was sent to willing parents and research team members made individual approaches. Thus, the research was distanced from the influence of the school. We were the ones who were negotiating with parents. Effectively, this allowed parents to be more open about conflicts they might feel over what their children may or may not be permitted to do, or the standards of education they were receiving. In one or two cases, there were dramatic criticisms of teaching and classrooms. These had to be borne by the researchers in order to move on into the parents' conceptions of what the child needed for healthy mental, emotional and physical growth. The following is a copy of the letter we sent to parents:

Dear

I am writing to ask you and your family for help with a research study currently being undertaken by a research team based at City College Norwich. This exciting project has the backing of the British Film Institute and the British Library.

We are interested in investigating the possible effects of various entertainment media (e.g., video and computers) on young children's thinking and understanding. As part of our study, we are hoping to observe and interview a hundred young children (4–9 years) drawn from schools in and around Norwich. This will provide us with valuable information about the ways in which children are currently using media equipment and how they are applying the skills acquired through these activities.

In order to obtain as much information as possible, we need to observe the children both at home and at school.

The headteacher and staff at your child's school believe that this is a worthwhile study that will provide useful information about future teaching and learning. They are happy to cooperate with the research based in school and will assist us as much as they can.

All children selected for inclusion in the project will be observed and interviewed in the school setting by one of the researchers over a period of a few days. One member of the research team will then visit the child at home to watch him/her playing. This will also be an opportunity to talk to parents and other members of the family about their attitudes to video, TV and computers.

The research findings from this high-profile project are likely to have nationwide importance. The project team consists of a small group of experienced researchers and teachers who will endeavour to conduct the study with as little intrusion as possible and with respect for your privacy and confidentiality. No information will be released which identifies your child without your permission and you will have the right to withdraw from the research project at any time.

We hope that you will allow your child to participate in this exciting project and we should appreciate it if you would complete the tear-off slip at the bottom of this letter and return it to your child's school as soon as possible. A member of the research team will then contact you to arrange a mutually convenient time to visit you at home.

If you would like any more information about the project, please contact the headteacher, who will be able to supply more details or, if you prefer, put you in touch with a member of the research team.

Yours sincerely

Professor Jack Sanger

✁ —
Reply Slip

I agree that my child .... can participate in the entertainment media project.
I understand that I can withdraw my child from the project at any time.

Signature of parent/guardian

Choosing Methods

Choosing what methods are needed to illuminate problematic areas of social life is, of course, the trademark of research. Methods should be chosen to fit particular circumstances: in this case, the delicate issue of working alongside young children in their homes and in their classrooms. Immediately the researcher is faced with this challenge, a sifting of possible strategies occurs. There is a need to negotiate access, careful procedures to protect both children and researchers against possible complaints of unethical practices, forms of interviewing which are appropriate to the very young, observation of environments of interest such as children's bedrooms and the realization that the research may have to employ innovative methods in order that participants in the study can articulate understandings which they may not have expressed before.

Interviewing

One of the first problems that we encountered concerned our desire to reach beneath the surface of children's immediate reaction to our presence. The early evidence suggested that children were used to giving answers which they thought would please adults. They are socialized in classrooms to try to appeal to what is in their teachers' minds. Consequently, initial interviews tended to have little of the unpredictability which we see in children's 'natural' behaviours.

The desire to please could be combined with a blurring of fact and fiction. For example, when Bryn Davies interviewed the following children, he discovered a wealth of apparent detail concerning his home, his family and his computer technology.

(*Bryn is talking with Ashley and Harry*)
B: Do you like playing with the computer?
A: Yes.
B: What computers do you have at home, Ashley?
A: Sega Mega Drive, Super Nintendo, Game Boy and an Acorn and a BBC.
B: And your dad has?
A: An Acorn and a BBC.
B: Have you got a computer at home, Harry?
H: No.
A: I thought you did.
H: 'Cause my mum's hardly got any money.
B: What do you mainly like doing at home then?
A: Mostly playing.
A: Playing with my 'puter and watching telly?
(*The boys are working on a badge for the class. They are both reasonably competent although Ashley has the air of being in charge physically in terms of having the lion's share of the mouse, etc.*)
B: What will you do when you get home tonight, Ashley?
A: Play on my 'puter.
B: Which one will you play on?
A: My dad's.
B: On the Acorn.
A: Yes.
B: What sort of things do you play on the computer at home, Ashley?
A: I play this? (*He is using a paint package on the school computer*)
B: What about games? Do you like playing them?
B: Which one's have you got?
A: I like playing *Batman*, that's my best game.
B: On what do you play that?
A: On the Sega Mega Drive.
(*There is a good deal of interaction between the children. The teacher prompts them and is clearly at home with the technology and the software. Her assistance takes the activity forward quite considerably*)
B: Do you get a go on this machine everyday?
A: No.
B: What about your computer at home, Ashley, do you play on that everyday?
A: Yes.
(*Ashley certainly is able to give the impression of being knowledgeable about the computer and the software as a result of his having them at home*)

B: What else have you got at home other than *Batman* and *Paint*?

A: I've got games, I've got some really good games. It's got everything you want on it.

(*Harry at this stage becomes a bit frustrated at Ashley's domination of the keyboard although the learning experience is certainly a happy one; generally both boys having a good time*)

B: Have you got any football games?

A: Yes, but my best game is Nintendo. That's a hundred and two thousand; that's a hundred. [£s]

B: Did you save up to buy that?

A: No, I got it for Christmas?

B: What's your favourite game on that?

A: Its like Sega Mega Drive.

A: I like *Tetris* but I haven't got it, I've only got one game for the Game Boy.

B: So do you play the computer everyday?

A: Sometimes.

B: What other things do you like doing out of school?

A: I like riding my bike with my friends.

H: Me, too.

B: Is your Nintendo in your bedroom?

A: Yes, and my Game Boy.

B: So you can play till late.

A: Yes, but my brother he's got . . . You know I've got a big brother. He's got the same games as me but he got another game.

(*Ashley has taken over the mouse again and Harry is showing a bit more frustration*)

B: Does your brother play a lot on the computer as well?

A: I never usually see him 'cause he goes out.

(*He asks me what games my son has*)

(*Harry, having had a turn on the computer, now asks for Ashley's assistance. In retrospect, the differences in ability between the two children are quite small. Mrs Smith comes in to offer assistance. She points to some new tools within the software package to develop the exercise. Ashley is questioned about whether he is letting Harry have a go on the machine. She then tells them to discuss beforehand what to do, and then come up with a finished 'product'*)

B: What do you like watching on television, Ashley?

A: I don't watch much telly.

(*Mrs Smith again comes along and moves the activity to its conclusion by offering some advice which entails moving to another part of the package. At this point the children input some text and demonstrate an awareness of the hardware by referring to the hardware in terms of the space bar, shift and delete keys. Ashley is dyslexic and Harry helps him out with the spelling*)

A: Where's the full stop again. My dad usually shows me where it is. What does the TAB key do? (*I try and explain and it doesn't do what I thought it should*)

(*Children then inform Mrs Smith that the exercise is complete and are congratulated on their efforts. They ask whether they can develop it further by adding some more patterns and she agrees. They both agree to do a pattern each*)

B: What are you going to do when you get home tonight?

A: Ride my bike.

H: Ride my bike.

B: Are you going to ride together?

A: No. No I'm not going to ride on my bike. I'm going to play on my 'puter.

B: What will you play on when you get home tonight?

A: Paint.

B: Game Boy.

A: I'll play my Nintendo.

(*The boys continue experimenting with the package and the conversation goes . . .*)

H: Yes, you're doing it Ashley.

A: I know, aren't I brilliant?

H: Yes, you are better than anyone.

A: Done it.

It sounds like basic, sound data. However, when Bryn visited Ashley's home, it was to discover he had neither computers nor elder brother!

Interviewing more than one child at a time, showed that it was perfectly possible for complicit misinformation to take place, so that the children might give a good account of themselves. Jane Willson (R1) and Roger Whittaker (R2) were interviewing a pair of 7-year-old girls, early in the project:

(*The children spoke with enthusiasm of their love of the Disney* Aladdin, *and without encouragement sang all of 'A Whole New World' from the film's soundtrack . . . Then things got even more interesting*)

R1:   I'd like to ask [Girl 1] because she told me earlier that one of her favourite films is *Strictly Ballroom* and it's got embarrassing bits in it.

Girl 2: Oooh!

R1:   You don't mind me saying this do you? Because there was kissing and stuff in *Aladdin* — isn't **that** embarrassing?

Girl 2: Not really, no . . .

R1:   Why?

Girl 2: Because really . . . it's not like *Strictly Ballroom* because *Strictly Ballroom*'s got loads of it. (*Laughter*)

R1:   Is there any difference between kissing in a cartoon film and when it's real people acting?

Girl 2: Well, I think that animation isn't really real so I don't really like it.

R2:   But (*to Girl 2*) you said you didn't like it in *Sleeping Beauty*, didn't you? That's why you don't like *Sleeping Beauty*, isn't it, because there's too much kissing?

Girl 2: Egh! (*Laughter*)

Suddenly, all was revealed. The two interviewees had known that the researchers were coming in to talk to them on this day, and had apparently planned accordingly:

Girl 1: She agreed that there was someone coming today so we had to all make up what we were going to say. I have to admit it, you see. (*Giggles*)

R1: Right! So this is all a load of rubbish that you're telling us?

Girl 1: No ⎫ (*Said together*)
Girl 2: Yes ⎭

Girl 1: No, we're not making it up as we go along. We ... we ... we ... erm ... actually wrote down our script. I know it off by heart now, so ...

R1: It's pretty good. Yep. We were pretty impressed.

Girl 1/Girl 2: (*Laughter*)

R1: Did you write each other's scripts or did you write your own scripts?

Girl 1: I wrote **her** embarrassing script and she wrote **my** embarrassing script.

R1: Right. Very good.

It seemed to us that a dependency upon questionnaire and interview-based research, in trying to elicit data from the young and very young, is riven with problems — and thus casts doubt upon much of the research which has occurred, hitherto. Theories of child development point up the gradual changes in the child as s/he grows up. For much of the age range we were interested in, children find it difficult to think and interact at a propositional level. That is, the more abstract the discussion, the less it means anything to them. Interviews and dialogue of a propositional type tend to be fantasy oriented, as in Bryn's interview above. In order to persuade children to reflect upon their experiences, interviews need to be embedded in more concrete realities. In other words, if they are to be interviewed about their bedrooms, you are far more certain of thoughtful and accurate representations of their feelings and understandings, if these interviews take place in the bedrooms, themselves. If you want to question them about their use of games machines, it should involve them using the said machines.

In fact our interviews with children underwent a rather fast metamorphosis. The face-to-face, albeit facilitative and gentle, approach quickly gave way to context-grounded interviews. The path this change of emphasis took, was significant. Words-only interviews were first replaced by interviews focusing on diagrams of computer hardware or video machines. These then gave way to 'location interviews', where the concrete actualities of hardware and software were present. Children touching video recorders or games machines were able to talk in a much more focused way.

When they were in their bedrooms, the researcher could point to details of the room, collections of magazines or pre-recorded and recorded tapes.

This was aided by the use of the aforesaid Polaroid instamatic camera. Here, a photograph could be taken in situ with the child in interaction. The child could then comment upon himself or herself in a rudimentary propositional way. Many children reacted in an excited and lively way to Polaroid pictures of their belongings. One 8-year-old boy, for example, looked at a photograph of his room and commented, 'That doesn't look like a sensible place to keep my books'.

In later case studies we used videotape as a means of precipitating self-evaluation, both with individual children and with their families and teachers. There were problems with interviews with teachers and parents, too. There was a tendency to 'toe the party line', at the outset of interviews. Parents, particularly, buying violent games for their children's computers or letting them see over-age videos, may still subscribe to the general consensus of disapproval for these activities in a public forum — which an interview can represent. The reason they publicly damn them seems to be because they gauge the likelihood that public opinion is against them.

Interviews were gradually focused, both in content and in method, as a result of regular debate among the research team. Reviews of what counted as significant evidence and what precipitated rich responses, enabled team members to vary and develop their interview strategies. This kind of corroborative dialogue meant that later case studies took less time than earlier ones. Progressive focusing on major issues took the place of the open-ended approach that was necessary at the outset to trawl for significant themes. Just as interview techniques were honed by earlier experience.

As well as interviewing them at school and at home, we interviewed their teachers and members of their families, to try to build up a more rounded picture of their abilities and preferred behaviours. As a central question in the research revolved around the degree to which learning is affected by screen-based entertainment technologies, other than television, it was important to build these pictures of children at home and at school in order to see how the experiences within one environment advantaged or disadvantaged the child when in the other. The following excerpt from Roger Whittaker's reflections upon interviewing, embodies many of the points we have just been making.

Video and the Domestic Experience

It may seem practical to take as a guiding principle the earlier advice of one of the headteachers: that 'we believe children because without any other evidence it's often dangerous not to believe them'. The starting point of many of these case studies was the testimony of the child. This could and would throw up particular avenues for further exploration at school and home. However, it wasn't always clear from the responses received, especially from the younger pupils, whether the picture being presented of the role TV and video played in their lives was being painted solely for the benefit of the researcher. In other words, to what extent were answers being given to please the questioner?

Here is an example of the pitfalls that can occur from the early stages of the research programme. The long interview extract is not edited, but is divided into key areas; along with commentaries. The conversation is with a 7-year-old girl.

1) Although the interviewer may be in a prepared and readied state for the task in hand, the child interviewee may just want to have fun:

R: I'm going to talk to you — or ask you — about videos. Do you have a video cassette player at home?
Girl: Yes.
R: And presumably you've got your own favourite videotapes that you enjoy watching?
Girl: Mmm ... I've got loads ... I've got nearly a million ... (*Laughs*)
R: Well, I think a million is quite a lot.
Girl: Yes. (*Laughs*)

2) The interviewer may have different knowledge about the topic from that of the interviewee. Due to lack of common ground, or just plain misunderstandings, negotiation of meaning may be difficult:

R: Let's concentrate on the few that you really like, to start off with. Your favourite videos that you watch over and over and over.
Girl: Well, I like *Strictly Ballroom* — it's a bit like *Dirty Dancing* — and I like *Silver Chair* and *Aladdin*.
R: Is that the latest *Aladdin* with Robin Williams as the genie?
Girl: Er ... yeah, I love Robin Williams, I like Robin Williams ... He's pl ... he's played ... erm ... and *Robin Hood* ... he plays the Sheriff of Nottingham in the real play.
R: Oh, does he?
Girl: Robin Williams. I like his films.
R: Right — I didn't know that. Tell me about *The Silver Chair* because I haven't heard of that.
Girl: Well, erm, there's this lion called ... Aslan.
R: Oh! Is it like *The Lion, The Witch and The Wardrobe*?
Girl: Where the children go in the wardrobe.
R: Right — so is it a film or is it a television series?
Girl: It's a film. We haven't taped it or recorded it or anything. It's a video. It's got Part One and Part Two.
R: So it was a television series, but it's been sold as a video tape?
Girl: Yes.
R: ... and *Strictly Ballroom*, that was another proper video?
Girl: Yeh ... that was ... that was taped.
R: That was taped ... off telly?
Girl: Yeh.

3) The question might lead in such a way that the interviewee is tempted to make statements which may be more wishful thinking than honest description — or a combination of the two:

R: Why do you like *Strictly Ballroom*?

Girl: Well ... 'cos it's got lots of views with ballroom dancing and I like ballroom dancing very much and ...

R: Do you go to dancing classes?

Girl: Well ... I am going to, soon.

R: What kind of dancing will you do?

Girl: I'll do ballroom dancing ... erm ... 'cos I've seen Ivan and Liz and Scott all on *Strictly Ballroom*. It's really wanted me to win the Pan-Pacific Champion — 'cos I want to be the Pan-Pacific Champion and be the Ballroom King and everything.

R: Right — it's got you interested in all that.

Girl: (*Smiles*)

4) The conversation may simply be at cross-purposes:

R: You mentioned *Dirty Dancing*, have you seen *Dirty Dancing*?

Girl: No, but my ... one of my friends has ... they're, they're ten or twelve, so.

R: The certificate?

Girl: Huh?

R: Oh! Your friends are ten or twelve?

Girl: Yes.

R: What certificate is *Dirty Dancing*? You know videos have the age certificate on, don't you? (*Long Pause*)

R: What certificate is *Strictly Ballroom,* do you know?

Girl: Erm ...

R: Is that PG?

Girl: I don't know really.

R: Or 12?

Girl: It's got 9, 12. 9, 12.

5) Anecdotes can arise from the asking of the most straightforward factual questions; stories which illustrate the way in which people might perceive particular media texts. The rich and personal nature of the revelations can leave the questioner somewhat nonplussed:

R: Oh, right. Have you ever watched any films that are 12 or 15?

Girl: (*Pause*) Well, I have ... I have ... erm ... well, my friends told me about the *Chippendales*.

R: Right . . . is that the video of the *Chippendales?*

Girl: Yes . . . my mum's got it. She secretly put it on when she was going to the Seventies Disco. (*Laughs*)

R: And what happens in that then?

Girl: Well, I don't really know.
      (*Pause*)

R: It's just men dancing, isn't it?

Girl: Yeah — sort of . . . (*Laughs*) I don't really know. (*Laughs*)

R: What did your friend say about it?

Girl: Oh, she . . . along with my sister, she . . . erm . . . er . . . well, Naomi, she's from Japan, she was watching it too and . . . erm . . . my sister said, 'Please don't tell Dad, he'll kill me', and she said 'Oh, no, no, no . . . I am too embarrassed to myself' (*in mock Japanese*). (*Laughs*)

R: What was she embarrassed about?

Girl: The *Chippendales.*

R: Why?
      (*Pause. Cough.*)

R: Because of the men?

Girl: Yes, because of the men?

R: Oh, right. (*Laughs*)

Girl: And all her face lit up like this, 'Oh, no, no, no I am too embarrassed myself'.

R: (*Laughs*) Have you seen any videos that you've been embarrassed watching?

Girl: Well . . . I have been embarrassed about *Strictly Ballroom.* (*Laughs*)

R: Why?

Girl: Because (*Laughs*) of all the kissing in it.

R: Oh, right. But people kiss, don't they?

Girl: (*Long laughter*)
      (*Pause*)
      (*Cough. Cough*)

6) So nonplussed, that the questioner really isn't clear about the information that is being shared:

R: Have you seen any videos that have had scenes in that have upset you — made you feel awkward . . . or . . .

Girl: Well, I have. It was one . . . erm . . . well, not really videos but . . . (*sigh*) about my Grandad. He's died now . . . that makes me upset.

R: Yes.

Girl: I watch videos of when I was two. He died when I was first born and when I was two he died . . . erm . . . and er . . . we went to erm . . . this club and . . . we . . . erm . . . we were sitting down and he let me have a drink of his beer. (*Laughs*)

R: That's nice, isn't it?
Girl: (*Laughs*) . . . and erm . . .
R: But I was asking you about videos, wasn't I?
Girl: Yes. It was.
R: Oh. This was on the video, was it?
Girl: Yeh.
R: Oh, I see. I'm sorry. So it was like a home video?
Girl: Yeh.
R: So somebody had a camera?
Girl: Yes.
R: And it makes you sad when you see it?
Girl: Yeh . . . 'cos . . . erm . . . he died when we were at the pub . . . and we've got that on tape . . . he . . . erm . . . he actually split his eye there.
R: Oh, dear.
Girl: There were no friends, so he died.

7) If the interview, in the eyes of the researcher, is not going particularly well, it is tempting to over-empathize, and in so doing step too far into the interviewee's personal space:

R: That's very sad, isn't it?
Girl: Mmmm.
R: Do you have a lot of videos of your family?
Girl: Well, yeh, we have . . . erm . . . the one that's really happy . . . it makes me cry 'cos I'm happy . . . 'cos erm . . . I was a bridesmaid and erm . . . the best bit was when we had our basket of flowers in one hand . . . we had our confetti in, in . . . about three thousand packets of confetti in our . . . erm baskets of flowers.
R: And you've got that on videotape . . . do you keep watching it over and over?
Girl: Well, sometimes. It really depends on how much time we've got because they are quite long.

8) By this stage of the interview, the questioner is desperate to convey as accurately as possible the content of the question; not, however, as succinctly as possible. It is to be remembered that the interviewee is a 7-year-old girl:

R: Now I must ask you. You must have your favourite television pro-grammes?
Girl: Oh, yeh. I have.
R: But, I'm not going to ask you that — what I'm going to ask you is: what television programmes do you like so much that you have on

videotape; and you watch them when they're on videotape because you like them so much?

Girl: *Strictly Ballroom.*

R: Right — that was a film though; I was thinking more of programmes, if you know what I mean.

Girl: Ah . . . Mmm.

R: Are there any children's programmes or . . . ?

Girl: Yes. There's the *Splash . . . Splash.*

R: Yes. That's the film about the mermaid?

Girl: Yes.

R: Right.

Girl: And . . . she's got a lovely dolphin . . . and it follows her around.

R: Well, was it a TV series as well then?

Girl: Yeh, it was.

R: Right.

(*Pause*)

R: How many episodes of that have you got?

Girl: Well it's . . . We've only got Part 1 and Part 2.

R: Right . . . and . . .

Girl: 'Cos it's only been on twice, so . . . really . . . it comes on every 1 January . . . but . . . er . . . (*Laughs*)

R: I don't know why that is . . .

Girl: 'Cos it comes on it once a year.

9) Collapse of interview:

R: Right . . . and other things . . . like comedy? Do you . . . or children's programmes? That you have on video to watch?

(*Pause*)

Girl: *Garfield.*

R: *Garfield*! That's the cartoon . . . off BBC is it?

Girl: It's on BBC 1, BBC 2, BBC 3.

R: And you have that on videotape?

Girl: Yep.

R: And you watch it a lot? Or from time to time? When you feel like it?

Girl: When I feel like it. When I feel happy, I do.

The full interview was twice this length — overlong considering the content, context and the age of the interviewee. It is interesting to note the annexation of the term 'embarrassing' from the researcher's previous questions. Much was revealed by these exchanges — concerning research techniques, strategies and procedures — not to mention the strategies, imaginations and intellects of the children. So as not to encounter insurmountable difficulties, the researcher has to utilize the benefits of the triangulation of child, school and home to the maximum. Each interview/

observation session is informally structured, but with care taken to maintain the full agenda (it may be inconvenient to return because of a missed point) and to provide enough openings for the unanticipated responses to be followed.

Observing

Because of the pressures to do research and evaluation as quickly as possible, owing to time and financial constraints, there has been a growing tendency to rely upon interview when trying to understand social behaviour. As has already been pointed out, interview-based research has its problems. Some of these may be lessened when observations are undertaken of individuals to check whether what they say is happening is actually happening, as in Bryn's story above.

All the individual studies relied upon detailed observation for cross-referencing respondents' perceptions and introspections. Field notes were taken within school and classroom milieux, the home and, in particular, rooms where entertainment media were located. In many cases these notes provided a basis for separate lines of enquiry which illuminated some central issue within the research. So, for example, where a computer is placed in a classroom (or outside it!) may give a good indication of the teacher's competence with it, school resourcing issues, and so on.

The sorts of 'educational' and other collections (tapes, magazines, toys) which children have and how and when they are used and positioned within a bedroom helped indicate their function within parental theories of the education process. A good example of this concerned a parent saying in interview that her child had been bought some educational magazines on how the body works. Observation in the bedroom showed that the complete set of magazines was still in it's monthly cellophane covers. We thought of this as an example of 'osmosis theory' in learning. Many of our parents appeared to believe that providing the materials were in the environment, then learning would occur. This was particularly true of computer-based technologies. Indeed, some of our teachers paid lip-service to the National Curriculum, by having computers present in the classrooms or corridors and using them merely to provide fair copy of children's work, so that the work could be put on walls for parents to see.

Cross-referencing and Analysing

Gradually, of course, we began to gather large amounts of data from our interviews, observations and the photographs and videos. In order to cross-reference all this data, it was filed in hard copy in the following way. The key first category area was 'school'. All children who attended a particular school were filed under their school name. This meant that the same contextual details of the school could be applied to each of these children. Then, of course, under school the sub-categories were the 'children'. All the data related to a particular child was kept together under the child's name.

In order to help each other as researchers, we constantly analysed themes and took personal responsibility for them. In general terms, Bryn Davies maintained a grip on information handling in school and home, Jane Willson on computers, computer games and gender issues, Roger Whittaker on matters relating to video technology, censorship and popular culture, and Jack Sanger maintained an overview and advised upon issues concerning the research methods we were using and developing. These were also sub-divided as major themes arose, such as gender, skills development, isolation, role-modelling, critical awareness and moral awareness. As each of the team added more data to our files, they colour-coded it into various categories so that other team members were guided into what might be significant material.

Writing

The broad basis for each chapter in this book was the responsibility of the field researcher for that subject area. However, each chapter was subjected to the critique of the Project Director, Jack Sanger who drafted and redrafted chapters as a result of this dialogue. This, we hope, has meant that the book is cohesive and more easily accessible.

Bibliography

ATKINS, M.J. (1993) 'Evaluating interactive technologies for learning', *Journal of Curriculum Studies*, **25**, 4, pp. 333–42.

BANDURA, A., ROSS, D. and ROSS, S.A. (1963) 'Imitation of film-mediated aggressive models', *Journal of Abnormal and Social Psychology*, **66**, pp. 3–11.

BANDURA, A. and WALTERS, R. (1963) *Adolescent Aggression*, New York, Ronald Press.

BANNISTER, N. (1995) 'Playing computer games is just a phone call away', *Guardian*, 20th September, p. 19.

BOWLBY, J. (1951) *Maternal Care and Mental Health*, Geneva, World Health Organisation.

BRIGHT, M. (1995) 'Schools develop CD-ROMance', *Guardian: Education Supplement*, 27th June, p. 8.

BROUCH, V. (1994) 'Navigating the arts in electronic sea', *NASPP Bulletin*, **78**, April, pp. 43–9.

BUCKINGHAM, D. (1993) 'Towards new literacies', *The English & Media Magazine*, Summer, p. 23.

BUCKLEY, N. (1995) 'Rapid growth forecast in home on-line shopping', *Financial Times*, 26th June.

CALDERA, Y., HUSTON, A. and O'BRIEN, M. (1989) 'Social interactions and actions and play patterns of parents and toddlers with feminine, masculine and netural toys', *Child Development*, **60**, pp. 70–6.

CARVALHO, A.M.A., SMITH, P.K., HUNTER, T. and COSTABILE, A. (1990) 'Playground activities for boys and girls: Developmental and cultural trends in children's perceptions of gender differences', *Play and Culture*, **3**, pp. 343–7.

CATTELL, R.B. and CATTELL, M.D.L. (1975) *Handbook for the Jr.–Sr. High School Personality Questionnaire*, Champaign, IL, Institute for Personality and Ability Testing.

COLE, G. (1995) 'Don't be a sheep when choosing RAM', *Observer*, 10th September, p. 15.

COOPER, J. and MACKIE, D. (1986) 'Video games and aggression in children', *Journal of Applied Social Psychology*, **16**, 8, pp. 726–44.

COX, J. and FREAN, A. (1995) 'Internet generation lifts computer sales sky high', *Times*, 22nd July, p. 7.

CRISP, S. (1996) 'Towards a wider horizon', *Guardian: Education Supplement*, 6th February, p. 6.

DAVIS, C. (1995) ' "Edutainment" and no seams', *Guardian: Education Supplement*, 5th September, p. 11.

DIPIETRO, J.A. (1981) 'Rough and tumble play: A function of gender', *Developmental Psychology*, **17**, pp. 50–8.

DOMINICK, J.R. (1984) 'Videogames, television violence and aggression in teenagers', *Journal of Communications*, **34**, pp. 134–47.

DRABMAN, R.S. and THOMAS, M.H. (1974) 'Does media violence increase children's toleration of real-life aggression?' *Developmental Psychology*, **10**, pp. 418–21.

DROTNER, K. (1989) 'Girl meets boy: Aesthetic production, reception and gender identity', *Cultural Studies*, **3**, pp. 208–25.

DYRLI, O.-E. and KINNAMAN, D.E. (1994) 'Preparing for the integration of emerging technologies', Technology-and-Learning, **14**, 9, pp. 92–100, May–June.

ECCLES, J.S. (1989) 'Bringing young women to maths and science', in CRAWFORD, M. and GENTRY, M. (eds) *Gender and Thought: Psychological Perspectives*, New York, Springer-Verlag.

FAVARO, P.J. (1982) 'Games for co-operation and growth — An alternative for designers', *Softside*, **6**, pp. 18–21.

FESHBACH, S. and FESHBACH, N. (1973) 'The young aggressors', *Psychology Today*, **6**, 11, pp. 90–5.

FISHER, S. (1990) 'The use of fruit and video machines by children in the UK: An analysis of existing research', *Society for the Study of Gambling Newsletter*, **16**, pp. 13–39.

FLING, S., SMITH, L., RODRIGUEZ, T., THORNTON, D., ATKINS, E. and NIXON, K. (1992) 'Videogames, aggression and self-esteem: A survey', *Social Behaviour and Personality*, **20**, 1, pp. 39–46.

FREUD, A. (1928) *Introduction to the Technique of Child Analysis*, New York, Nervous & Mental Disease Publishing.

GARDNER, J.E. (1991) 'Can the Mariro Bros. help? Nintendo games as an adjunct in psychotherapy with children', *Psychotherapy*, **28**, pp. 667–70.

GARVEY, C. (1977) *Play*, London, Fontana/Open Books.

GOLDSTEIN, J.H. (1994) 'Sex differences in toy play and use of video games', in GOLDSTEIN, J.H. (ed.) *Toys, Play and Child Development*, Cambridge University Press, Cambridge.

GRIFFITHS, M.D. (1993) 'Are computer games bad for children?' *The Psychologist: Bulletin of the British Psychological Society*, **6**, pp. 401–7.

GRIFFITHS, M.D. and DANCASTER, I. (1995) 'The effect of Type A personality on physiological arousal while playing computer games', *Addictive Behaviours*, **20**, 4, pp. 543–8.

GUNTER, S.-A. and WINSTONE (1994) *Television: The Public's View 1993*, London, John Libbey.

HEPPELL, S. (1995) 'Weaned on the screen', *Getting Wired: Part 2, Sunday Times*, 7th May.

HYDE, J.S. (1981) 'How large are cognitive gender differences? A meta-analysis', *American Psychologist*, **36**, pp. 892–901.

HYMAS, C. (1994) 'Lost for words', *Sunday Times*, 10th April.

JENKINS, S. (1995) 'The death of the written word', *Journal of Information Science*, **21**, 6, pp. 407–12.

JOHNSON, C.S. and SWOPE, K.F. (1987) 'Boys and girls using computers: Implications for the classroom', *Arithmetic Teacher*, **35**, 1, pp. 14–16.

JOHNSON, D.C., COX, M.J. and WATSON, D.M. (1994) 'Evaluating the impact of IT on pupils' achievements', *Journal of Computer Assisted Learning*, **10**, p. 138.

JOHNSON, R.T. (1988) 'Story retelling: Innovation in a learning technology context', *Early Child Development and Care*, **32**, pp. 53–8.

KAY, J.J. and MELLAR, H.G. (1994) 'Information technology and new primary school teachers', *Journal of Computer Assisted Learning*, **10**, pp. 157–67.

KIESLER, S., SPROULL, L. and ECCLES, J.S. (1983) 'Second class citizens', *Psychology Today*, **17**, 3, pp. 41–8.

KOCH, M. (1994) 'No girls allowed', *Technos*, **3**, pp. 14–19.

KNOWSLEY, A. (1995) 'Love at first byte', *Sunday Mirror Magazine*.

LEVY, M.R. and GUNTER, B. (1988) *Home Video and the Changing Nature of the Television Audience*, London, John Libbey.

LLOYD, C. (1994) 'Publisher predicts final chapter for the printed word', *Sunday Times*, 22nd May.

MACCOBY, E.E. and JACKLIN, C.N. (1974) *The Psychology of Sex Differences*, Stanford, CA, Stanford University Press.

MARGOLIS, J. (1995) 'A man created cyberspace', *Sunday Times,* 26th February.

MORROW, L.M. (1985) 'Reading and retelling stories: Strategies for emergent readers', *The Reading Teacher*, **35**, pp. 870–5.

MORROW, L.M. (1984) 'Reading stories to young children: Effects of story structure and traditional questioning strategies on comprehension', *Journal of Reading Behavior*, **16**, pp. 273–88.

NEUSTATTER, A. (1991) 'Keyboard junkies', *Independent on Sunday Review*, 17th November, p. 64.

NEUSTATTER, A. (1992) 'Girls and boys stay in to play', *Observer*, June, p. 42.

NOVEMBER, A. (1992) 'Familyware (home technology and literacy)', *Electronic Learning*, **11**, 7, pp. 50–64.

PLANT, S. (1995) 'How to Spend IT', *Financial Times*, 9th September.

PROVENZO, E.F. (1992) 'The video generation', *The American School Board Journal*, **179**, 3, pp. 29–32.

RAMESH, R. (1995) 'Children "drugged" by computer game's hidden messages', *Sunday Times*, 8th October.

SCHEIBE, K.E. and ERWIN, M. (1979) 'The computer as altar', *Journal of Social Psychology*, **108**, pp. 103–9.

SCHUTTE, N.S., MALOUFF, J.M., POST-GORDEN, J.C. and RODASTA, A.L. (1988) *Journal of Applied Psychology*, **18**, pp. 454–60.

SERBIN, L.A. and SPRAFKIN, C. (1986) 'The salience of gender and the process of sex typing in three to seven year old children', *Child Development*, **57**, pp. 1188–99.

SILNOW, G.W. (1984) 'Playing video games: The electronic friend', *Journal of Communication*, **34**, pp. 148–56.

SLUCKIN, A. (1981) *Growing up in the Playground*, London, Routledge and Kegan Paul.

SMITH, P.K. (ed.) (1984) *Play in Animals and Humans*, Oxford, Blackwell.

SNYDER, I. (1994) 'Writing with word processors: The computer's influence on the classroom context', *Journal of Curriculum Studies*, **26**, 2, pp. 143–62.

SPENCE, J. (1988) 'The use of computer arcade games in behaviour management', *Maladjustment & Therapeutic Education*, **6**, pp. 64–8.

STUTZ, E. (1995) 'Is electronic entertainment hindering children's play and social skill development?' Unpublished paper.

TAVRIS, C. and WADE, C. (1984) *The Longest War: Sex Differences in Perspective*, 2nd edition, London, Harcourt Brace Jovanovich.

WARD, R. (1985) 'Girls and computing', *Computer Education*, **49**, pp. 4–5.

WAVELL, S. (1995) 'Has parent power ruined childhood', *Sunday Times*, 6th August, pp. 1–10.

WHITEHOUSE, C. (1995) 'Refashioning boys' toys', *Times Higher Educational Supplement*, 12th May.

WINKEL, M., NOVAK, D.M. and HOPSON, H. (1987) 'Personality factors, subject gender, and the effects of aggressive video games on aggression in adolescents', *Journal of Research in Personality*, **21**, pp. 211–23.

WINKLE WILLIAMS, S. and MATILE OGLETREE, S. (1992) 'Preschool children's computer interest and competence: Effects of sex and gender role', *Early Childhood Research Quarterly*, **7**, pp. 135–43.

WOBER, J.M. and FAZAL, S. (1994) 'Age and involvement with computers and their games', *The Psychologist: Bulletin of the British Psychological Society*.

ZILLMANN, D. (1982) 'Television viewing and arousal', in PEARL, D. BOUTHILET, L. and LAZAR, J. (eds) *Television and Behaviour: Ten years of scientific progress and implications for the eighties (Vol 2). Technical Reviews*, Washington, DC, US Government Printing Office.

ZIMBARDO, P. (1982) 'Understanding psychological man: A state of the science report', *Psychology Today*, **16**, p. 15.

Index